# The Story of the

# Fylde

First published in Great Britain in 2000 by
The Breedon Books Publishing Company Limited
Breedon House, 44 Friar Gate, Derby, DE1 1DA.



Researched, compiled and written by
David Pearce
Editor of The Gazette's weekly Memory Lane feature.

Additional contributions:
Jacqueline Morley, Elizabeth Gomm, Craig Fleming Jonathan Lee, Barry Band

Edited by
Steve Singleton

Acknowledgements

A book of this sort can only be written with the co-operation of many people, both professional and amateur. We would like in particular to express our thanks to the following:

Ted Lightbown, secretary of the Blackpool and Fylde Historical Society and Aviation historian Russell Brown of St Annes; Ralph Smedley of Thornton-Cleveleys, Christine Storey of Poulton, Jacqueline Turner of Kirkham and Bill Curtis and Richard Gillingham of Fleetwood along with Barry Shaw of Blackpool Civic Society.

Thanks particular go to the generations of Gazette photographers for preserving this historical record. Other members of the Gazette team who made vital contributions were librarian Carole Davies, page designer David Upton, photographic assistant Andy Smith and Keith Taylor of technical services.

In addition, many Gazette readers loaned photographs and supplied information. The part some of them played in the Story of the Fylde is told in these pages.

ISBN 1 85983 207 5

Printed and bound by Butler & Tanner Ltd., Selwood Printing Works,
Caxton Road, Frome, Somerset.

Colour separations and jacket printing by GreenShires Group Ltd, Barkby Road, Leicester.

# The Story of the Fylde

A **Gazette** Millennium Souvenir

# The story of

WEST LANCASHIRE EVENING GAZETTE

LAST EXTRA

THE CUP'S HERE

WEST LANCASHIRE EVENING GAZETTE

STREAMLINE TAXIS 23535

Two policemen wounded in North Shore gun terror

BLACKPOOL POLICE CHIEF SHOT DEAD IN GEM RAID CHASE

SUPT GERALD RICHARDSON, chief of Blackpool sub-division of Lancashire Constabulary, today died in Blackpool Victoria Hospital after being shot by a gunman following an armed raid on a Blackpool town centre jewellers. He was 38.

LATEST NEWS

## Chapter 1:

The Early Years: The first chapter sets the scene by giving a thumbnail sketch of the Blackpool and Fylde story through the years to the birth of the 20th century and beyond.

For centuries the whole area was a very rural place. It was dominated not by towns like Blackpool but by much older settlements such as Kirkham and Poulton.

## Chapter 2:

The Twenties: Blackpool was flying high as a leading aviation centre but the story had started much earlier when the town made flying history.

The resort was in carnival mood as the dark clouds of World War 1 rolled back and the first Illuminations lit up the scene but serious flooding wrecked the town of Fleetwood. We tell the early story of the Pleasure Beach.

## Chapter 3:

The Thirties: Bright and breezy Blackpool was the capital city of seaside fun But not everyone approved of the raunchy Golden Mile where scandalous shows got the resort into the Sunday paper headlines. And we take a look at the galaxy of stars who had built Blackpool's reputation as the major entertainment town outside London.

## Chapter 4:

The Forties: Wartime turned Blackpool into a vast training camp for the RAF and then the Americans invaded South Fylde. Wartime brought tragedy to the Fylde but Blackpool also kept a smile on the face of war-weary northeners .

West Lancashire Evening Gazette

THURSDAY, MAY 24, 1984

PRICE 15p

DISASTER SPECIAL

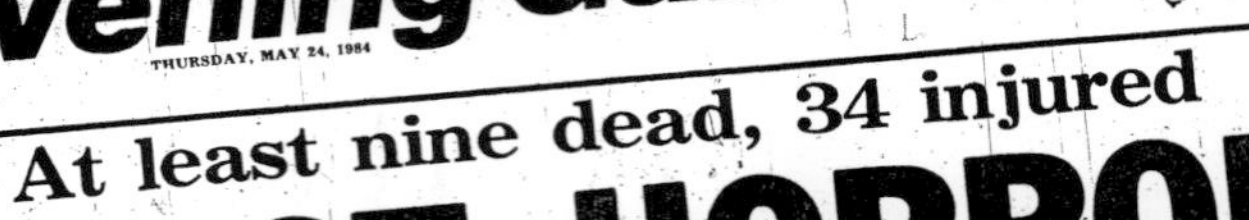

At least nine dead, 34 injured

BLAST HORROR STUNS VILLAGE

STUNNED villagers in St Michaels were today taking in the full

EVENING The Gazette

THURSDAY, OCTOBER 1, 1998

No. 22,018

AVROE HOUSE SPECIAL

NEWSPAPER OF THE YEAR North West Newspaper Awards '98

Prime Minister Tony Blair gives Avroe House the official seal of approval

WE MAKE THE NEWS

YOUR Gazette made the news itself today! Tony Blair took time out from his hectic conference schedule to pay a visit to our new headquarters.

In a week when Blackpool has faced criticism about its beaches and poor quality hotels the Labour leader also revealed during his visit that the Saudi Arabia ambassador had described the resort last night as "Britain's answer to St Tropez"!

The Gazette

SATURDAY, JANUARY 1 2000

28p

No. 22,530

SOUVENIR EDITION

A CENTURY IS BORN

MEET Erin, Blackpool's first citizen of the new millennium, who arrived minutes after midnight.

■ Full story and more pictures: Page 12.

The Gazette

SEE YOU IN THE NEW MILLENNIUM

DON'T MISS TOMORROW'S SOUVENIR EDITION

FRIDAY, DECEMBER 31, 1999

No. 22,529

20th CENTURY FINAL

28p

TONIGHT

Prize patroller

BLACKPOOL lollipop lady Margaret Brown was today celebrating after receiving the MBE in a spectacular Millennium New Year Honours List along with a dazzling array of showbusiness and sporting stars. Dame Elizabeth Taylor tops the bill.

■ Pages 20 and 21

ONE GREAT GRANDAD'S WISH: A PEACEFUL 21ST CENTURY FOR LITTLE MOLLY

FACE TO FACE WITH

# the Fylde

## Chapter 5:

The Fifties: Blackpool bounced back as the resort's soccer heroes twice took the road to Wembley and came home with the Cup. A Blackpool man helped to conquer the world's highest mountain but a major fire wrecked one of the jewels in the town's entertainment crown. Ernie was born in Lytham St Annes.

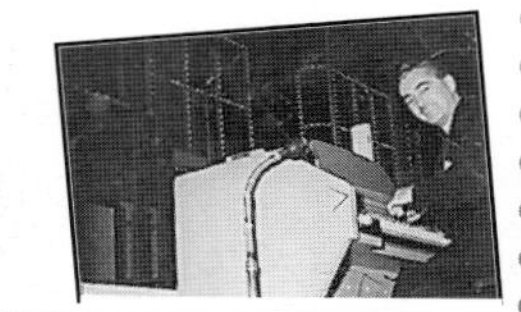

## Chapter 6:

The Sixties: As a tide of Mersey music rolled into the resort we take a second in-depth look at the Blackpool entertainment scene from World War Two to the age of the Beatles. Steam trains were on the way out but Blackpool welcomed a new era as more liberal laws saw the birth of today's late night club scene. Planemakers brought new prosperity to the Fylde and there were dreams of a new town for Kirkham.

## Chapter 7:

The Seventies: As Blackpool celebrated 100 years of progress and major new attractions were opened, Mother Nature hit back. A ferocious storm wrecked much of Fleetwood and the rest of the coast took a terrific battering. And violence flared as gunmen brought mobster murder to the streets of Blackpool. Road links to the Fylde were boosted by the opening of the new M55 motorway.

## Chapter 8:

The Eighties: Changes were on the way in the holiday towns of the Fylde coast – and in the villages too.A giant party greeted the 100th birthday of Blackpool trams.

## Chapter 9:

The Nineties: A ferocious fire wiped out a whole section of South Shore and Blackpool decided to go it alone at the Town Hall. Old traditions like the rugby league club disappeared but new investment arrived like The Pepsi Max Big One ride on the Pleasure Beach.

## Chapter 10:

The Fylde Coast celebrates the dawning of a new year and a New Millennium with the biggest party ever seen. As the face of the Fylde changes look forward to the next chapter in the story of the 21st Century

# INTRODUCTION

WELCOME to The Story of the Fylde. Step back in time and leaf through the pages of life in Blackpool and the Fylde during the 20th century.

Revisit the news stories of joy and tragedy that captured the headlines of the Fylde Coast's favourite evening newspaper - The Gazette.

Gazette Memory Lane Editor David Pearce and a team of writers have delved into the archives to bring together a fascinating collection of landmark stories – to form a lasting souvenir of the region's remarkable history.

Everyone has an image of Blackpool. For some, it conjours up a picture of the Tower and the Golden Mile. Others think of the trams, the Illuminations and Piers.

It was the Northern mill workers who helped make Blackpool what it is today - Britain's premier resort. They came in their droves to sample its unique atmosphere and bracing sea breezes.

Further along the coast, what fun it must have been to witness and enjoy the growth of the near neighbours of big, bold and unashamedly brassy Blackpool. The splendour of Victorian and Edwardian life was all to see in genteel Lytham St Annes and also in Thornton Cleveleys.

Meanwhile Fleetwood thrived as a fishing port and there were bustling historic markets and industry in the inland towns of Poulton and Kirkham.

Each chapter of The Fylde Story traces the changing decades, culminating in the biggest Millennium party the Fylde Coast has ever seen and a look forward to the 21st Century. Gazette readers also recall some of the major events of the century which they have witnessed. The stories and pictures are certain to jog the memories of residents and holidaymakers alike.

CRAIN ELEVATOR
LANCASHIRE & YORKSHIRE RAILWAY COY
BOVRIL
MARKET
AQUARIUM
MENAGERIE
FR 5523

Chapter One

# The Early Years

# Mapping out the Fylde

WHEN the man who designed and drew this illustrated map was a schoolboy he came bottom of the class in an art examination – and got a thrashing from his father.

Now 71, David Peirse never forget the incident from his Durham childhood.

At his Preesall home the retired headmaster recalled: "My father was a blacksmith and he was a good father and not a man who ever hit me. He rarely raised his voice. But he was angry that day because he knew I had the talent to do much better."

David got the message and was soon top of the art class. He planned to study the subject at a higher level. But when his Dad died young he went to work instead to support the family.

After national service in the Royal Navy he went to teacher training college to study geography and history. Art became a hobby but his knowledge of the British Isles and the story of its peoples was to come in handy later.

David found relaxation at the easel from the stresses and strains of a teacher's life. And he developed a special form of art – the illustrated map.

It combined his talent for drawing and painting with his knowledge of geography and history.

A huge amount of research and plenty of trial and error drawing goes into the finished product.

Although he enjoys this arduous and painstaking work, David knows that to get a project finished there has to be discipline in the artist.

He agrees with Michaelangelo when the Italian genius said: "The statue is in the block of stone and I have to get it out."

David was the first head teacher at St Aidan's CE High School in Preesall in 1961 and retired nearly 30 years later. The arts wing bears his name. He was awarded the MBE and is heavily involved in the world of Rotary and the church.

His home in Lancaster Road overlooks St Oswald's where he has been a Reader for nearly 40 years.

Now his knowledge of the Bible helps him design stained glass windows – a new outlet for a remarkable artistic talent.

The skeleton of the elk, dating from about 10,000 BC, is now on show in Preston's Harris Museum

# Harold the unlucky elk of pre-history

AN unlucky elk, later nicknamed Harold by historians, gave the earliest clue to human life in the Fylde. The unfortunate creature was on the menu for local residents 12,000 years ago and they hunted it with a variety of weapons – harpoons, spears or arrows, a club, an axe and maybe a trap.

The injured animal blundered on to an ice-covered lake but was drowned and lay, undiscovered in the mud at the edge of the water as the centuries rolled by.

At the time the elk died great sheets of glacial ice were ebbing away but round the lake were sub-arctic trees and shrubs.

In 1970 Mr Tony Scholey of Blackpool Old Road, Highfurlong peered into a hole which had been dug that day near his home on land owned by Mr Jonathan Devine of Tebay Avenue, Cleveleys.

He saw bones in the side of the trench and the full story was unearthed by archaeologists.

What made the find so important was the discovery among the bones of the barbed tips of two harpoons made from bone.

This proved the giant beast – looking like a stag complete with antlers – had been hunted by humans.

It remains the earliest evidence of mankind in the north west

In those days of the Ice Age hunters Highfurlong was an inland site with the sea 300 miles to the west. Britain was then linked to mainland Europe and those primitive people had already been around for thousands of years.

Eddie Green with his garden find

# Romans at the bottom of Eddie's garden

THERE are Romans at the bottom of the garden where Ann and Eddie Green live in Dowbridge, Kirkham.

The couple's fascinating link with the past began soon after they moved into their home nearly 25 years ago and began to find fragments of pottery in flower bed soil.

In 1985, when British Aerospace worker Eddie was making the foundations for a garage he discovered more evidence.

Archaeology experts from Lancashire County Council were called in for a proper dig and discovered evidence of a cobbled surface, iron nails and pottery which had been made in Gaul – modern France.

But a large sycamore stood in the way of further investigation – until 1997 when it was removed.

Eddie explained: "In 1985 we did not know if the cobbles were part of a long strip or road but now it's been confirmed they were part of the floor of a house.

It was probably lived in between AD90 and AD140 and would have been made from wood with a heavy tiled roof. Evidence shows it may have been on fire twice and rebuilt."

Perhaps the builder left his boots behind because hob type nails have been found!

He certainly enjoyed roast lamb for rib bones bearing knife marks have turned up.

Eddie said: " I am happy we know what it is. It has been well documented and now it's back under the garden so it won't deteriorate in the open air."

One day, Ann and Eddie hope their collection of fragments and photographs will be on display for the museum which local history enthusiasts are planning for Kirkham

It seems Dowbridge was a 'des res' area long before the Roman Legions marched north from Chester.

Eddie has found a flint which was dated at 1800BC and which links in with other finds.

He said: "It is amazing to think people could have been living around here 5,000 years ago."

The Bellman worked for the Lord of the Manor and was the ancient equivalent of the evening news bulletin. This picture was taken in Freckleton Street at the turn of the century

Modern architecture has crept into The Square at Kirkham but the ancient circular Fish Stones remain. However, the Catch of the Day is no longer sold there.

# Piggery jokery in Kirkham

## *Rough justice in first capital of the Fylde*

THE pigs were the problem in ancient Kirkham. Some people kept them tied up but practical jokers cut the ropes and they dug up the streets with their snouts.

One local was fined by the forerunner of the local council – the Court Leet – for keeping his porkers next door to his neighbour's bedroom.

The official on the street imposing the rules was The Barleyman and when he reported a resident for not looking after his pigs properly he got some "evil speech" from the accused's wife. So she got fined as well . . .

That was life 400 years ago in Kirkham – the first capital of the Fylde.

The action really began i 1296 when the monks of Va Royal in Cheshire owned th manorial rights to the town.

The Abbot granted a charte to hold a market and fair an that put Kirkham firmly on th map.

Children at play in Moor Street, Kirkham, a century ago

For centuries the church was a powerful force in the life of Kirkham. Before the present parish church of St Michael it is thought another existed on Carr Hill.

Founded on the old industry of making sailcloth, cotton textiles became important for Kirkham as this busy scene from Progress Mill shows. It is now an industrial estate in Orders Lane.

Now converted into a modern home the Kirkham windmill stands beside Dowbridge near the site of the Roman fort.

Like other Fylde locations it was mentioned in the earlier Doomsday Book

But the charter gave the population new rights to control trade and to live as freemen, not serfs.

They could graze their animals on land around the present grammar school known as The Moor – a name which survived with older residents until modern times.

Strips of land called Burgage Tofts, and used for early farming, survive as the back gardens of homes in Preston Street while Orders Lane derives from Old Earth Lane.

Tradition says Kirkham had a church at Carr Hill about 650 AD but the modern town grew up around St Michael's which was in existence at Doomsday time. The parish was a vast agricultural district and took in half the Fylde area between the Ribble and the Wyre.

Fifteen locations from Hambleton to Salwick each sent two representatives to the Thirtymen committee who governed church affairs. They were also involved in the early days of Kirkham Grammar School which is 450 years old this year.

Kirkham suffered at the hands of soldiers from both sides in the Civil War who robbed and plundered the area.

But in its aftermath, around the year 1700, merchants in Kirkham and Poulton started to trade with ships from the Wyre which journeyed as far as the Baltic and the West Indies.

From the former came flax which families like the Hankinsons, Hornbys, Langtons, Shepherds and Birleys used to make Kirkham an industrial town where linen sailcloth and rope was made. Such goods powered Nelson's navy to victory in the Napoleonic wars.

Cotton weaving was a cottage industry until the railway arrived from Preston in 1840 and Kirkham's character changed again.

Now it was a cotton mill town like Preston.

But many of the workers lived in slums. In 1851 a health inspector's report highlighted the horrors. In Marsden Street 16 people lived in two rooms. There were 12 in another house and none of them had a bed or bedding.

Sewage was dumped in the street along with all sorts of other rubbish.

Textile magnate Thomas Langton Birley moved out to Fleetwood for a while to get away from the smell.

Later he lived at Carr Hill. This old house was demolished to make way for Carr Hill High School but not before Eddie Sergeant, who had bought the manorial rights, lived there in the '60s. His Lower Deck strip club was a famous Fylde night-spot of the time.

With cotton no longer king Kirkham was set to double in size in the same decade as a debate raged around the building of hundreds of new homes on the RAF camp site. Instead, it became an open prison.

The M55 motorway breathed new life into the town which has retained some industry and now has a new, more vibrant atmosphere.

The Langton family who made their fortune in the textile trade lived in this imposing house (above) in The Square. Later it was a church community centre and is now a doctor's surgery

Founded by the clergy, Kirkham Grammar School celebrated 450 years of education in 1999

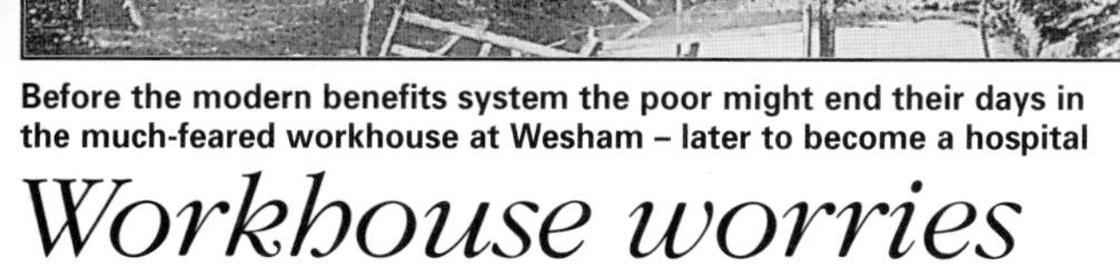

Before the modern benefits system the poor might end their days in the much-feared workhouse at Wesham – later to become a hospital

# Workhouse worries

**For years Kirkham was famous – or infamous – for its workhouse. Older generations all over the Fylde dreaded the thought of ending their days under its roof. The first was built in Marsden Street in 1726 and its able-bodied inhabitants had to earn their keep by breaking stones.**

**A new one in Moor Street in 1834 held 260 people but was soon overcrowded. This site later became a childrens home for Lancashire youngsters after the workhouse moved to Wesham in 1900. That building later became Wesham hospital.**

**BEFORE THE BOOM**
**Until major housing wor began in the 1960s, Poulto looked like this for decade with the church shrouded i trees and fields close to th centr**

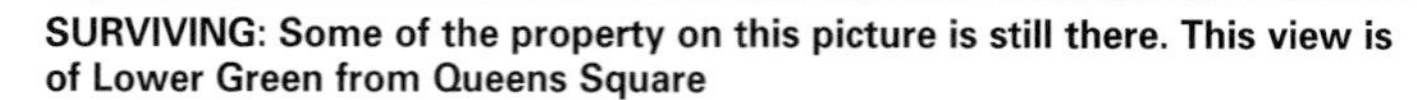

**SURVIVING: Some of the property on this picture is still there. This view is of Lower Green from Queens Square**

**GATHERED IN: Through the centuries the church collected payments called tithes and used some of the value to help the sick and needy. Tithe goods like corn were stored in this tithebarn where the Teanlowe car park now stands**

# Potts and

## Alley way of life was ruled off limits

POTTS ALLEY was not exactly a des res. The people at one end had a nasty habit of emptying their chamber pans into the churchyard, which made a mess of the tombstones.

And then there were the goodtime girls who hung out down there not to mention the open sewer and the rats scampering about.

It was so bad that when public health inspectors ran the rule over Poulton-le-Fylde 150 years ago they decided Potts Alley was off limits.

Poulton had a rather raunchy image back in those Victorian days.

Being a centre for the vast agricultural lands all about it was the headquarters of itinerant labourers over from Ireland and men tramping the lanes of England. It was a temporary base for pedlars and drifters. Some lived at the Twenty Steps lodging house. Some ended up in the establishment that gave Queens Square the nickname Workhouse Square.

And you can bet they drank in long gone pubs like the Spread Eagle or the Wheatsheaf or bought their ale from beer sellers who brewed at home and traded at the front door.

And they rubbed shoulders with the sailors who traded from Skippool Creek or Wardleys on the River Wyre bringing in flax for the sailcloth mills of Kirkham, tallow and timber and sometimes taking emigrants to a new life in the Americas.

Built around the ancient church of St Chad which probably goes back more than 1,000 years, Poulton grew up as a market town. In its muddy streets everything from livestock to produce was sold.

SQUARE DEALS: Horses lined up for sale (left) in the square at Poulton

TAKING IT EASY: Relaxing beneath the market cross (above) nearly 100 years ago

THE VICARAGE: Built in the early 1800s the tree-shrouded vicarage (top left) was demolished in the 1950s and replaced by the present house on Vicarage Road

# Poulton pans

EARLY VIEW: From St Chad's tower more than a century ago (left) only fields can be seen north of the Golden Ball

NEW AND OLD: Workmen pause in the destruction of the original Thatched House pub with the present building completed behind it

## history in brief

### *Thatch, match and disaster*

DISASTER struck in 1732 during the funeral of a local worthy, Geoffrey Hornby. Torches from his funeral procession set fire to the thatch of buildings in the Market Square and the final bill came to £1,032 – a lottery jackpot figure then.

Churches as far away as Bedfordshire sent what they could afford to help.

### *The Baines endowment*

THE town's most famous son was a woollen merchant called James Baines.

Perhaps his heart was softened by the sight of wretches confined in the stocks or savaged at the whipping post outside his front door in Market Square.

When he died in 1717 his fortune ensured education for the poor. His endowed schools have survived for juniors in Marton and Thornton and as a high school in Hardhorn – all parts of the parish of Poulton in those days.

Later, stagecoaches came through on their way to Blackpool and the magistrates held their court in the Golden Ball.

### *Last stop Poulton*

IN 1840 the railway arrived in Poulton and holidaymakers completed their journey to the sea in horse-drawn wagonettes.

### *World war wrangle*

AFTER a 10 year wrangle about compensation much old property around St Chad's was demolished just before World War 1 to create the streets we can still see.

And Poulton settled down to take it easy for more than half a century until a building boom began to swallow up the surrounding fields in the 60s and the town took on a new image as a trendy suburb of Blackpool.

This is how Blackpool measured up in a map of the 1890s

The Crystal Palace was Blackpool's first public building. It started life in 1837 as the Victoria Promenade. Looking up Victoria Street the house Bank Hey can be seen. It was built in 1846 on the site of the future Winter Gardens

. . . and here's how the beach looked to early Blackpool visitors

This is Great Marton Road – better known now as Central Drive. On the left is the junction with Chapel Street. The white buildings on the left are Bonny's, a farm which provided early accomodation. The date is 1890

NEARLY 400 years ago a clergyman mad history in the Fylde. He was the firs person to write down the word Blackpoo when filling in the record of a baptism at Bispham parish church.

But the Blackpool story had started long befor that day in 1602.

Back in the 12th century the powerful Butle family, Barons of Warrington , controlled th parish of Layton cum Warbreck.

And in 1257 Henry III granted William Butle the right to hold a market every Wednesday i Layton and an annual fair from November 29 t December 1.

This was the first permission granted for market in the whole of the Fylde.

The Butlers built a manor house for some o their family members close to the present da Hollywood Avenue in Layton.

In medieval times there were just a few farm scattered about the present day resort.

Le Pull was a stream draining Marton Moss an Marton Mere into the sea near Manchester Square The peat stained the water and gave rise to th name Black Poole.

The original stream, Spen Dyke, runs in culvert now under Rigby Road.

Around 300 years ago Blackpool got its firs major house. The name Foxhall lives on in famous promenade pub but the original dwelling there was built by Edward Tyldesley, the Squire o Myerscough and son of the famed Sir Thoma Tyldesley who supported the Royalist cause in th Civil War.

Probably the first visitors to Blackpool wer friends of the Tyldesleys who enjoyed riding on th beach, hunting, and plenty of eating and drinking

By 1754 a clergyman staying in Poulton wrot in his diary: "At Blackpool near the sea there ar accommodations for people who come to bathe."

It is said the first hotelier was Edwar Whiteside who lived at Fumblers Hill near th

This painting shows Blackpool as it was in 1750. The building on the left was known as Mr Forshaw's bathing place and the detached building to right was the Lane Ends Hotel at the corner of Church Street

# The early days

present Cocker Square and owned a well full of sweet water.

Another character of those times was Tom the Cobbler who served bread to his guests from his greasy apron.

As the year 1800 drew near Blackpool had four substantial hotels – Bailey's (now the Metropole); Forshaw's (Clifton Arms) Hudson's (on the promenade site of Woolworth's, formerly Lewis's) and Hull's (the site of Pricebusters, formerly Woolworth).

Other accommodation sites included Bonny's (the King Edward pub in Chapel Street) and the original Gynn Inn which then stood nearer the sea beside a creek running inland from the beach.

Healthy fresh air and the growing fashion for sea bathing and even drinking seawater brought the customers rolling in.

A bell rang when it was time for the ladies to bathe and any man caught having a peep was fined a bottle of wine.

The only genuine shows in town were staged in a farm barn.

The resort took a big step forward thanks to Henry Banks who could be called the Father of Blackpool.

In 1819 he bought the Lane Ends estate which included the Lane Ends hotel in Church Street where he had been landlord for nearly 20 years.

His son-in-law Dr John Cocker built the town's first assembly rooms, called the Victoria Promenade, at the north west corner of Victoria Street and Bank Hey Street.

It took visitors from Yorkshire two days to reach Blackpool in those stagecoach days and a whole day to travel from Manchester.

But all that changed in 1840 when the Preston and Wyre railway was built to link Fleetwood with Preston via Poulton.

It was the birth of the day tripper.

Cheap day excursion trains brought in the refugees from the smoke, grime and slums of industrial towns in the north west for fresh air and fun on the Fylde.

One of Blackpool's most famous pubs, The Talbot was built in 1845 at the corner of Talbot Road and Topping Street. Home of a famous bowling competition it was demolished in 1968

## Resort starts its meteoric rise to be top attraction

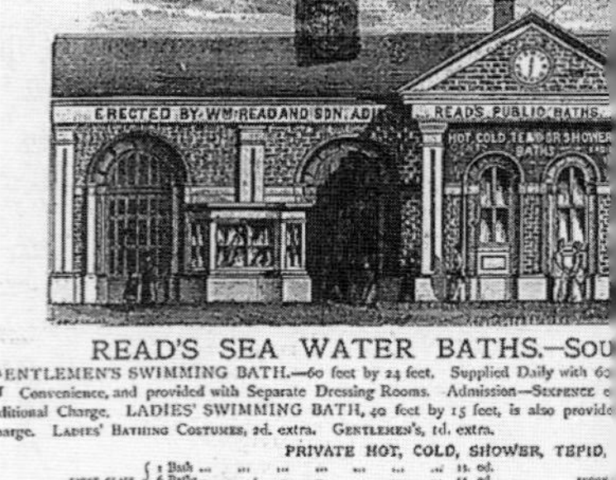


# Going up

AT first there was not a lot for the Victorian visitors to do in Blackpool.

And the cloth capped millworkers were not welcome when North Pier opened in 1863.

It was for "quality" visitors who liked to promenade along its length in their elegant clothes.

But the pier signalled the start of a building boom. In 1867 the Prince of Wales Arcade opened on the future Tower site and the following year the Talbot Road Assembly Rooms and Theatre Royal (now Yates's and Addison's night club) were built along with the present Central Pier then known as South Jetty.

It attracted little trade until 1870 when businessman Robert Bickerstaffe introduced Open Air Dancing for the Working Classes.

Some attractions of those times have completely disappeared.

Only a pub survives today to keep alive the name of the Raikes Hall Gardens. But in 1872 it was surrounded by extensive pleasure gardens. Later there was a lake, racecourse, football and cricket ground, skating rink, aviary, monkey house, ballroom, theatre and switchback ride. By the turn of the century Raikes Hall had lost its popularity in favour of the Golden Mile and the land was sold for building in 1901.

Dr William Cocker became the first Mayor of Blackpool in 1876.

He owned the Tower site and had turned the Prince of Wales arcade into an aquarium which survives in the present day complex.

To combat the British weather, the Winter Gardens company was formed in 1875 to build an indoor promenade and pavilion which opened with great razzmatazz three years later.

In 10 years, Blackpool had doubled its population and in 1877 the Borough Theatre (later known as Feldman's and the Queens, now the site of C and A) was opened.

Then came a slump which hit the town's tourist trade hard.

To boost things Blackpool staged a carnival to showcase its new electric street lighting system. A showpiece was a mock battle

**To combat the tremendous success of the Tower the rival Winter Gardens company looked for a new feature. In 1896 the Gigantic Wheel was constructed at the corner of Adelaide Street and Coronation Street. It was 220 feet high with 30 carriages each holding 30 or more passengers. When the rival Tower Company and Winter Gardens Company became one in 1928 the new board of directors closed down the Big Wheel in October, 1928. Some of the carriages survived locally as garden sheds and even a country cafe. The Big Wheel site is now the Olympia**

**The south-east foundation of the Tower upon which one of the four legs was to rest. The story that the structure was built on bales of Lancashire cotton was only a comment on where the takings at the turnstiles really came from**

Men and women bathed in seperate pools at Read's public baths on Central Promenade. It cost two old pence to hire a woman's costume and one penny for men

Between 1902 and 1905 the present promenade was built between North and South piers. It meant reclaiming 22 acres of land from the sea. Sand to fill in the foundations of the huge project was pumped from the beach at 165 tons an hour. In 1911, when Princess Parade was built around the Metropole, material was carried along the seafront from South Shore on a temporary steam railway called the Sands Express

on the beach between the piers titled A Naval Attack on Blackpool. They reckoned 100,000 people watched the show

Many of Blackpool's most famous attractions were developed in the 1890s.

They were set up to cater for an estimated 250,000 summer visitors.

The most famous was the Tower itself which opened at Whitsuntide 1894 complete with circus and ballroom . It mirrored the success of the Eiffel Tower in Paris which had led to a rash of tower projects in the UK although many never got off the ground. One that did was at New Brighton on the Mersey but Blackpool was the big success despite a rocky start for the Tower Company.

In 1837 Manchester banker Sir Benjamin Heywood built a splendid house called West Hey where Blackpool Tower now stands. Later The Prince of Wales Arcade opened there. Part of those old buildings can be seen to the right of this picture. Only the aquarium survived and is still an important Tower attraction. The foundation stone of the Tower was laid in September 1891 by the local MP Sir Matthew White-Ridley and it opened for business at the Whitsuntide Bank Holiday in 1894

When this photograph was taken from Victoria Street in 1893 the Tower had reached half its final height of 518 feet

To build the Tower contractors Heenan and Froude constructed an electrically-powered crane inside the framework. Each piece of ironwork was made at their Manchester factory

Other key developments around the time:

**1889 Original Opera House at Winter Gardens complex**

**1893 Victoria Pier (now South Pier)**

**1894 Grand Theatre**

**1895 Empire Theatre (later Hippodrome and ABC)**

**Tramway (opened 1885) extended**

**1896 Giant wheel at Winter Gardens**

**Empress Ballroom**

**1897 Golden Mile began when council banned traders from the beach and they re-located in promenade front gardens**

**1899 Tower Pavilion rebuilt as Tower Ballroom Alhambra opened (site of Woolworths) Reopened as the Palace in 1904**

**1898 Fleetwood – Blackpool tramway opened**

**1899 Completion of three-tier promenade between Cocker Square and the Gynn**

**The Banks family kept a shop in School Road, Marton and operated a travelling shop in the district. The business closed in 1980 when Uncle Arthur Banks (left) was killed in an armed robbery at the premises**

**Kitty Ellen Kirkham outside her cottage in Kitty Lane, Marton. It was demolished in 1958**

**The bearded man in this group at the old Shovels pub in Marton was Thomas Wade, a character know as Old Bonk**

**Last orders at the old Shovels pub in Marton**

# Rural retreats

AS Blackpool grew and prospered in the early years of the 20th century, the districts round about stayed rural just as they had been for centuries before .

Bispham was a village centred around its ancient church of All Hallows but the tramway link from Blackpool to Fleetwood encouraged more and more house building north of the Gynn.

The resort reached out to embrace Bispham and drew it inside the boundary of the County Borough of Blackpool which was created in 1904. The same happened to Marton.

But out in the mosslands south east of fast-growing Blackpool, rural life continued for decades. Its flavour still lingers, almost in the shadow of the Tower, despite the spread of bricks and mortar across the fields.

Marton was soon earning a nice living supplying greengroceries to the expanding tourist trade but life was often harsh for the families known as Mossers or Mossogs.

They had more in common in speech, custom and lifestyle with the folk in Pilling or Freckleton than the refugees from the milltowns in Blackpool itself.

When St Nicholas CE primary school was opened in 1874 the Gazette News reported: " It is as though Marton Moss was removed many hundreds of miles from the busy haunts of fashion or of trade. It is intensely rural in its aspect and the inhabitants have a certain primitive look about them."

Children were often kept off school by their parents to help with the planting and harvesting of crops as the school log shows in those early years.

Illness, like scarlet fever and diptheria, was a childhood killer.

Ironically, Marton is now criss-crossed by some of the busiest roads in the Fylde and much of its character has been changed by building development.

But local people are proud of their heritage and keep it alive with exhibitions of memorabilia and the publication of books recalling Marton's rural roots.

Nearly a century has passed since this picture was taken at Blowing Sands, the junction of present-day Common Edge Road and Squires Gate Lane

Bispham village retained its rural flavour well into the 20th century

'Coal Jack' Cardwell and family at Moss House Farm, Moss House Lane in 1905. When an assistant stole the takings from the coal round Jack sold two cows to pay his colliery bill

Pictured about 1900 are market gardener John Parkinson and his wife Emma with their nine children and John's mother Esther. They lived in a cottage in the Blowing Sands area of Marton off present day Squires Gate Lane

West Crescent, St Annes in 1900

Derbe Road in 1895

This 1906 shot recalls the days of trams in Lytham St Annes. It shows what is now Clifton Drive South

WHEN the world celebrated the birth of the new millennium there was an echo of a much earlier age down on the seashore at St Annes.

For the legend goes that the ghostly bell of Kilgrimol sounds beneath the waves on special occasions.

The story tells of a great storm when local people sheltered with the monks of Kilgrimol. The wind and tide wrecked the woodlands which covered much of the Fylde and the sands blew in to turn swamp and forest into farmland.

No doubt old Cuthbert Clifton heard the tale.

His family came from the Kirkham and Westby districts and in 1606 he bought the estate of Lytham from Sir Richard Molyneux of Sefton, in present-day Liverpool, for £4,300.

Lytham was mentioned in the Doomsday book and it changed little over the centuries. The Sand Grown'uns lived in simple cottages wringing a hard living out of the land and a harder one out of the sea.

The present-day St Cuthbert's Church was the third to bear that name. It was built in 1834 and worshippers often walked there across what is now Lowther Gardens but was then called Hungry Moor.

The Cliftons lived in their stately Georgian-style Lytham Hall designed by John Carr of York in the mid 18th century and their tenants sometimes wrangled with residents of Blackpool over grazing rights. One skirmish was known as The Battle of Mad Nook.

Shipwrecks were frequent when the prevailing westerly winds drove helpless sailing craft on to the lee shore. The cargo came in handy. A ship called the Susan Campbell was loaded with barrels of beer while the Annie Cooper carried tobacco. One called the Reuben had some useful timber onboard.

Those were the days when Highbury Road was Twiggy Lane and families were crowded into ancient cottages with names that belied the living conditions inside. One was called Fancy Hall.

For the housewife of the day it was a life of brutal toil bringing up a large family in tough conditions.

Gradually, modernisation crept in.

One rustic was asked what he thought about the advent of electricity.

He was delighted to be rid of the oil lamps and candles and explained: " Tha presses a wart on't wall and th'leet comes on in a bottle on't ceiling."

Long before that, of course, the arrival of the holidaymakers had changed life in Lytham.

Hotels replaced the early cottages and splendid homes were built within sound and sight of the sea.

Like Blackpool, the town drew visitors from the north west from around 1775.

No doubt Lytham would have liked to be the first Fylde coast town with a rail link to Preston but that honour fell to Fleetwood in 1840.

In 1846 Lytham got a branch line to the Preston-Fleetwood track near Kirkham and there was a huge celebration when the locomotive Little Queen ran for the first time.

Like other Lancashire seaside towns Lytham got a large boost from the railway

But a much older form of transport, the river Ribble, swung its silted course away from Lytham Pool in favour of Preston dock leaving Lytham to the fishermen, the leisure sailors and the boatbuilders. It was there they made the craft that starred in Humphrey Bogart's immortal cinema film African Queen.

At Easter, 1865, Lytham pier was opened. Pleasure steamers called there linking with Blackpool, Fleetwood, Southport and further afield.

Lytham boasted a floral hall which was later a roller skating rink and a cinema before it was burned out in 1927. During a gale in 1903 two barges smashed through the iron pier. It closed in 1938 and was scrapped in 1960.

For generations the traditional country lifestyle of the Fylde survived between Lytham and Blackpool.

But that all changed in 1874 when businessman Elijah Hargreaves from Rossendale hit on the idea of developing the town of St Annes

They called it the Opal of the West and we take a closer look at that story in a future edition.

# The wind blown 'uns

You can still recognise Park St Lytham, today from this 1900 shot

Idlers in The Square, St Annes 100 years ago

Ancient Lytham Mill (left) was a landmark in the days when the place was a sleepy fishing village

The Square in the early days of St Annes (below). Garden Street is on the right as you look towards the sea. Towards the centre of the picture is the Chaseley Hotel, now part of the town hall complex

An artist's impression of Fleetwood as envisaged by Decimus Burton who was hired to design it

There is neither a statue nor memorial erected in Fleetwood to the visionary man who created the town and gave it his name. Sir Peter Hesketh Fleetwood lost most of his fortune in the venture and his ancestral home became Rossall School

# A Victorian

AT first it was going to be called Wyreton. If Sir Peter Hesketh Fleetwood's original scheme had gone according to plan the geography of the North Fylde area would look a lot different today.

Instead the Victorian new town which the Squire of Rossall dreamed of creating from a greenfield site was not Wyreton on the banks of the river near Thornton but the port and resort of Fleetwood by the sea at the mouth of the river.

The Squire was a wealthy man who lived at Rossall Hall, the site of the present-day public school. He owned vast tracts of land in Lancashire including parts of what is now Blackpool, Preston and Southport.

But he lost much of his fortune making his new town dream come true.

He had been MP for Preston, was well known in London society, and was a favourite of the young Queen Victoria.

He shrewdly realised how important railways would become and set up the Preston and Wyre railway company to bring the tracks from Preston to the Fylde coast in 1840.

He hired a famed architect of the day, Decimus Burton, to design the new town and he produced the elegant stone structures which survive today. The best example is the North Euston Hotel with its gracious curving facade. Queens Terrace, now an apartment complex, is another, while lesser-known examples are to be found in locations like Dock Street.

Work began on the Fleetwood site in 1835 but prior to that Sir Peter even got so far as laying a foundation for Wyreton.

Even the keenest of local historians – like Mrs Bill Curtis who has written much about Sir Peter and his schemes – cannot pin down

Liverpool-based maritime artist John Herdman was invited by Sir Peter Hesketh Fleetwood to stay at Rossall Hall while he painted a series on the new town of Fleetwood. Cargo, packed in barrels, was unloaded on the beach before any quays were built and manhandled to waiting carts

Sailing trawlers called Smacks tied up at the Stone Quay beside the present-day P and O shipping compound. They laid the foundation for Fleetwood to become the country's third biggest fishing port

In winter time conditions on Fleetwood docks could match the deck of an Arctic trawler but a sense of humour and comradeship kept men going in harsh conditions

# How one man's urban dream moved downriver new town

the shift of opinion that moved the location to the coast.

But part of it must have been pressure from Sir Peter's wealthy pals in the textile trade. They wanted a port to handle shipments of cotton, timber and grain. Decimus Burton tucked it away behind the town.

Kind hearted Sir Peter knew what life was like in the slums of industrial Preston and other mill towns and he wanted workers there to enjoy the fun and fresh air of the coast. The railway let them do that at Fleetwood. But it was the growth of entertainment facilities in Blackpool that drew the big crowds away and left Fleetwood a much quieter style of seaside holiday town.

When it came to housing the workers Sir Peter insisted on wide streets and decent homes which have stood the test of time.

But his grand design proved too grand even for his deep coffers and he was undoubtedlyduped by some he trusted with the practical side of his ideas.

While Wyreton upriver turned into the industrial hamlet of Burn Naze, Wyre Dock at Fleetwood handled the biggest cargo ships of the day until it was forced into decline by the growth of Preston docks, the Manchester Ship Canal and competition from Liverpool.

Around the turn of the century fishing sailed in to save the day. Always a traditional local industry, it boomed as steam trawlers switched from Hull and Grimsby and later from other ports like Milford Haven.

The industry grew to dominate life in Fleetwood for decades until its collapse around 20 years ago.

Now, after years of decline, Fleetwood is beginning to re-invent itself with a new look for the 21st century.

Fleetwood beach in 1902. The building on the left is the railway station

Sail & Steam: Wyre Dock, Fleetwood about 1890 when cargo trade was booming

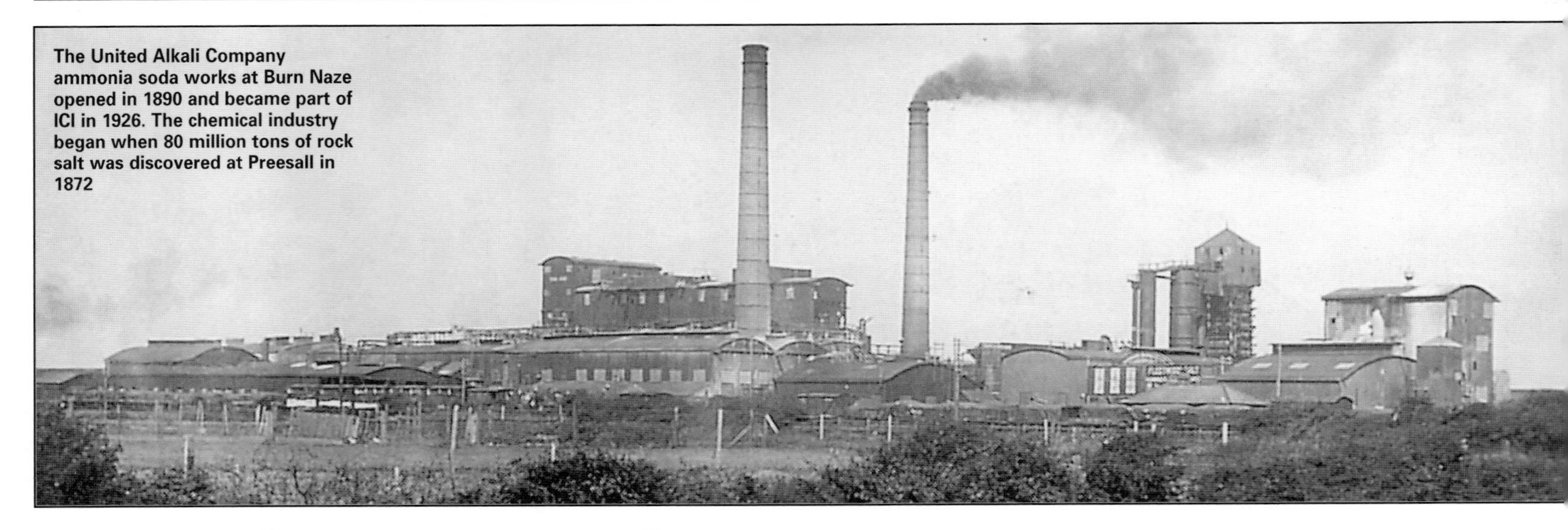

The United Alkali Company ammonia soda works at Burn Naze opened in 1890 and became part of ICI in 1926. The chemical industry began when 80 million tons of rock salt was discovered at Preesall in 1872

# The Chemic men

Complete with top hat and morning suit landlord Smethhurst of the Gardeners Arms prepares to join the Thornton gala procession in 1912

THE Chemic men were a tough bunch. When they were on night shift at the Thornton Alkali works they sometimes walked along the railway line to wet their whistles at the Bay Horse pub.

And Fleetwood publicans did a roaring trade shipping barrels of beer into the growing district of Burn Naze to eager new customers before the local pub was built.

A worker in 1901 recalled: "There were Irishmen, Poles, ex-public school boys and shabby, genteel alcoholics along with a nucleus of skilled and experienced men from Widnes."

Conditions were appalling and gas victims were often walked around the yard until they could breathe properly again. The pay was 2p an hour for an 84-hour session.

The impact of the giant factory shook Thornton awake from generations of slumber beside the river Wyre.

Despite the march of bricks and mortar you can still get a feel for that old, rural atmosphere in the lanes down near the river at Stanah.

The nearby 70-foot tower of Marsh Mill stands witness to the days when the Fylde was known as Windmill Land.

More than 40 windmills once studded the plain which was a huge granary. Farmers were more interested in corn then than they are today in milk, eggs and bacon.

Marsh Mill was built in 1794 by Bold Fleetwood Hesketh, the Squire of Rossall and the millstones kept on grinding until 1922.

A chequered career followed including spells as a cafe and a false teeth factory and no one wanted to know when the mill was auctioned in 1950. It might have been demolished but the council saved the day with a cheque for £2,250. Enthusiastic volunteers preserved the machinery and now it's a tourist attraction.

Built in 1794, Marsh Mill (below) stands 70 feet tall and ground corn until 1922. Later it was a false teeth factory and a cafe until it was revamped at the heart of the Marsh Mill village

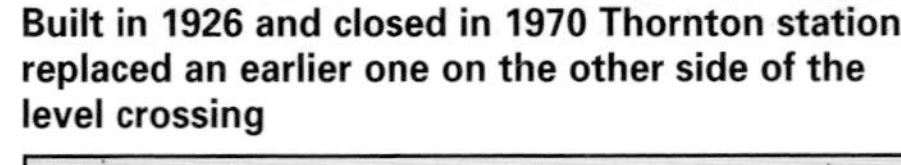

Built in 1926 and closed in 1970 Thornton station replaced an earlier one on the other side of the level crossing

Now occupied by Hastings Road, Thornton, Enderley Gardens was a favourite spot for afternoon teas where visitors admired the shrubs and flowers

Starting life as a house called Eryngo Lodge, Cleveleys Hydro (left) became an elegant seaside hotel. A chauffer-driven Rolls Royce met guests at Thornton station

Cleveleys seafront looked more like a building site at the turn of the century

# and Tom Lumb

In 1906 a competition showcased the latest in house design at Cleveleys and helped to put the place on the map

UNTIL Thornton's industrial revolution there was very little to write a postcard home about in Cleveleys just up the road.

They say the name came from a publican called Cleveley whose ancient inn stood at the top of present-day Slinger Road. It must have been a wild old spot and may have been a smuggler's den linked to the Isle of Man.

In 1783 the landlord advertised in Manchester that he catered for visitors by the sea. But until the turn of the century Cleveleys was just a few cottages and farms.

The man who changed all that was Tom Gallon Lumb.

The Manchester-born engineer planned and supervised the building of the tramway from Fleetwood to Blackpool. He was Mayor of Blackpool but never lived there.

His home was The Towers off present day West Drive and reached by a footpath with seven stiles from the trams. He and his friends went out hunting, shooting and fishing in the district with a gamekeeper and you can bet the Chemic men did a bit of poaching too.

Tom Lumb dreamed of a City of the Fylde uniting the whole coast and he later campaigned for Blackpool to swallow up Thornton-Cleveleys and Poulton.

He greatly admired the new-style architecture of Letchworth Garden City.

And when he and his colleagues bought thousands of acres of land in the Fleetwood and Thornton Cleveleys area they brought in the architect Sir Edwin Lutyens, the designer of modern Whitehall.

In 1906 an exhibition was staged with prizes for the best home designs.

You can see the results around West Drive, Stockdove Way, Whiteside Way and Cleveleys Avenue.

And the crowds who flocked to see these modern homes were charged sixpence each.

Many came by train and although the station was in Thornton it was at first named Cleveleys. Plans for a branch line to Cleveleys itself never happened.

The exhibition put the growing seaside town on the map.

In 1906 there were 850 houses and less than 4,000 people. By 1937 that had grown to 4,252 houses and nearly 13,000 people.

Cleveleys was trendy and it had a thriving holiday industry.

A showpiece was the Cleveleys Hydro fashioned from an old house called Eringo Lodge on the shore at the Blackpool end of the town.

When it was demolished in the 1950s, local historian Ralph Smedley was a local policeman and supervised the use of dynamite by the demolition men.

He recalls: " The walls were so thick they had to be blasted. Little did I think in those days that in the future I would be collecting pictures and researching its story."

Cleveleys Hydro was home to hundreds of civil servants driven out of London in World War Two. Many stayed on at the new government offices of Norcross and Warbreck Hill.

Ralph recalls: "Many were billeted with local landladies and they got 10s 6d (52 and a half pence) for their keep so they called them the half guinea people."

The Savoy complex on Victoria Road West housed a ballroom and cinema as welll as a cafe and various shops

# Over the river

WHEN THE Over Wyre district was a sleepier place than it is now and Red Ribble buses connected it with the outside world the conductor had to collect two sets of fares from the passengers.

First he sold the tickets.

Then, as the bus approached the Shard toll bridge he asked for "Bridge Pennies" to pay the toll collector.

The old iron bridge was built in 1864 at a cost of £13,000 but people had been crossing the Wyre at that spot for centuries before that.

The bridge was built at the site of Aldwath – the old ford that linked with Kate's Pad which was a trackway of logs through the Over Wyre area.

Later there was a ferry and Civil War troops used it.

Probably named from the Celtic word gwyr, meaning pure and fresh, the river Wyre is born in the wild fells north east of Garstang.

Before the M6 was built Garstang was slap bang on the north-south route through western England. Neolithic tribes, Celtic people, Roman legions, the Jacobite rebels of Bonnie Prince Charlie all marched through Garstang's streets and enjoyed varying degrees of hospitality from its residents. Greenhalgh Castle was one of the ruins that Oliver Cromwell 'refurbished'.

Now Garstang remains a busy market down by the river and a great centre for exploring the surrounding countryside. Its streets are cleaner now than in 1805 when 3,000 head of Scottish and Irish cattle were driven through the town.

The Wyre flows through St Michaels. The village church was old when William the Conqueror arrived in England.

In the last 30 years the atmosphere of Over Wyre centres like Hambleton, Stalmine and Preesall has changed. Hundreds of new homes have been built for commuters who want to live in the country and people who want to retire there.

But step off the beaten track a little and you can still feel the atmosphere of an older, rural way of life which was once widespread throughout the whole of the Fylde – white cottages, old dialect and all.

And it's a heritage showcased in a fascinating way by the Fylde Country Life Preservation Society in their living museum at Farmer Parr's Animal World in Fleetwood.

Farming is a way of life in Over Wyre but there was a time when the men of Preesall spent their days underground mining salt. The vast underground salt beds gave life to the chemical industry at Thornton across the river.

**Garstang's Thursday Market is still popular. Here's how it looked in the High Street in 1900**

**Moss Cottages (left) are still standing in Moss House Lane, Pilling. The tall lady was Mrs Betty Isles**

**Progress came to Preesall in 1906 (below) with piped water. This is the switch-on ceremony**

**The Pilling Pig railway which ran between Knott End & Garstang**

**A view (below) looking across the old Shard toll bridge to Over Wyre**

Mrs Ellen Townsend was postmistress of Warton for 60 years and retired aged 69

Workers at Balderstone Mill, Freckleton before World War I. Some wear clean white aprons known as brats while the boys have clogs on their feet

# Heading South . . .

THERE have been many plans for dams and bridges across the River Ribble to link the Fylde with its old holiday town rival, Southport.

But there was a time when hardy travellers needed no bridge to cross the river.

Guides Lane, Warton led to Guides House – a pub from which a guide would escort parties through a ford at low tide to Hesketh Bank.

But when Preston docks were developed training walls were built in the river to keep the channel clear of silt and the detour through Preston became the norm.

Long after that the Ribble bank was home to a fleet of houseboats.

They finally disappeared when nearby land was requisitioned by the Air Ministry in 1940 for the building of Warton Aerodrome – now the British Aerospace complex.

There'll be more about that in a later edition of these supplements.

The same area yielded the plant known as Poor Man's Asparagus – the Lancashire delicacy Samphire – much loved by the old country folk of the Fylde.

The Ribble has played a vital part in the life of Freckleton and Warton.

Historians believe Romans from Chester landed there in their first exploration of the Fylde by boat.

In Freckleton, Bunker Street gets its name from the days when coal from Wigan came across the Ribble in barges and was dumped there for collection.

The Ship Inn nearby is thought to be the oldest pub in the Fylde with a licence from 1677. Freckleton had eight pubs when the population was 900.

Boat building and repair were local industries and commercial fishermen once took salmon from the river.

An ancient toll road linked the villages with Preston crossing the marshes by Newton and Clifton.

One of the most ancient features was the Warton peg mill – an early windmill made of wood. Every time the wind changed the miller had to swing the whole structure back into the wind. The wooden structure arrived from Rufford across the Ribble in 1717 but legend says it originated far away in the Fens.

Changes came slowly.

When the parish council discussed the installation of streetlights one worthy remarked: " There's enough leets in Warton – trouble is they're all in Townsend's garage."

Balderstone Mill was probably Lancashire's most westerly example of the cotton trade.

It closed in 1980 after a century of weaving with 320 looms.

Memories live on with Mill View and Balderstone Road street names for houses on the site.

The farmer and his wife: Mr and Mrs Richard Bickerstaffe of School Farm, Bank Lane

Baby Mary Sumner with her mother at Blackfield End Farm, Church Road, Warton

BLACKPOOL
LMS
JOY FLIGHTS
by Machines of the
RAILWAY AIR SERVICES
TO-DAY
5/- & 10/-
from
STANLEY PARK AERODROME
NO ADMITTANCE WITHOUT AUTHORITY
NO SMOKING
PROGRESS
S.S. MINDEN BLACKPOO
MOTHERS TRY PRITCHARD'S TEETHING POWDERS
SUNLIGHT SOAP
PALATINE BAZAAR
GOOD FITTING CORSETS
ALLINSON'S
GAZETTE AND NEWS
FOR BLACKPOOL AND FYLDE DISTRICT

Chapter Two

# The Twenties

# Taking shape

THE biggest single development on the Fylde coast in the early years of this century was the huge civil engineering project to create the modern promenade along Central Beach.

Work began in 1902 and it took 170 workmen three years to complete the awesome task of recapturing 22 acres of land from the sea.

This epic picture was taken as the work neared completion.

It is featured in the excellent book: Circular Tour – Seaside Pleasure Riding By Tram by Brian Turner of St Annes.

On the right are houses which later became the Golden Mile and the narrow width of the old promenade – complete with trams – can easily be seen.

To fill in the vast expanse of new promenade thousands of tons of sand were used.

On the left a constant stream of horse drawn carts can be seen coming up the slade – the slope from the beach – with cargoes of infill.

But much of it was pumped into the workings through equipment mounted on a specially-built jetty just south of North Pier.

The pump was powered by electricity from the tramway supply and could shift 700 tons an hour.

The work was finished by Easter, 1905 but it was not until Whitsuntide that the tidying up was complete and the Talbot Square tramway junction opened. This made it possible to take a circular tram tour via Marton. In those days the lines ran inland through the resort.

During World War One Squires Gate became the King's Lancashire military convalescent hospital. The structure in the middle of the picture is left over from the days of the Clifton Park racecourse. The area is now Blackpool Airport

Time for a trip to the cookhouse for these soldiers in training at Weeton Camp

During World War One the Blackpool district was a major army training area.
Here's how Weeton Camp looked in those days

# ...but as the world prepares to

AS the 20th Century dawned, Blackpool continued to build on its growing reputation as a major holiday resort.

The promenade, as it appears now between North and South Piers, was constructed by reclaiming 22 acres from the sea.

Rail services to the resort were improved to cope with the growing number of visitors.

When World War One broke out Blackpool kept the home fires burning in three different ways.

As usual the resort provided much needed rest and recreation for the workers of Lancashire including the thousands of women who found themselves in a new role as they stepped into the shoes of men who had joined the forces.

Secondly, Blackpool – and other parts of the Fylde coast – were used for military training.

The area had long links with the military going back to the days of the militia – the forerunner of the territorial army

These volunteers had come to the Fyld coast for years for annual camps and trainin exercises.

During World War One, this training too on a deadly new image with 14,000 troop billeted in the town.

Central Beach, as we know it today, was pieced together nearly a century ago

# Other key dates from the early years:

**1904:** Blackpool becomes a County Borough with its own emergency services and education department
**1909:** Historic aviation meeting at Squires Gate
**1912:** First static illuminations when Princess Louise opens Princess Parade
**1913:** Record breaking successful holiday season

*After the war:*

**1923:** World's largest open air bath opens at South Shore
**1925:** Completion of Colonnades and seafront improvements at North Shore
**1926:** Opening of new South Promenade and Stanley Park
**1927:** Huge crowds see total eclipse of the sun. Later Fleetwood devastated by flooding
**1928:** Merger of Tower Company and Winter Gardens triggers demolition of Big Wheel and building of Olympia
**1929:** Municipal aerodrome opens at Stanley Park

World War One trenches were dug on land off Watson Road by Army recruits as part of their basic training – and later opened to the public

Soldiers from the temporary hospital at Squires Gate showed the public what life was like in the Blackpool version of the trenches

The modern roadway of Yeadon Way runs along the embankment in this picture. When it was taken – more than 80 years ago – the route carried the train track from Central Station

# go to war, Blackpool must adapt

On land in Watson Road, South Shore, trenches were dug just like those in France and Belgium – but without the real-life horrors of the front.

Later these model fortifications were open to the public. Today, the site is Watson Road Park near the junction with St Annes Road.

Meanwhile the harsh reality of war reached into Blackpool.

The Clifton park racecourse – an unsuccessful project on the site of today's Blackpool airport at Squires Gate – was earmarked as a hospital.

It took 15 weeks to build rows of huts and modify some of the racecourse buildings. The bill came to £26,000.

The Kings Lancashire Military Convalescent Hospital catered for men who were recovering from their injuries but would be fit for active service again in six to eight weeks.

It closed in 1919 by which time nearly 6,000 officers and almost 32,000 other ranks had been treated there.

Then the site became a rehabilitation unit where the maimed survivors of the conflict learned skills to help them cope – from the use of artificial limbs to practical craft training for a job. It closed in 1924.

**At the 1910 Blackpool Flying Carnival aviation pioneer A V Roe (extreme right) flew his triplane past Layton Hawes Farm (left) which stood on airport land opposite Abbey Road. Above he is on the right showing off his plane at the 1909 aviation meeting**

# Those

**RAF planes (left) at the Blackpool Air Pageant in 1928. It was not long into the history of aviation before Blackpool was offering pleasure trips (right) and queues formed for joy flights at Stanley Park (below)**

**Budding pilots learned to fly from Blackpool in planes like this Avro 548A**

**The scene at Squires Gate (left) just before the outbreak of World War One, when it was the Clifton Park racecourse. By the 1920s the resort could boast the latest in transport at the new Stanley Park airport pictured above**

Intrepid pilots at the 1910 Blackpool meeting line up on the rear of a horse-drawn trailer

Staying aloft by good luck as much as good management, a flimsy aircraft from the 1909 show

One horsepower was enough to get the early flying aces on their way

# magnificent men

FLYING in Blackpool took off early – just a few years after the Wright Brothers in America discovered the trick.

But one of the most important flights ever made in the resort was in 1927 when air ace Sir Alan Cobham touched down at Squires Gate.

He had targetted 100 towns and encouraged them to build municipal airports.

Blackpool was a natural choice because it was one of the first places in Britain where aircraft were flown.

The town first took off in 1902 when astonished crowds watched a gas-filled airship take off from Rigby Road on a flight to Leyland.

Bright and breezy Blackpool was quick to cash in on the new wonder of the age.

Just seven years later, in 1909, the resort staged an aviation meeting.

France was leading the way in European flying and, with backing from newspaper tycoon Lord Northcliffe, the council took a bagful of cash to Paris and signed up some top fliers.

They also had a long running row with Doncaster where the council staged a similar meeting on the race-course famous for the St Leger

Blackpool's chosen site was Squires Gate Fields – 40 acres of grassland south of the town and owned by the Clifton family of Lytham Hall.

Those Magnificent Men in their Flying Machines had the impact of modern-day space travel and attracted crowds of 200,000 prepared to brave appalling weather for a glimpse of the action.

Cash registers jingled and someone advertised a cure for Aviation Headache – caused by staring at the sky.

Frenchman Hubert Latham, known as the Storm King, provided a death-defying display in bad weather one afternoon . . . so as not to disapoint guests of Squire Clifton he had met the evening before!

"Come down, you splendid fool" chorused the worthies from the grandstand. They were relatives of the Russian royal family.

The Brits, represented by the legendary A V Roe were defeated by technical problems rather than lack of courage.

Nevertheless aviation in Blackpool went on the back burner and the Squires Gate site became the Clifton Park racecourse from 1911 to 1914 before a military hospital was built.

In the 20s pleasure trip flying began again and In 1928 the Blackpool Air Pageant was staged.

It featured displays by 80 RAF planes. These included simulated dogfights and bombing raids using bags of flour.

Boys from Arnold School played the role of rebel tribesmen who received a severe thrashing from the RAF while Blackpool TA volunteers manned anti-aircraft guns.

Other highlights included stunning upside down aerobatics from Gerhard Fiesler, a World war One German fighter pilot and a demonstration of his wares by parachute designer Leslie Irvin whose work saved thousands of Allied airmen in World War Two.

Then, after Sir Alan Cobham's visit, local worthy Sir John Bickerstaffe agreed to sell land beside the newly-developed Stanley Park to the council.

And there Blackpool's municipal airport was built for £82,000. There was already talk of a white elephant when it opened in 1929.

But it was used as a stopover in the Kings Cup Air Race which had been instigated by George V.

Down at Squires Gate other attractions included a mini TT course for motor cycle racing and a forerunner of modern speedway.

But plans for a zoo at Squires Gate were rejected in 1929 and so was a £250,000 scheme to build a Roman-style sports arena.

Despite complaints about noise and Sunday flying aviation continued at both sites as the 30s dawned.

*No one knew then that the airman's finest hour was still to come.*

Flying ace Sir Alan Cobham leaves Squires Gate in his De-Havilland 50. He came for talks about the new Stanley Park airfield . . . and nearly crashed on landing

# Let there be

## They Called It The Clown Hall

### "Where are the other Fifty?": Joke and, its Sequel

**There has been comedy behind the scenes of this year's Illuminations.**

IT is concerned with the comic tableaux which are to add humour to this year's spectacle. The result has been a secret meeting of Councillors, representations to the Mayor, and a hurried removal of two figures from the Town Hall front.

THE Men behind the Lights are always on the look-out for something new, and they decided to replace the golfers on the front of the Town Hall with something fresh.

**They chose—two clowns!**

And so the juggling figures with their comic noses and faces duly took shape, and very novel they looked on the front of Blackpool Civic Hall, overlooking Talbot Square.

Then there was a ripple of uneasiness. People could be seen asking the City Fathers a question in the street. And the City Fathers would either grin or laugh outright, or go red in the face, or white with rage, according to their varied temperaments. The question was:

**"Where are the other fifty?"**

There was a rumour that Doodles and Fiery Jack protested against amateurs getting so much publicity for a rival show.

Worse still, people began to call it "The Clown Hall."

Out of the fifty-two members of the Town Council there were several who did not relish this clown joke. *Something*, said they, *must be done.*

A leading Alderman last night presided over an indignation meeting of councillors, and as a result urgent representations were made to the Mayor, who agreed that *something must be done.*

It has been. Men worked into the late hours of last night, under the twinkling stars and a moon which seemed to be wearing a faint grin, removing the civic figures.

To-day the fair face of the Town Hall is unsullied by any unseemly jest. Instead of the clowns, the erstwhile occupants of the Town Hall front are returning. The place of honour is again occupied by golfers, who are, of course, the soul of respectability.

To dedicate the Civic Palace to golf, that refuge of statesmen and tired business chiefs, is one thing.

But clowns—well, no. The Blackpool Council's reputation would not stand that. So Punchinello did what is vulgarly termed a "midnight flit" to Bispham.

**—This Is Official!**

Here is the cream of the joke. To-day, "The Evening Gazette" asked for an official explanation of all these mysterious doings. And this was it:

*"There is so much light in Talbot Square that the figures were not shown off to advantage, and they have been removed to a darker background at Bispham."*

Well, well!

**Waves**

**Royal visitor the Duke of Kent (above) switched on the lights in 1937. Watching is Town Clerk Trevor Jones**

**There were red faces at the Town Hall the year two clowns were displayed as part of the Illuminations – on the front of the Talbot Square building. The figures were moved to Bispham after locals laughed at the councillors' expense . . .**

BLACKPOOL Illuminations bega to take shape as a moder attraction in 1925 after the reso had remained in darkness for yea through World War One and its aftermat

It seems hard to believe now but whe holidaymakers first tripped the Ligh fantastic in Blackpool they stood in awe just EIGHT arc lamps.

This artificial sunshine, as it w described, became a crowdpuller in 18 and the basic idea is still much the sa 120 years later.

But, it has to be said, the style, sca and sheer professionalism of the 19 version will have little in keeping wi that first electric lighting experime

Gone are the days when the ligh went out as the tide came in because water leaked in to the ca iron wiring pipes on the seafront

These days hi-tech has replace high tide as the main talking poi of the annual Illuminatio extravaganza.

The nearest to modern-d displays was staged on Prince Parade in May 1912 to ma the first royal visit Blackpool.

Princess Louise officia opened the new section the promenade subsequently known Princess Parade.

As part of th celebrations for this even the Blackpool electric engineer was instructe to decorate the Prom what was then a nov fashion with festoons garland lamps.

About 10,000 bul were used and t results were

**Mr Blackpool himself, and one of the period's most popular entertainers, organist Reginald Dixon kept the crowd happy in 1956**

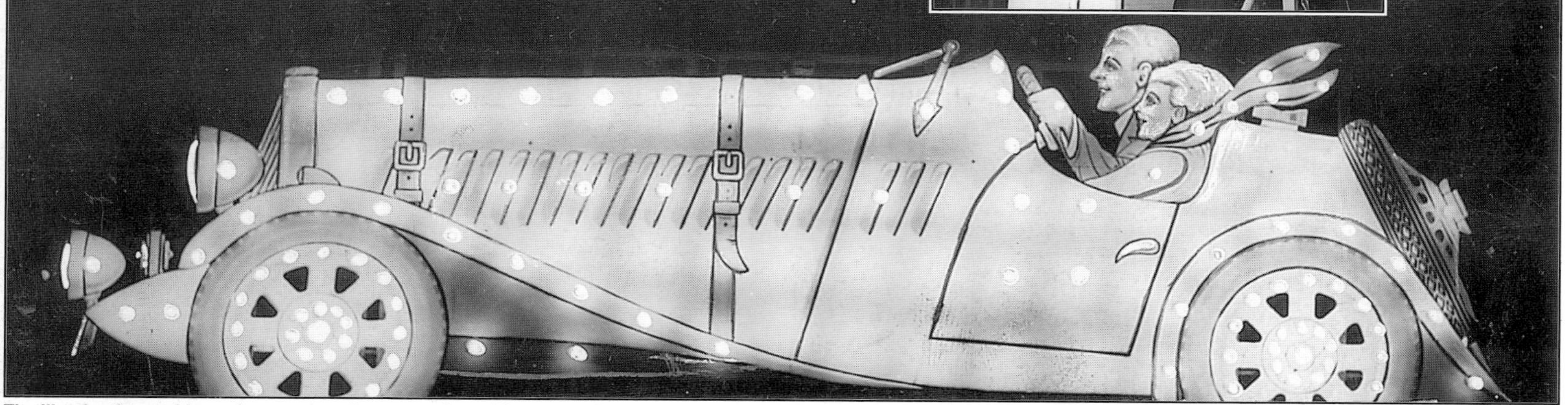

**The illuminations tableaux have come a long way since this car was featured more than 60 years ago.The handsome Gondola tram on the facing page appeared when the lights came on again in 1949**

impressive that the local chamber of trade and other business people in the town persuaded the council to stage these Lights again in September of that year.

Thousands of people visited the resort to see the Illuminations and the event was judged a commercial success.

In 1913 the council was again encouraged to stage the Princess Parade lights as an after-season event in September.

The response from the public was nothing short of astonishing but hopes of building on this success were shortlived with the outbreak of the First World War the following year.

Illuminations were back in 1925 on a more ambitious scale with lights festooned along the Promenade from Manchester Square to Cocker Square.

It was appreciated that Blackpool Illuminations were a worthwhile tourist attraction and they continued to be staged annually for many years.

By 1932 animated tableaux had been added and these were erected on the cliffs linking North Shore and Bispham. The length of the Lights was extended to its present length – just under six miles – starting at Squires Gate and finishing at Red Bank Road.

In 1939, although the Illuminations were ready for staging, they were prevented by the outbreak of the Second World War.

There was a full-scale preview on August 31, complete with a giant searchlight sweeping wide from the Tower top. By the next night the blackout had been enforced and the only colour to be seen was inside hotels and boarding houses where landladies had coloured their light bulbs with Dolly blue.

Even after the war had finished there were restrictions on the use of fuel, and decorative lighting, such as the Illuminations, remained prohibited.

The austere climate of post-war Britain meant the Lights did not come on again until 1949 when Anna Neagle pressed the switch.

Even then there was a 'cliffhanger' as the council waited for government permission to burn the required amount of electricity.

The scale, density and content of the Lights has improved year by year and the development of new ideas and new themes is continuous.

In particular the use of electronic controllers, fibre optics, non-neon and lasers has added a new dimension to the fabulous autumn crowdpuller.

The Pleasure Beach area in 1905 when gypsies still camped nearby

# From this

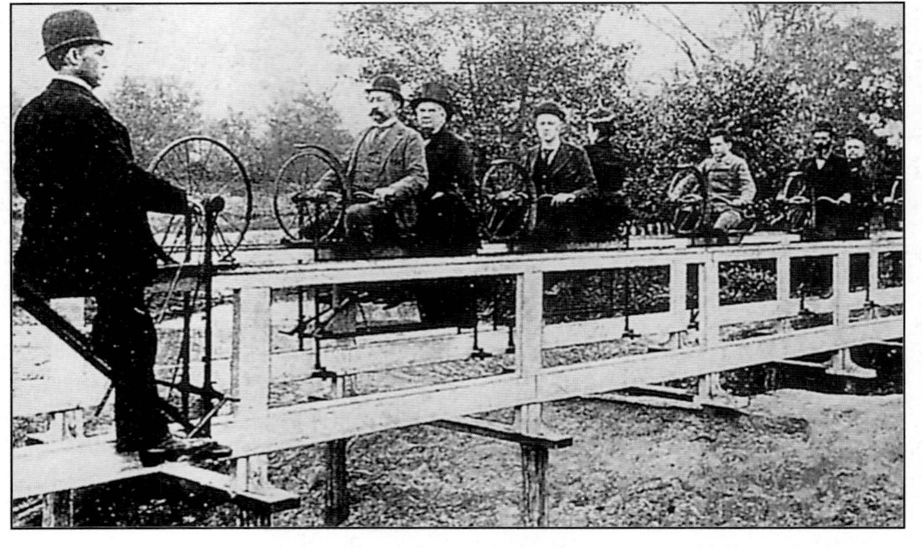

Victorian visitors (above) enjoyed the Bicycle Railroad. It was the first ride on the Pleasure Beach site operated by William Bean and was invented in Mount Holly, New Jersey, and used there as public transport

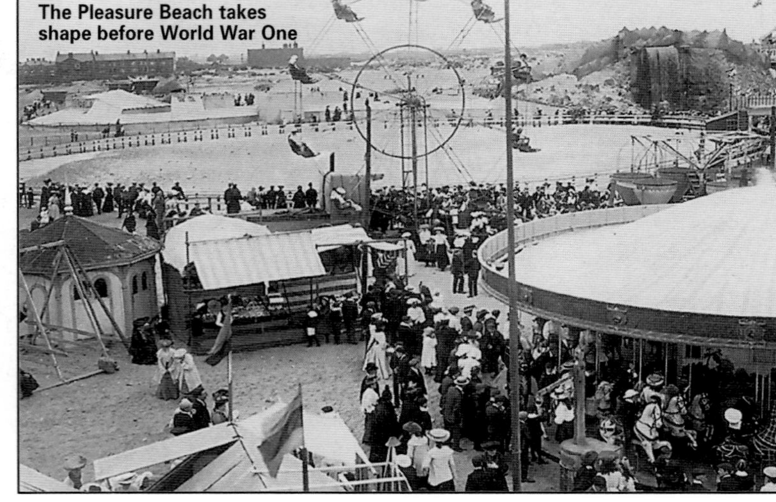

The Pleasure Beach takes shape before World War One

IN 1929 one of Blackpool's founding fathers died on a cruise which he had hoped would improve his failing health.

The tremendous energy and business skill of Chelsea-born William Bean had fuelled a world-famous attraction.

He discovered amusement parks when he went to America and was impressed with places like New York's Coney Island.

By 1896 he was operating a ride among the sand dunes of South Shore.

So Blackpool Pleasure Beach began more than a century ago with an American-designed attraction – the Hotchkiss Bicycle Railroad – where travellers "pedalled" furiously with their hands to move around an oval track.

This early form of white knuckle fever gripped the resort and things have continued roller coaster-style since.

*But with many more ups than downs.*

It all started out on sandhills and today remains on that same South Shore site, albeit now dwarfed by the man-made steel mountain that is the Big One.

The Joy Wheel, the Bowl Slide and even the world's first Rainbow Wheel are all long gone. But each new arrival has been at the cutting edge of leisure technology.

Amazingly, two of the earliest attractions still survive, Sir Hiram Maxim's Flying Machine from 1904 and the 1922 Noah's Ark, given a new lease of life since empty space beneath became the fun park's entrance.

The attraction remains in the hands of the family whose vision saw the Watson's Estate grow beyond anyone's imagination – even those businessmen who sank their money into the famous Tower.

William Bean, who became an Alderman on Blackpool town council, was grandfather of the present managing director Geoffrey Thompson.

Before the turn of the century the sar dunes near the Starr Inn an neighbouring farmland owned by th Watson family had become the home temporary booths and stalls, fairgrour rides and a gypsy encampment.

Various operators ran attractio there and William Bean worked for time with businessman John Outhwai to expand operations at South Shore. I 1904 William Bean owned the land ar the Pleasure Beach began to grow.

With Bean's death in 1929 ma agement was taken over by the founde son-in-law, Oxford graduate Leona Thompson, then newly-married to Dor who, at 96, remains chairman.

She has travelled most of the ride visits the site most days and has a sha memory stretching back to the ear years of this century.

The outbreak of war in 19 frustrated plans for expansion but, at th Home Office's request, the par remained open at weekends all ye round.

Expansion continued throughout th 60s and 70s with new rides proving constant attraction: The Cableway, Ali in Wonderland, Monorail, Log Flum Monster, Astroswirl and Gold Mine.

Geoffrey Thompson took control o his father's death 23 years ago and h first new ride was the Steeplechase, horseback roller coaster.

Many others have followed, eve upward to the world's tallest, faste rollercoaster, the Big One, and later th PlayStation.

The new Millennium saw the late attraction opened on the site of th Fun House (destroyed by fire in 199 called Valhalla a spectacular state-o the-art dark ride guaranteed to brin in even more white knuckle thr seekers.

The old Casino building (below) made way for the present day Art Deco design by Joseph Emberton

The scenic railway in 1907

# . . . to this

By the end of the 1920s the Pleasure Beach looked like this. On the left is the original Casino building and behind it the zig zags of the Virginia Reel. A handsome array of vintage trams are ferrying crowds along the Prom

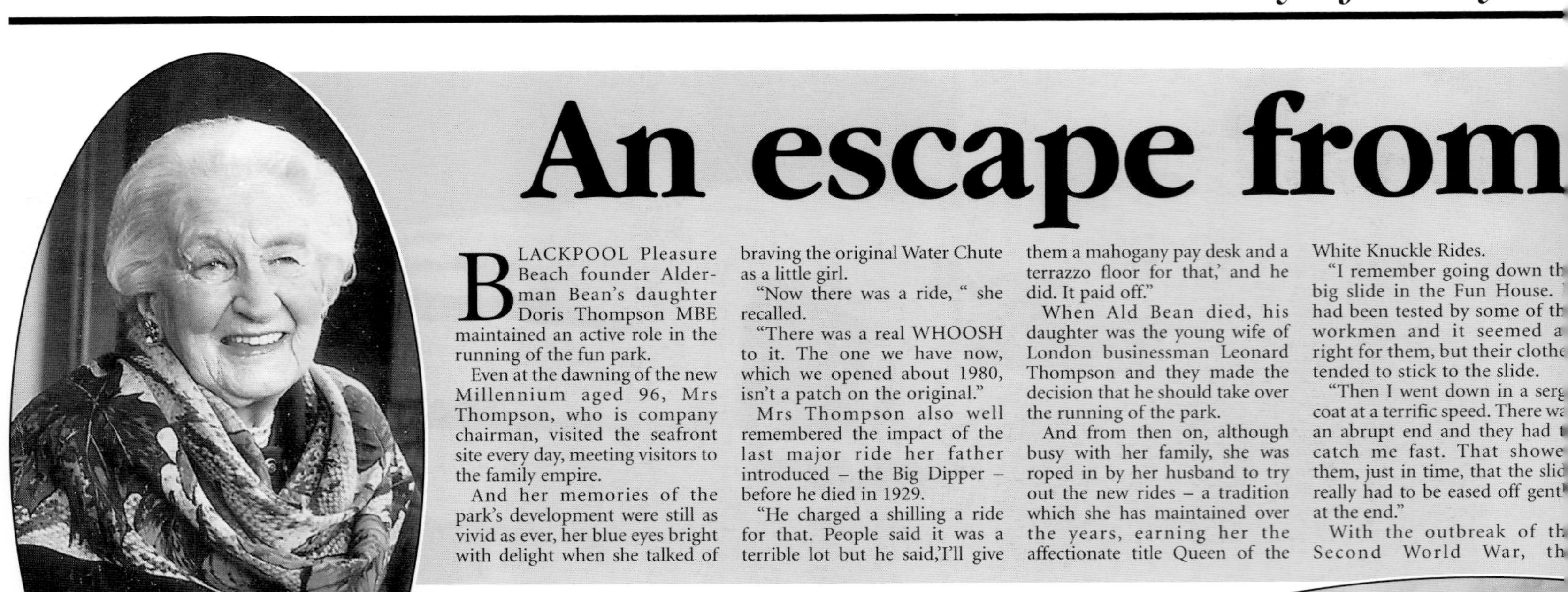

# An escape from

BLACKPOOL Pleasure Beach founder Alderman Bean's daughter Doris Thompson MBE maintained an active role in the running of the fun park.

Even at the dawning of the new Millennium aged 96, Mrs Thompson, who is company chairman, visited the seafront site every day, meeting visitors to the family empire.

And her memories of the park's development were still as vivid as ever, her blue eyes bright with delight when she talked of braving the original Water Chute as a little girl.

"Now there was a ride, " she recalled.

"There was a real WHOOSH to it. The one we have now, which we opened about 1980, isn't a patch on the original."

Mrs Thompson also well remembered the impact of the last major ride her father introduced – the Big Dipper – before he died in 1929.

"He charged a shilling a ride for that. People said it was a terrible lot but he said,'I'll give them a mahogany pay desk and a terrazzo floor for that,' and he did. It paid off."

When Ald Bean died, his daughter was the young wife of London businessman Leonard Thompson and they made the decision that he should take over the running of the park.

And from then on, although busy with her family, she was roped in by her husband to try out the new rides – a tradition which she has maintained over the years, earning her the affectionate title Queen of the White Knuckle Rides.

"I remember going down th big slide in the Fun House. had been tested by some of th workmen and it seemed a right for them, but their clothe tended to stick to the slide.

"Then I went down in a serg coat at a terrific speed. There wa an abrupt end and they had t catch me fast. That showe them, just in time, that the slid really had to be eased off gent at the end."

With the outbreak of th Second World War, th

**Queen of the White Knuckle Rides Doris Thompson MBE**

**Below: crowds pack the Pleasure Beach on a Bank Holiday**

**Designed by Sir Hiram Maxim – who invented the machine gun of the same name – The Flying Machine (above) is another old Pleasure Beach favourite**

**Whizzing down the Virginia Reel**

# reality

leasure Beach was kept ınning during the winter eekends.

Mrs Thompson recalled: There were so many people ho needed to be entertained etween service stints – soldiers ıd airmen, civil servants and vacuees.

"For them it was an escape om reality."

But there was no time for xpansion.

"All we could do was keep the xisting machinery going well ıd safely."

Thrills and spills on the old Water Chute. Doris Thompson maintained it was better than the more modern version

oah's Ark remains a popular ttraction

The Carnival programme and (below) bathing belles on one of the floats made by craftsmen from Nice

# Carnival comes to town

A bevy of beauties complete with pierrot

## The French connection packs them on the prom in 1923

IN 1923 Blackpool went Carnival Crazy when the City Fathers hit on a bright new idea to pull in the crowds.

Councillors took a trip to Nice in the South of France – three days each way on the train – to see how it was done.

And they made a good job of organising a Blackpool replica of the French event.

Technicians from France built some of the tableaux.

It was estimated that in eight crowded days of activity about two million people visited Blackpool.

More than 200 special trains and 50,000 vehicles brought in the visitors.

It almost started with a tragedy when King Carnival – played by Blackpool Tower clown Doodles – and his Queen (comedian Frank Walmsley in pantomime drag) arrived by plane.

It landed on the sands and promptly flipped upside down.

But 'royalty' was unhurt and joy was unconfined.

One of the major attractions was the huge processions featuring bizarre designs and decorated floats entered by many local companies and organisations.

Thousands of people wore fancy dress and the route was decorated with flowers and banners.

The new open air swimming pool at South Shore, which cost £70,000, was opened by the Mayor, Coun Harry Brooks and there was a gala involving Olympic class swimmers.

Motorcycle speed trials we[re] held near the Gynn and th[e] winner, on a Brough Superio[r] machine, clocked 76.5mph.

There was a carnival ball [–] even a carnival song. An[d] prizes for everything fro[m] flower decorated cars to fanc[y] dress outfits. One woma[n] appeared as a red and whit[e] barber's pole.

More royal regalia for a Carnival participant

The parade (above and top picture) wends its way along the promenade

King Carnival – played by Blackpool Tower clown Doodles – and his Queen (comedian Fred Walmsley) with their jester

STANLEY PARK
AND THE
NEW PROMENADE, SOUTH SHORE
Opened To-day, October 2nd, 1926.

# More resort fun and games in new park

THE opening of Stanley Park in 1926 by Lord Derby was a big milestone in the story of Blackpool and the Fylde.

For it opened up a whole new vista of lesure activities for local people. Those without the energy to play tennis and bowls could take a cruise on the lake or simply stroll among the lawns and flower beds or take in the views from seats among the trees and shrubs.

In a typically bold gesture, Blackpool council created a green alternative to the brash promenade from 288 acres of land which included farm fields but also a huge shanty town of rickety sheds, caravans , pig sties and hen runs dotted with stagnant ponds.

The scheme was masterminded by architect E Prentice Mawson and it gave new hope to many unemployed men who earned a wage for their families labouring to turn the wasteland into a wonderland.

The only cloud on the horizon was the cost. It shot up from an estimated £110,000 to £250,000 largely because of problems concerning the building of the lake which turned out to be the bed of an ancient river.

# Oh they did like to bestride the seaside

A typical Blackpool pleasure steamer, the Wellington

# The end of

North Pier after the fire. The rebuilt Indian Pavilion is on the right hand side towards the sea

Sightseers crowd the pier (left) as a huge column of smoke billows on the breeze, but the wooden Indian Pavilion blazed like a furnace

ON SEPTEMBER 12, 1921, a huge fire devastated part of Blackpool's North Pier.

The dying notes of Sam Speelman's North Pier orchestra had barely drifted away on the Sunday afternoon air and the crowds from the pier were heading for high tea.

One of the last to leave the handsome Indian Pavilion where the orchestra played was Bill Borland from Moss Side in Manchester who saw smoke coming from the woodwork.

He raised the alarm but it was already too late.

The handsome building near the end of the pier was made of pitch pine and by the time the fire brigade arrived it was a raging inferno.

Then came two explosions which might have been caused by bottles of spirits or fire extinguishers explodin

The venue was destroyed in half a hour along with kiosks nearby.

Workmen toiled feverishly to r up planks and make a firebreak stop the spread.

The only good news was the wir keeping the flames away from the re of the structure.

As a huge column of smoke ro into the sky crowds forgot the appetite and packed the Promena to watch the action.

And even when the fire died dow not everyone went home.

By the light of the moon in t early hours of the following morni crowds of local people crept about t beach with oil lamps collecting to of firewood from the wreckage of t pier which had crashed on to t sands.

The Speelman orchestra had l

EARLY visitors to Blackpool liked to sit by the sea, paddle and swim in it, fill hot baths with it, even drink it. And they liked to sail on it.
Until modern times sailing and motorboats plied for hire on the foreshore taking trippers out on the briny.
But some liked to travel further and in more style.

The Bickerstaffe family, who started out as fishermen and became moguls of the Blackpool holiday industry, had a pleasure steamer called Bickerstaffe operating in 1879.

By 1894 they formed a company to build Queen of the North but this ship was lost on war service in 1917.

The steamers were always linked with the piers where they tied up to load and unload.

They linked with resorts from Llandudno to Morecambe and ships like the Lady Evelyn took passengers to Barrow so they could catch trains and explore the Lake District.

In 1895 the Blackpool North Pier Company got in on the act buying the paddle steamer Greyhound which was 230 feet long and competed directly with the similar Queen of the North. Greyhound got as far as Douglas in the Isle of Man.

A Morecambe-owned steamer called Robina was often seen at Blackpool but in 1923 both Robina and Greyhound were sold for work on Belfast Lough.

The Greyhound was later sold to Turkish owners.

Another well-known Blackpool steamer was Deerhound which arrived in 1901. Four years later she went to Cornwall then out to Canada.

In 1928 the Bickerstaffes scrapped their namesake boat but in 1933 the Blackpool Pleasure Steamers firm was formed. The ex-Mersey ferry Bidston was renamed Minden then a former minesweeper turned survey ship was re-christened Queen of the Bay.

They were both scrapped after the 1937 season leaving the Atalanta as the last surviving Blackpool steamer until she joined the Royal Navy for World War Two.

**Loaded with passengers, the steamer Minden cruises in Morecambe Bay**

# the pier show

their instruments and sheet music library on stage and it was destroyed.

So was the luggage and props of a visiting concert party.

Like many theatrical people they had spent Sunday travelling and their baggage had been stored in the pavilion just in time to be burned to a cinder.

The pavilion was added to North Pier in 1877 on one of two wings which added nearly an acre of space to the pier surface.

The building could seat 1,500 people and was modelled on different aspects of real-life Indian architecture in Delhi and other locations.

At the back of the stage was an inscription in Arabic which meant: "The hearing falls in love before the vision."

Sir Charles Halle was one of the stars of the concert stage who had appeared in the Indian Pavilion and it was sometimes used for church services as well as classical music concerts.

**Here's how Central Pier looked in earlier days**

**South Pier pictured in Victorian times**

The timber lighthouse which stood on the dunes at what is now the corner of Lightburne Avenue and South Promenade. The lighthouse was erected in 1865 following the collapse of its stone-predecessor two years earlier. It became a well-known landmark, popular with picnic parties from Blackpool

The wilderness that was St Annes in 1880. Sand dunes, spartina grass and rabbit warrens abounded on windswept undeveloped land occupied by farmers and fishermen. Pictured centre is St Annes Parish Church built in 1873

# A flash of inspiration

SQUIRE John Talbot Clifton of Lytham Hall, who died in 1928, made history at the age of seven when he laid a foundation stone that marked the birth of the town of St Annes.

But the story started back in 1874 when a stroll on the beach changed the whole course of Fylde coast history.

Businessman Elijah Hargreaves was on holiday in Blackpool.

He came from the Rossendale Valley – a part of Lancashire known as the Golden Valley because of the wealth created there from the textile trade.

And Elijah, like the prophet he was named after, saw a golden future among the sand dunes and farmlands that lay between Blackpool and the ancient town of Lytham.

He got the idea as he walked along the shore. It was wild and windswept with few signs of life.

A wooden lighthouse stood where Lightburne Avenue is now. Church Road was a rough track called Common Lane and Highbury Road East was quaintly named Twiggy Lane complete with Twiggy Hill Farm.

It all belonged to the Clifton family, fabulously wealthy local squires who lived at Lytham Hall.

But they liked Elijah's idea of a new town and gave their blessing to the ambitions of the nine men who formed the St Annes Land and Building Company soon after Elijah strolled down the coast towards Lytham and visualised the town they called The Opal of the West. It was named after the chapel of St Anne.

At first the image was anything but u market.

Wooden huts housed the workforce wh slept on the trestle tables from which they a their food.

A railway branch line into what is no The Square brought in bricks, timber an cement.

Work began in February, 1875 and b March 31st, the foundation stone of the S Annes Hotel was laid.

The VIP with the trowel was master Joh Talbot Clifton then just seven. He died i 1928.

There was a huge wave of publicity for th new town for most of the mayors and gentr in Lancashire had been at the stone-layin ceremony.

But the early years were difficult an investors lost a fortune.

Slowly the place developed and grew Property built as houses and called Hydr terrace was changed into the shops of St Anne Square.

A major benefactor was Lord Ashton, th linoleum tycoon from Lancaster

"Little Jimmy" Williamson liked golfin holidays on the Fylde coast and paid mo than £26,000 to give the town the park th now bears his name, Ashton Garden although the deal was surrouded by cloak an dagger secrecy.

He spent £10,000 on a war memorial an gave as much to help start the hospital in 192

Elijah, who saw his dream become realit died in 1904.

South Promenade before the many improvements that were to transform the resort int the Opal of the West.

The first sandgrown'uns lived off the land and the sea. Women folk spent many back-breaking hours raking up cockles on the beach

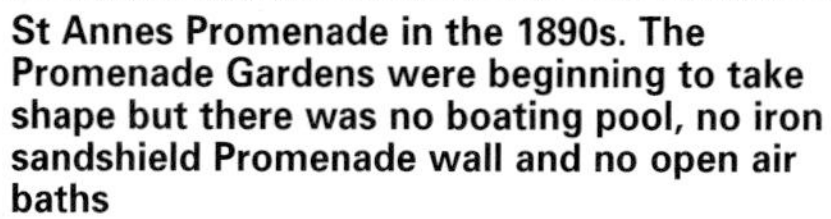

St Annes Promenade in the 1890s. The Promenade Gardens were beginning to take shape but there was no boating pool, no iron sandshield Promenade wall and no open air baths

Newly built St Annes Parish Church. Lady Eleanor Cecily Clifton provided the money for the building of the chapel of ease with a small spire which opened in 1873 to serve the isolated West End farmers and fishermen

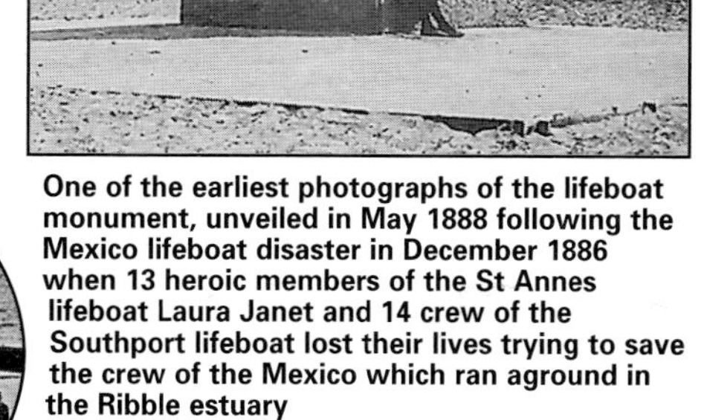

One of the earliest photographs of the lifeboat monument, unveiled in May 1888 following the Mexico lifeboat disaster in December 1886 when 13 heroic members of the St Annes lifeboat Laura Janet and 14 crew of the Southport lifeboat lost their lives trying to save the crew of the Mexico which ran aground in the Ribble estuary

St Annes Pier has been the town's central seaside attraction for more than 100 years. Hundreds of people crammed the pier to witness the official opening on 15 June 1885, by Lord Derby, Col. Fred Stanley MP. Generations have since been drawn to stroll along its wooden decking

St Annes Hotel was the first of the new buildings in St Annes, its first turf being cut in February 1875. Squire John Talbot Clifton was only seven years old when the following month he laid the foundation stone which launched the new town

Among the first homes in St Annes were Clifton Cottages in Church Road, then known as Common Lane. The properties were originally thatched

The pier was originally 315 yards long with a 40-foot jetty that reached out into the channel. It was used by fishing vessels and a variety of sailing craft and pleasure boats – including steamers which ran regular trips along the coast, to Lytham, Southport, Liverpool, Morecambe and Fleetwood

The heartbreaking task of salvaging a home

# Fleetwood

THE FYLDE COAST is no stranger to devastation from the sea but nothing in recorded history can match the violence of the storm that blew up on the night of October 28, 1927.

The town of Fleetwood was the worst hit and became a national disaster area where five people died and thousands were left homeless.

Noah himself would have been horrified at the monstrous power of the elements which sent a wall of water rushing through the town just after midnight.

People said the tidal wave sounded like a roaring lion as it ripped through their homes and left water 10 feet deep in places.

In those days there was little in the way of sea defences and Fleetwood was a much smaller community.

Districts like Rossall, Larkholme, West View, Flakefleet and Broadwater were open fields occupied by a few farms and isolated houses.

Near the present Fleetwood fire station on Radcliffe Road were allotments and smallholdings where families lived in crude wooden caravans.

Lashed by a hurricane-like wind that was well over Force 12, the 25 foot tide was boosted by more than seven feet and just after midnight the sea swept unhindered from the West Side between Rossall School and Rossall Point to link with the river Wyre in the east. Fleetwood, at the end of its peninsula, was cut off from the outside world and became a devastated island.

The swirling flood waters overturned some of the caravans.

Trawler mate Thomas Chard and his family lived in one.

He found himself in the water holding his youngest child Ellen, aged four. He lost his grip on the youngster and she was drowned along with his wife Mary, aged 34, and sons James, 11 and Richard 7.

Mr Chard was washed hundreds of yards into Gordon road where he clung to the wall of a half-built house.

Another caravan resident, Lily Bailey, a 34-year-old widow, also lost her life.

At least one other death in the port which occured soon afterwards was put down to the trauma of that fateful night. One victim was so shocked she could neither walk nor speak.

But three babies were born. One became a famous trawler skipper – the late William Gregson known as Bluey because of his piercing eyes. His middl name was Storm.

As the wind reached 78 miles a hour Peter Wilson and his wi clung to the roof of a pig sty o their Peel Road smallholdin Lashed by the driving rain the were rescued by boat three hou later.

Another caravan dweller o Copse Road spent two hours o the roof then paddled to safety on home-made raft.

At their home on Broadway young couple used a coal fire pok to break through the bedroom wa to comfort an hysterical woma trapped next door with fou

**Crowds at the water's edge around Ash Street**

**Rescue boats in Blakiston Street opposite Milton Community Centre**

**This shop at the corner of Warrenhurst Road and Oak Street is still open!**

**A mark showing the height of the flood still exists at the Strawberry Gardens on Poulton Road**

## DIARY OF DISASTER

Floods created a 2,000 acre lake

Council surveyor William Melvillle put the initial damage bill at £250,000 plus

The ferry to Knott End was Fleetwood's only link with the outside world for days

On the night of the storm a passenger steamer struggled through to Fleetwood from Belfast

Floating furniture bobbing on the water smashed ceilings and windows in many houses

Old salts at the Seaman's Mission on Dock Street gave up their beds for homeless people

The damage was caused by 130 million gallons of seawater

15,000 candles were distributed before power returned

People all over the country sent money and clothing to a disaster fund.

Leeds sent a special relief convoy. A woman there handed over the clothing of her baby which had died.

Cash totalling more than £108,000 was received.

More than 3,200 claims were made against the fund. Householders were paid in full and businesses at an average of 75 per cent

Crooks came into town pretending to be local people in order to claim from the funds

Railway fireman John Roberts recalled the first train into the port with the track still underwater. Years later he said: " The streets were like rivers with many boats between the houses. At Wyre Dock station people cheered us."

The Fleetwood Chronicle summed it all up with the comment: " Widespread misery and distress has been occasioned."

Tucked away in the same issue was a commentary on the weather by Countryman. It said: "November is here with chilling blasts and overflowing pools."

**Hundreds of logs high and dry in Dock Street**

**Rescue teams on rafts cruise the streets as people watch from bedroom windows**

**Workmen check one of the caravans where five people died**

# disaster

children. In Willow Street Captain James Calvert, concerned about his prize Pekinese dogs, went downstairs only for a tidal wave to burst open the front door and wash him out into the street. He was carried 150 yards into Poulton Road and grabbed bushes outside the bay window of a house.

He was dragged inside but later joined rescue teams.

In Cambridge Road a mother and her three children were poisoned by gas from a pipe fractured in the flood and were taken to hospital for oxygen.

The rescue effort swung into action and police and volunteers worked for 24 hours and longer at a stretch without a break.

Dawn broke to find 5,000 people trapped on the first floor of their homes. Cold, wet and hungry they were supplied with emergency rations from a fleet of rowing boats many of which were brought as far as Rossall School from Blackpool on lorries. There was no electricity for five days.

St John Ambulance volunteers and Fleetwood scouts did great work and emergency centres were set up in the London Street schoolrooms – now a furniture warehouse – and the police station.

Many of those rescued during the first hours had only sodden nightclothes to wear. One policeman handed over his entire wardrobe – except for his uniform and his best suit.

As the water slowly receded it left behind tons of stinking mud and raw sewage in homes and streets along with many dead pigs and chickens which had floated from allotments and gardens.

And 2,000 tons of giant pitch pine logs had been washed out of Alec Keay's sawmill on Copse Road and were left high and dry in Lord Street, Dock Street and Station Road.

**Brown paper and string ties up the welfare parcels.**

Boots
Boots

Chapter Three

# The Thirties

Holiday town Blackpool was booming in 1936 for this August Bank Holiday Monday picture at the Pleasure Beach. Plenty of hats and coats about though!

# The calm before the storm

THEY called it the hungry Thirties. But Blackpool defied the economic doom and gloom and embarked on a massive building programme throughout the decade.

The resort's upbeat image, in line with the town's motto Progress, started in 1931 when Prime Minister Ramsey Macdonald opened the municipal airport at Stanley Park.

Work began on the Technical College in Palatine Road – forerunner of the huge Blackpool and the Fylde Çollege of today.

The vast Woolworth store, with its equally vast cafe, opened on the Prom and, inland, so did Carleton Crematorium.

Gracie Fields was in town to declare the Squires Gate holiday camp open and the Duke of Kent unveiled the promenade between Little Bispham and Cleveleys, Victoria Hospital and the lifeboat station all in one day.

The Co-operative Society emporium opened on Coronation Street along with St John's Market.

The Talbot Road bus station was completed in 1939 along with the Odeon cinema in Dickson Road.

The North Pier theatre, destroyed by fire the year before, was rebuilt.

And the curtain went up at the "new" Opera House with Jessie Matthews and Sonny Hale topping the bill.

Then, in July that year, one of Blackpool's most famous landmarks opened its doors for the first time – Derby Baths.

Demolished in 1990 in a move that sparked a major political row, the pool was on a grand scale and seemed to sum up the defiant spirit which had led Blackpool to invest so much over the decade.

Everything from bridges at Layton and Squires Gate to libraries and new schools had been built in a few short years.

But in September 1939 the tide of history turned for Blackpool and the rest of Britain.

The country was at war.

The Blackpool Regiment, a group of local territorial army volunteers, marched away to a grim fate as prisoners of the Japanese on the infamous Railway of Death in Burma.

And the resort became RAF Blackpool, a vast training camp where 770,000 RAF personel were to undergo training – as the next issue of the Fylde Story will show.

**Central Beach was a sea of humanity in the last summer of peace in 1939**

**The Gazette breaks the news of the Nazi invasion of Poland in 1939 – and Britain and Blackpool prepare for war**

# Curtain up!

**Lancashire's idol Gracie Fields made annual summer variety appearances at the Grand Theatre from 1932 to 1938 inclusive**

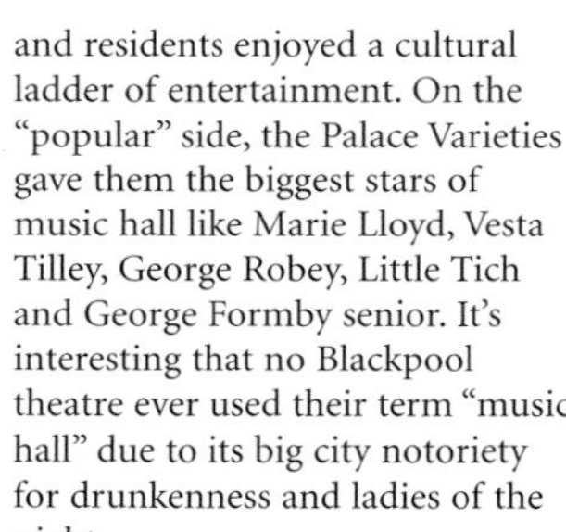

**Unruly comedian Frank Randle was already a local resident when he made his name in Blackpool**

**The top concert artist in 1930s Blackpool was the American bass Paul Robeson, who gave shows at the Opera House in 1931 and 1936**

THE golden future that had been meticulously planned for the Blackpool entertainment world was beginning to gleam in 1939.

Biggest and best had been the aim, extending the thread that stretched back to the 1890s, and it emerged in handsome art deco style with the nation's biggest Odeon, the biggest provincial theatre with the Opera House, and perhaps the most distinctive of seaside edifices, the new Casino building at the Pleasure Beach, designed by the eminent architect Joseph Emberton.

It all came to a halt with the declaration of war on September 3. But the war did at least produce a quick dividend for the resort's showmen. They made fortunes from holidaymakers seeking a safe haven, and from the thousands of service personnel and civil servants who were dazzled by the finest entertainments menu in the country, not excluding London.

Blackpool's growth to its premier position at the end of the 1930s had been 50 years in the making, from the day the first Opera House opened in 1889, followed by the Tower and the Grand Theatre in 1894, the Empire in 1895 and the Alhambra in 1899.

Everything in the resort's burgeoning entertainment heirachy was privately owned.

The borough council was never involved. And so, when ventures failed, there was no municipal safety net. Investors lost their money.

The first disaster in the ambitious 1890s was the Empire, a large variety theatre that went broke after 18 months and had brief spells of success as the Hippodrome under various managements until it was relaunched as a movie house in 1910.

The second failure, the Alhambra, was a whopper. A huge Italianate building on the promenade block to the north of the Tower, it housed a variety theatre, circus and ballroom but had been oversubscribed by investors at £370,000. A reckless management spent the lot in an attempt to emulate the success of the Tower.

The Alhambra went broke in 1902, was picked up for a bargain £140,000 by the Tower Company, and relaunched as the Palace in 1904.

As these rival managements fought their way into the new century, the patrons basked in the privilege of seeing the country's top stars and shows at keen prices. Blackpool in the 1900s boasted a wonderland of entertainment that was not surpassed in later decades, no matter what later generations believed.

We should be aware that in those days, before affordable recorded music, when radio was 20 years away and TV existed only in HG Wells' imagination, the visitors' priority in personal spending was on live entertainment.

The nerve centre of the resort was live music. Hundred of instrumentalists – probably more than 1,000 – provided music in orchestras and ensembles of various sizes and styles in the Tower, the Winter Gardens complex, the theatres, ballrooms, piers, restaurants and the larger hotels. Even modest cafes had a pianist and sheet music sales were "plugged" by demonstrators in song booths on the prom and in music shops.

**Contralto Clara Butt**

In those halcyon days visitors and residents enjoyed a cultural ladder of entertainment. On the "popular" side, the Palace Varieties gave them the biggest stars of music hall like Marie Lloyd, Vesta Tilley, George Robey, Little Tich and George Formby senior. It's interesting that no Blackpool theatre ever used their term "music hall" due to its big city notoriety for drunkenness and ladies of the night.

A step up the cultural scale, the Grand Theatre and the Opera House presented top London musicals, like The Merry Widow, The Arcadians and The Chocolate Soldier, plus regular chances to see leading actors and actresses like Ellen Terry, Lillie Langtry, Mrs Patrick Campbell, Frank Benson, Beerbohm Tree and Mr and Mrs Kendal in the entire spectrum of drama and comedy from Shakespeare to Oscar Wilde.

Stage shows held such an important place in the holidaymaker's week that afternoon matinees were as important as evening shows and larger venues would add a morning show if business looked promising.

Touring opera companies were regular visitors to both theatres but the jewels in Blackpool's Edwardian crown were the superstar Sunday concerts at the Tower and the Winter Gardens, whose general managers –George W Harrop and Jonathan R Huddleston respectively – fought a 'culture war' by paying huge fees to stars of opera and classical music. Special Sunday trains brought well-heeled patrons from all over Lancashire.

The Tower's illustrious regular star for a period of 20 years was the tall and elegant Clara Butt, whose powerful contralto voice rattled teacups at 50 paces and was one of the undoubted legends of Blackpool's musical life. Other prestige-seeking bookings included the great Polish pianist Paderewski (1902) and legendary opera names like the Spanish soprano Luisa Tetrazzini (1910).

The Winter Gardens Company more than matched the Tower in the years prior to World War One with several appearances by the Australian soprano Nellie Melba, and the Austrian violinist Fritz Kreisler, while other superstar bookings included the Italian tenor Enrico Caruso and the Irish tenor John McCormack (both in 1909).

From 1901 to 1911 the Gardens also presented the American "march king" John Philip Sousa.

In this charmed environment another form of entertainment arrived. It was the essence of seaside fun and gaiety, the pierrots in their silken, ruffled costumes could be seen in a dozen outdoor locations on the Fylde Coast, on piers, in parks, and on rickety stages in the sandhills.

Several names emerge from the past as popular figures; Bobby Allandale at the Central Pier, Cousin Freddy at St Annes and Tommy and the Jolly Tars at Cleveleys, but none were bigger than Fred Walmsley, who headed his Tonics concert party on the South Pier from 1909 to 1925.

Astonishingly, Fred then led the revolution to what could be termed modern season shows. In 1927 he became the comedy kingpin of Lawrence Wright's annual On With The Show at the North Pier, which had broken the mould the previous year with a fully-staged show that included a big orchestra, concert vocalists, and dancers.

During the war years the theatres did well. New stars were in

Gentlemen of the orchestra in the early days of The Palace

Happy-go-lucky George Formby became a Fylde Coast resident and starred in four Blackpool summer shows in the 1930s

The first of John Gielgud's three starring appearances in Blackpool was in September, 1939

Lively Tessie O'Shea settled in Poulton after making a name in Blackpool summer shows in the 1930s – three at the North Pier

the making; Jack Hulbert and Cicely Courtneidge appeared twice at the Opera House, the young Jack Buchanan at the Grand.

The younger generation, whose attitudes to life, love and the universe had been brutally changed by the carnage, which bereaved every family, led the revival in the mid 1920s by following everything American; short skirts, jazz, dance parties, chewing gum and, in the theatre, anything by George Gershwin and his contemporaries.

"Popular music" that would be today's chart material was everywhere. Gracie Fields and George Formby (junior ) made their first appearances at the Palace in 1923 but the biggest variety sensation of the decade was Bolton-born Jack Hylton and his band with their syncopated music and comedy in a slickly rehearsed show. More than any other bandleader, Hylton proved that not all the good tunes came from Vienna!

The American "King of Jazz," Paul Whiteman, brought his orchestra to the Winter Gardens in 1926, stimulating the public's appetite for the new music. The traditional Sunday classical concerts slowly began to lose their appeal.

The Grand and the Opera House fought to get the latest American musicals – which went on tour only months after the West End openings. The names are now legend: Sigmund Romberg's Rose Marie and The Student Prince, Rudolf Friml's The Vagabond King, Vincent Youmans' No No Nanette and Hit the Deck, George Gershwin's Lady Be Good, Tip Toes and Oh Kay, and probably the blockbuster of the decade, Jerome Kern's Showboat.

The glitter and razzmatazz of the decade comes over strongly in the local newspaper adverts and reviews and social gossip.In 1928 the resort buzzed with excitement at the merger of the two largest entertainment operators, those old rivals the Blackpool Tower Company (with the Tower, the Palace and the Grand) and the Blackpool Winter Gardens Company. It was a formidable force in local entertainment.

It came just in time for, although success seemed to shine from every theatre front, it was due mainly to the hundreds of thousands of visitors who flocked to the resort in the summer. Out of season the owners often resorted to showing films for economy.

Radio was becoming more popular and for the first time there was an option to braving the Fylde Coast's wet and windy nights in the search for entertainment.

And when the movies began to talk – The Jazz Singer came to the Hippodrome at Easter, 1929 – the rapidly-expanding cinema industry dealt a crippling blow to live entertainment. The Winter Gardens Pavilion and the Palladium were converted for sound the following month.

By the end of the year, in a desperate bid to hold the line against "the flicks," there were five repertory companies in Blackpool, including the Grand Theatre and the Tower Circus. By mid-1930 all the resort's cinemas had converted to talkies and the theatre slump continued.

Stage shows disappeared from the Winter Gardens Pavilion in 1930 (and didn't return until 1949). At the end of 1930 the Grand was switched to a policy of winter films and a short summer season of weekly plays and musicals.

As the Depression took its grip on the public's purse, the winter of 1932-33 was the leanest period ever experienced by Blackpool's theatre owners. Touring shows were in short supply as productions went broke. In January, 1933, only Feldman's variety theatre had a live show in the resort. Even the Palace Varieties had to show films until Easter.

Inland towns lost some theatres for ever. In Blackpool, however, the summer holiday trade held up and businesses survived.

Big names continued to appear in weekly shows during the season, for summer season shows were still an idea waiting to hatch. These were led by daring investment from independents like Bert Feldman, who launched a season show at his theatre in 1932, and by local producer Jack Taylor who, in the same year, used the Palace Varieties for Variety Fantaisie, a summer season of what was termed "cabaret variety."

He repeated the exercise in 1933 with George Formby as the comedy host of Variety Fair and in 1934 Taylor produced the first of his five summer shows at the Opera House, George Forby starring in 1936, 37 and 39.

Alongside the star-studded spectaculars in the big theatre there came a revival of the pierrot scene, which had always been there, if somewhat anonymously. Major producers now put the follies indoors and gave them orchestras. Manx comic Harry Korris came to the resort to lead The Arcadian Follies at the South Pier, a success story that ran for nine seasons, while the Royal Follies had a similar track record at the Central Pier.

The sweet smell of success drifted down the variety profession. Big stars began to buy houses on the Fylde Coast; George Formby, Frank Randle, Dave Morris, Norman Evans, Tessie O'Shea, Harry Korris, Sandy Powell.

The ever-present Tower Circus, and Leonard Thompson's spectacular new ice shows at the Pleasure Beach, rounded off the transformation of Blackpool showbiz as the economy gradually threw off the bad old days of the Depression.

Blackpool's sold foundation of "straight theatre" also made a recovery, the Grand Theatre being returned in 1938 to live shows all year round. At the Grand and the Opera House great names like Sybil Thorndike, Evelyn Laye, Fay Compton, Marie Tempest, John Gielgud, Ivor Novello, Leslie Henson and Lupino Lane could all be seen as the decade reached its climax.

Good times were back and the showmen began to look to the future, typified by the Tower Company's commitment to a beautiful new 3,000-seat Opera House.

*The mind can easily boggle at what might have been had there been no Second World War.*

The stylish lines of the Pleasure Beach Express station by Joseph Emberton. It faced Watson Road and was modified in the 60s then replaced by a Victorian design in 1970.

# Art of the possible

BLACKPOOL went Art Deco daft in the Thirties. Probably the most famous architect who set his stamp on the resort was Joseph Emberton who was hired by Pleasure Beach boss Leonard Thompson.

The amusement park covered a smaller area then and had fewer rides. But there wasn't a corner of the place that Joseph didn't alter in some way.

Elsewhere in the resort local architects followed Joseph's lead.

One was John Christopher Derham whose father had been Chief Constable.

He created wacky designs like the Little Vic pub in Victoria Street and drew up plans for Olympia.

That is not an art deco building but it used the exterior tiled finish called faience so popular with art deco architects. Another example was the former Gazette building in Victoria Street.

A few remnants of the style can still be found at first floor level on buildings in Topping Street and Market Street.

They are the work of another Blackpool architect Halstead Best. He designed the Castle Hotel on Central Drive and the Fleece in Market Street.

The former Blackpool lifeboat house near Central Pier and the Rigby Road transport offices are other projects.

But the lavish Fylde Coast hotel envisaged for a seafront site south of the solarium was never built.

Blackpool architect Charles Mackeit created the Opera House with its art dec interior and other local classics were th Odeon frontage on Dickson Road an Woolworth building on the seafront.

The most prolific designer of the time wa John Charles Robinson, the Blackpoo Corporation Architect from 1920 to 1944.

Although his name is recalled only by loca historians he left a huge imprint on the resor

Some of his biggest and grandest scheme are long gone.

They include the South Shore swimmin pool which was the biggest of its kind in th world but was knocked down in 1983 to mak way for the Sandcastle.

Perhaps his best known piece of work wa Derby Baths.

The giant pool complex, complete wit tiled exterior, went up in 1939 and wa demolished 51 years later to make way for th Stakis Hotel.

From public lavatories to schools, fro libraries to bridges, his designs both great an small are found throughout the resort.

He designed his own home, Lockeridge a 50 Newton Drive.

Historian Ted Lightbown, secretary of th Blackpool and Fylde Historical Society said: The name of J C Robinson should be muc more widely known because he really did pla an enormous part in the development o Blackpool before World War Two.

"After that the appearance of the town di not change a great deal until the 1960s whe the Palace building was knocked down on th Prom to make way for Lewis's. That was th signal for major changes in the town."

**History Note:** Art Deco was a design style bor in France. Its roots lay in the world of ballet an painting.
Examples were seen in Britain in the 1920s i the design of posters but it really came to th fore in the '30s

The Gazette office of 1934 designed by Blackpool architect Halstead Best and demolished in 1987

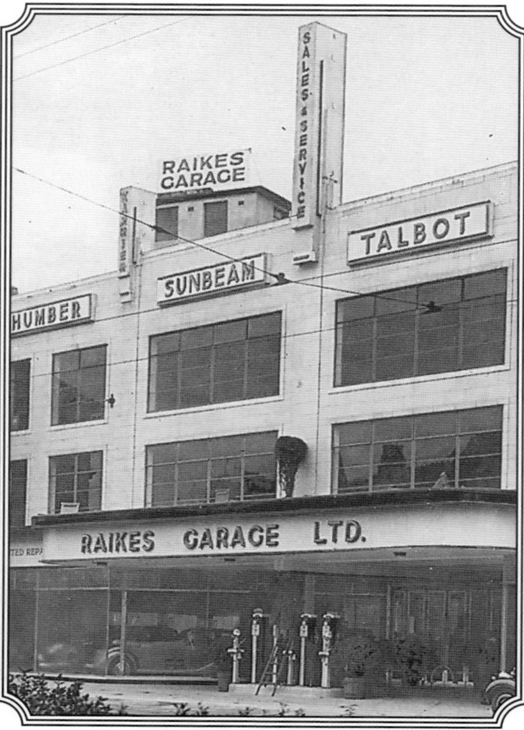

This building, in Church Street, was typical of the time. After decades as a garage it is now a solicitors' office

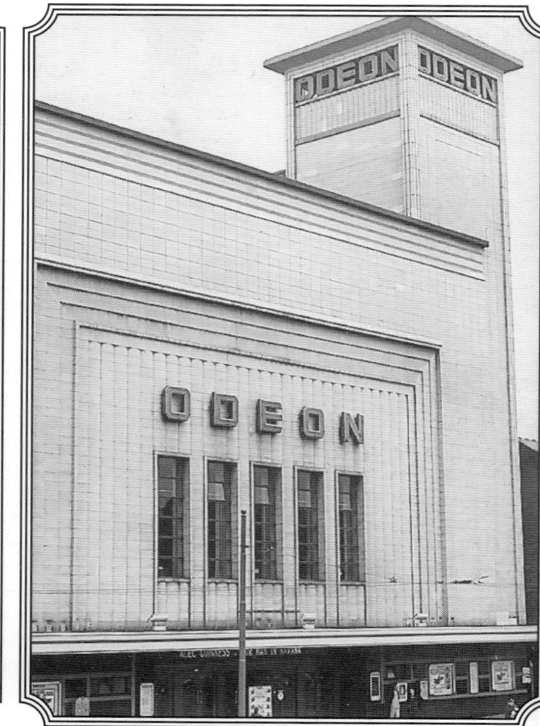

The Dickson Road Odeon opened in 1939 and closed down in 1998

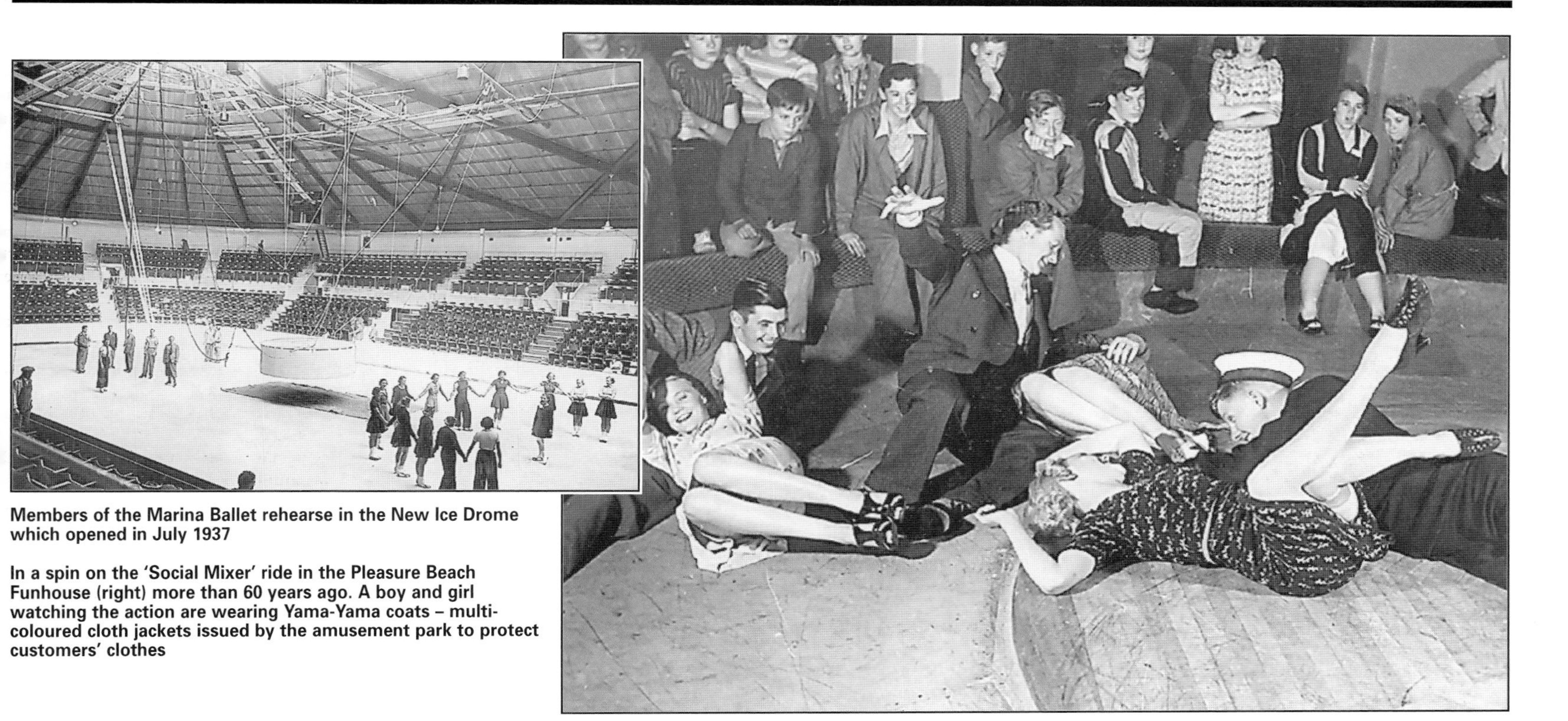

Members of the Marina Ballet rehearse in the New Ice Drome which opened in July 1937

In a spin on the 'Social Mixer' ride in the Pleasure Beach Funhouse (right) more than 60 years ago. A boy and girl watching the action are wearing Yama-Yama coats – multi-coloured cloth jackets issued by the amusement park to protect customers' clothes

# Fun & flames

BLACKPOOL Pleasure Beach was a well-established part of the Blackpool entertainment scene in the 1930s.

In 1937 the Ice Drome was opened as the Thompson family continued their policy of investment which has seen so many changes at the site over the years.

But it wasn't all plain sailing.

In 1934, there was a serious fire which destroyed the Chinese Theatre and miniature railway station and workshop. The new one was re-designed by Joseph Emberton.

The Chinese Theatre had been known as the Indian Theatre and started out in 1910 as an early Pleasure Beach attraction.

In those days it was the Naval Spectatorium in which were depicted various sea conflicts including the World War One Battle of Zeebrugge.

Badly damaged in the blaze was the miniature engine Carol Jean named after a daughter of Pleasure Beach chairman Leonard Thompson.

And in 1938 Emberton's new Casino building was under construction when a floor collapsed killing four workmen and injuring two others.

But such disasters have always proved only a temporary setback to life at the amusement park.

In the funhouse young people in the 1930s enjoyed themselves with fewer inhibitions than their parents would have sanctioned.

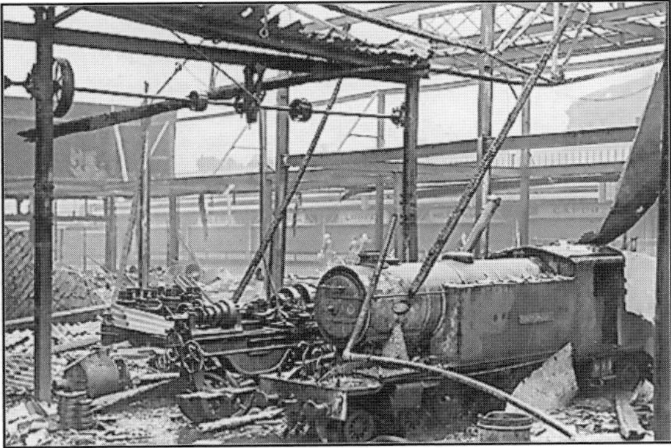

All that was left when fire gutted the Pleasure Beach Express station in 1934

Here, a fire, started by a discarded cigarette, broke out in the Indian Pavilion in 1938.

# A giant among spielers!

THEY called him The Admiral. Dressed up to the nines in a smart naval style uniform, William Robinson was the top spieler of the '30s on Blackpool's Golden Mile.

His job was "get a pitch" – draw a crowd for the various showmen who worked along the seafront.

He brought his family to Blackpool from Bradford and was a friend of Harry Ramsden, the fish and chip tycoon.

The Admiral's son, Ken Robinson of Garstang Road, Blackpool, recalls happy days on the Golden Mile as a young man.

He said: "My Dad could have sold cigars in Cuba. He had all sorts of jobs in publicity and showbusiness and certainly had the gift of the gab."

Ken spent most of his working life at the old Catterall and Swarbrick brewery in Blackpool but his Dad's magic rubbed off for he is a noted magician, a talented entertainer and still appears as a lookalike of his hero, the famous Blackpool clown Charlie Cairoli.

He vividly remembers some of the seafront shows of the '30s where his father worked.

On Central Pier they crowded in to watch German artiste Erika, the Stratosphere Girl who climbed a 200-foot pole and swung by her feet to the oohs and aahs of the crowd.

She had a young brother who was seen wearing the uniform of the Hitler Youth movement.

Says Ken: "I often wondered what happened to him in the war."

Central Pier also featured an escapologist who leapt into the sea inside a burning sack only to surface unscathed to the delight of the crowd.

Ken remembers the Luna Park building on land now occupied by Mr B's near what is now New Bonney Street.

Australian-born Bevis Walters worked from there under the stage name Explorer Evans.

Complete with immaculate white suit and pith helmet he packed them in to see a menagerie that included snakes and lizards.

He also had an attraction called The Invisible Ray Machine.

"That was very popular" recalls Ken Robinson. " Perhaps people were more gullible then but there was no shortage of people willing to get into a cabinet which apparently made them disappear. "

But the fun at Luna Park came to an end in 1937 when the place was destroyed by fire.

It was operated by businessman Harry Kamiya and his brother Monzo who had received a threatening letter, critical of the Japanese, just before the fire.

Nearby on the Prom was Fairyland which was demolished in 1970 for the widening of Chapel Street.

Re-built in 1931 from a buiding of 1907 it contained a roller skating rink. This ancient site was once the location of a bathing house for patrons of Bonny's-in-the-Field – an early place for visitors to stay where the King Edward pub now stands.

**Those were the days! Crowds pack Central Beach in the 1930s and Admiral William Robinson (top picture) was pulling them in . . .**

**Ken Robinson recalls a host of sideshows.**

The Giant Rat
- probably a mongoose

Jolly Alice
- a very large lady billed as One Ton of Fun

The Tattooed Man and Woman
- they certainly were; all over

The Mermaid
- she once left a sign saying gone for dinner. Was it to the fish shop?

**And a Gazette survey on the Golden Mile more than 60 years ago came up with:**

A teenage stripper known as La Belle Eve

An Irish woman called Mavourneen who weighed 33 stone

A man called Alf Pyott from Stockport who stood one inch short of two feet and weighed 24 pounds.

Animal exhibits included a flea circus and Billy the World's biggest pig who sported a gold tooth.

Those far off times saw other shows in which humans were exhibited as curiosities. There were the Giraffe-necked women of Africa and plate-lipped people from Burma..

Mary Ann Bevan was described as the world's ugliest woman and Lobster Man Andy, who had no arms, did balancing and juggling tricks with his rudimentary hands.

Many people worked long and hard on the Golden Mile for £1 a day which was considered a very good wage.

Publicity for Harold Davidson suggested the fires of hell awaited the ex-cleric

Trippers (below) queue at Luke Gannon's Golden Mile Show at the corner of Brunswick Street

A typical scene on the Golden Mile in 1934

# Headline-maker Luke could read their minds ...

SHOWMAN Luke Gannon often hit the headlines in the 1930s and upset Blackpool's "fathers."

But he loved the publicity because it brought the crowds flocking in.

Luke had been working a mind-reading act with the beautiful Madame Kusharny on the site of the old Red Lion pub where Yates's South now stands on the Promenade.

Then he persuaded a local character known as Bandy – because of his bow legs – to take part in the first of many starving stunts.

He lived only on liquids for 60 days and each day a doctor entered the glass case in which he was exhibited, handed over his day's pay, checked his condition and then re-sealed the case with tapes which the public signed to guard against secret feeding.

The trippers queued up at twopence a time.

A Dutchman billed as The Great Sacko died after fasting in a shop on Church Street. With black irony it became a tea room. And that started a craze for starving people exhibits at resorts around the country.

Luke Gannon pressed on at a new pitch on the Golden Mile where he exhibited a woman called Joyce Heather.

Newly-wed Joyce had to live in a large barrel while the crowds peered in through a glass window.

She had to survive 10 days without food or water – the first of the Starving Brides.

The prize was £200 – but Joyce quit on day nine.

Speculation about whether she had received anything for her ordeal angered the crowds and Luke faced an angry mob on the forecourt.

The crowd rolled the barrel across the Prom and on to the beach and the commotion blocked the Prom.

Luke loved every minute.

Next summer the barrel was back with its most famous resident the Reverend Harold Davidson.

When he was the Rector of Stiffkey, a parish in rural Norfolk, Harold was in the habit of visiting London and found himself in the Sunday papers over what he claimed was pastoral work with prostitutes.

He was de-frocked from the church after a lengthy church court hearing where he was charged by a bishop with immoral behaviour.

On his first trip to Blackpool in the 1930s he was booked to go without food for 14 days.

On the first day 10,000 people blocked the Prom and paid nearly £850 at 2d a time to see the former cleric in his barrel.

The following day Luke and the Rector were fined £2 each for obstruction.

Opposition to the Golden Mile shows was growing and the council waged war on Luke Gannon.

In 1935 they had Harold Davidson arrested for attempted suicide – then a criminal offence – as he lay in a glass-topped coffin on the Mile.

But a doctor told the court that 10 days rest had done Harold good and he was fitter than when he began. Case dismissed.

In 1937 he appeared in Skegness and was addressing a crowd from inside a cage containing two lions when one attacked him. He died later from his injuries.

Meanwhile Luke organised a number of starving and freezing bride stunts but when the crowds had gone, living conditions improved for the stars of the show.

He paid a midget, aged 28, to pose as a pupil at Claremont Junior School. The authorities thought she was 10 and when the truth was revealed the headlines ensured that Luke's latest attraction was in the limelight – the girl that hoaxed the teachers.

And he bought a fishing boat called Girl Pat which had been stolen from Grimsby and sailed round the world using only a schoolboy atlas and creating huge publicity.

The craft was later tied up at North Pier and again the visitors paid a fortune to see it ...

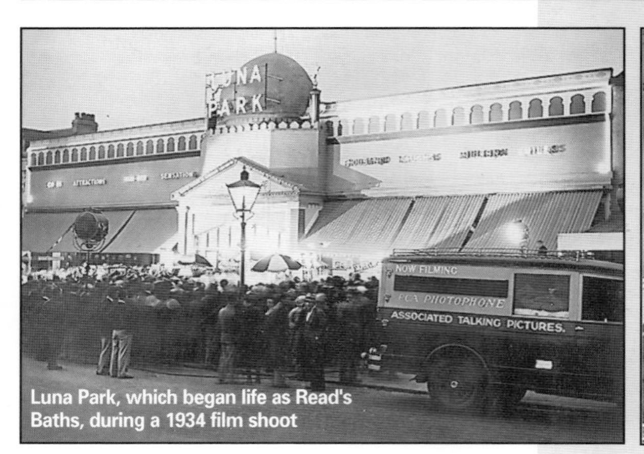
Luna Park, which began life as Read's Baths, during a 1934 film shoot

Fire on The Mile. The stall on the left offered Hot Pies! The Ellis Family were long-established Palm Readers, while Lawrence Wright staged summer shows and published sheet music sold from the song booth and 'plugged' by singers

Apart from song booths to promote sheet m 30s Blackpool featured non-stop contests lik piano-playing marathon

# The Gold

IT WAS rough and it was raunchy. But to millions of visitors the old-style Golden Mile from the Thirties to the Sixties was as much a part of Blackpool as the Tower, the piers or the Pleasure Beach.

The story started more than a century ago on the sands of Central Beach.

Victorian visitors spilled out of the trains at Central Station and were bombarded by an army of get-rich-quick characters after their hard-earned cash.

There was Professor Toole who sold hair restorer – you could tell it was good, he had plenty of thatch himself.

Charlie Sennett had a voice like a parade ground sergeant. People said he had been struck off as a doctor in the army. He sold a product called Nervous Cordial and had a 'spiel' filled with long and strange-sounding words which baffled the average tripper.

His medicine could cure: "The itch, the titch, the palsy and the gout; the plague within, the plague without."

And there was Billy Muggins who threw sticks of rock into the audience to build up a crowd. Then he started to sell his wares.

In 1879 the council reacted to complaints about the hassle caused on the beach and brought in local laws to control the army of hustlers.

They looked for a new pitch and found it in the front gardens of the houses lining the promenade. The roadway was much narrower then.

Legend has it that the first Golden Mile stall sold bric a brac but things soon changed. Visitors packed the sands shoulder to shoulder in the summer sunshine and there was a ready sale for jugs of tea, chips, sandwiches and ice cream before the days of candyfloss and burgers.

Then the amusement caterers moved in with roundabouts and slot machines and the Mile developed the familiar higgle-de-piggledy shanty town look which it kept for decades.

Then came the third phase of the Golden Mile's development as the showmen arrived with their freak exhibits and animal attractions which made the Mile notorious.

The scene was set for the scandalous times of the Thirties, the days of Starving Brides and naked showgirls when Blackpool hit the headlines with an image that was far from seaside family fun.

An early Golden Mile food operation – before the days of burgers.

he Victoria was a famous promenade pub on
e Golden Mile which later became the site of
ipley's Odditorium

Was this a very early example
of closed-circuit television
on the Golden Mile?

## Central Beach and the Golden Mile in the Thirties

# en Age

Off to the Isle Of Man from Squires Gate in a 1930s De Havilland Dragon

Night-flying at Stanley Park (below) involved lights like these

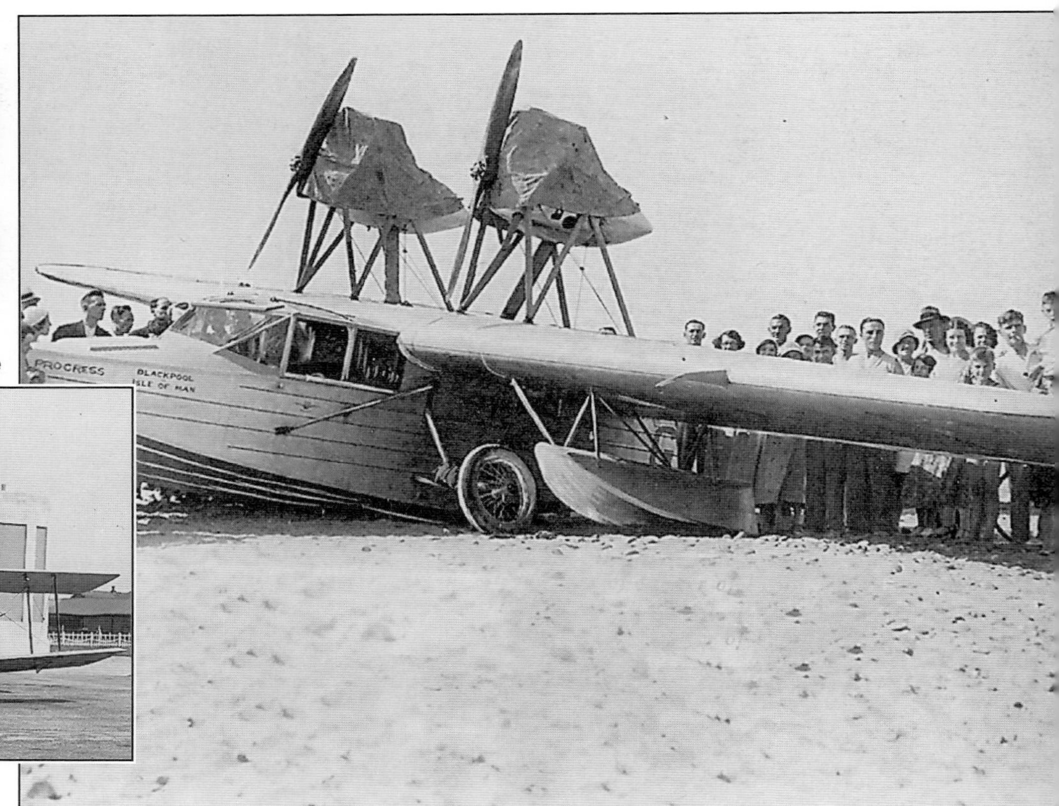

# The perils of the early air pioneers

PRIME Minister Ramsey Macdonald officially opened Blackpool's municipal airport at Stanley Park in 1931.

There were many complaints from residents about noise and the issue of whether it was right to operate flights on a Sunday.

In 1935 there was a brief ban on joy flights on the Sabbath but even that was quickly withdrawn.

However, down at Squires Gate private enterprise was forging ahead with regular services to Liverpool and the Isle of Man.

Although many holidaymakers could afford a quick flip round the Tower, travelling any distance by aircraft was strictly for the wealthy.

And, since only a handful of the population ever went abroad for holidays or on business, taking to the skies was still like flying to the moon for the man in the street.

It could be dangerous too.

In 1933 a seaplane which also had undercarriage wheels took off from Stanley Park for the Isle of Man.

But when the pilot realised the undercarriage had been damaged he landed in the sea off South Shore.

He and four passengers escaped but the sea nearly claimed the plane.

After a struggle lasting until midnight it was dragged to safety higher up the beach.

The following year an Avro 504 crashed into a Westland Wessex aircraft over Blackpool.

The Wessex was part of Sir Alan Cobham's Flying Circus which was a fleet of planes operated by the noted air ace.

This plane landed safely at Squires Gate.

But two sisters who were taking a pleasure flight in the Avro were thrown out and fell to their deaths and the pilot was killed when the fragile machine crashed to the ground in Swainson Street.

Wreckage in Swainson Street, North Shore after three people died in a mid-air collision

Firemen preparing to enter the blazing building put on their breathing apparatus

Earlier the fire had quickly destroyed shop awnings

# Boots ablaze

\ steam- lriven oad roller vas rought in o help a rane pull lown langerous rickwork right and elow)

\t its eight rowds stimated t 10,000 vatched he ragedy nfold

ONE of the most serious fires in Blackpool's history broke out on October 7, 1936.

And it was one of the most tragic and poignant.

For it claimed the life of a young firefighter who had just returned to duty the day before from his honeymoon.

The body of Ray Laycock, who was 25, was found hours later in the cellar of the Boots Building between Market Street and Corporation Street.

He had been carrying a hose to the seat of the blaze when he was overcome.

Two of his colleagues were treated in hospital for breathing problems caused by heat and smoke.

Big crowds watched as flames rapidly took hold of the large building next to Blackpool Town Hall.

There were municipal offices above the groundfloor shops area and many valuable records were destroyed.

The blaze started in the Boots photographic department in the basement which was packed with inflammable chemicals and celluloid film.

Firemen worked through the night but the building was left a smoking shell.

Parts of it had collapsed damaging a shop in the market complex which then stood next door.

The heat had cooked fish and rabbits in the neighbouring building.

Fire Chief Tom Varley and his men were praised for their gallant efforts in preventing the fire from spreading to the town hall and other nearby buildings.

He said: " The firemen were often working under very great danger and difficulty."

He escaped death by inches the following day when part of a wall collapsed into West Street.

After a stint of more than 12 hours the Blackpool firemen were allowed to rest while colleagues from neighbouring towns took over.

Teams of workmen toiled all night digging in the rubble until Fireman Laycock's body was found.

Sightseers stood with heads bowed and hats removed as he was lifted clear on a covered stretcher. Many were in tears at the tragic scene.

# Shape of things

THIS is the brave new face of Blackpool envisaged by the city fathers just over 60 years ago.

And it might have happened if a certain German politician hadn't given Britain other things to think about.

For years the council had been unhappy about the Golden Mile with its shabby shows and ramshackle stalls.

The Central Beach Clearance Scheme was proposed in 1938 to sweep away the entire Golden Mile area.

With it would go the little alleyways and terraced cottages that huddled behind the Mile around Bonny Street and all sorts of slum property in one of the oldest parts of the resort.

This sweeping £2 million plan would clear a giant triangle bounded by the Promenade from Coral Island to Central Pier, by Chapel Street and by Central Drive.

Central Station would have been moved south to front on to Chapel Street and would be given a totally new frontage.

The rest of the giant site would house a bus station, municipal offices, shops, gardens and various other buildings.

It would have been the biggest single change to Blackpool at any time in its history.

But although Parliament granted Blackpool powers to make it possible, it never happened.

Future developments were to alter the same area in a less dramatic way.

**Central Station (foreground) and the Golden Triangle that would have been home to the new-look Blackpool**

# — to come?

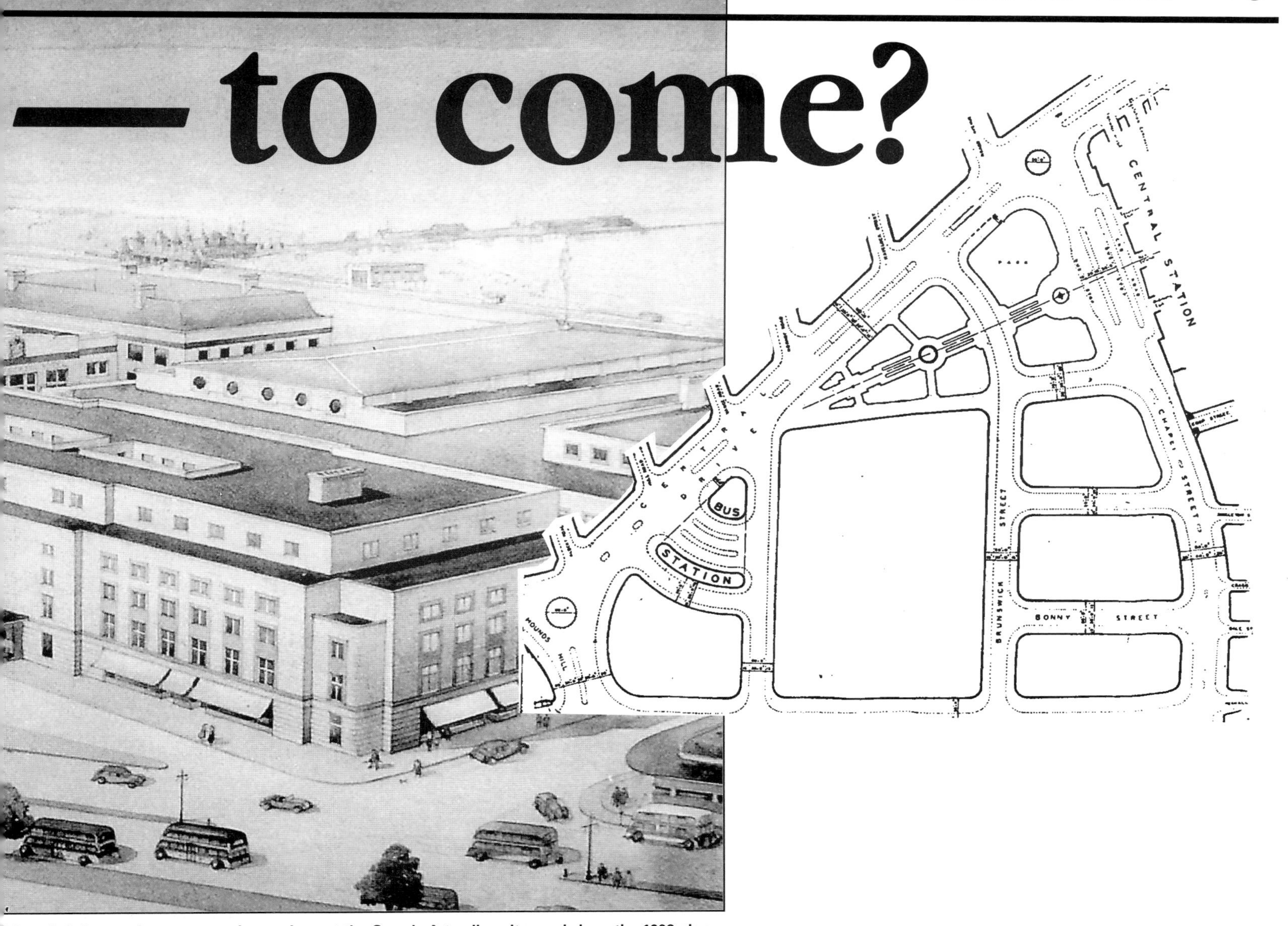


This artist's impression may soon be on show at the Grundy Art gallery. It reveals how the 1938 plan would have changed the face of Blackpool. Above right is a plan of the Central Beach Clearance scheme

# ...and the £1m revamp that never left the drawingboard

THE biggest ideas of all for revamping Blackpool in the 1930s got no further than the drawing board and the council debating chamber.

Imaginative ideas came from Councillor Harry Evans and could still strike a sympathetic chord with many people today.

His plan was to spend £1 million on a giant re-vamp spread over 10 years.

His fellow councillors humoured him by discussing the schemes but took no action.

Projects included:

- Ban ugly buildings from the promenade.
- Create sunken gardens and hothouses on the seafront
- Lay down a velvet walk of spongy rubber
- Provide new sea bathing facilities including hot showers
- Improve the entrances to all three piers
- Build a luxury lido centre for swimming, sunbathing and boating

Not since the early years of the century, when the promenade was widened along Central Beach, had such bold visions been made public.

Coun Evans wanted to excavate giant underground car parks and build an elevated tram track between Gynn Square and Starr Gate.

He thought the trams would run faster that way with less stress for drivers who did not have to look out for wandering pedestrians.

And the scheme would clear the decks for the sunken gardens and sun saloons.

## *One man's personal recollection of a boarding house upbringing in booming Blackpool of the 1930s*

# VACANCIES

# ...but the bath's taken!

Ivor Jones takes a trip down memory lane to visit the house was born in on Bairstow Street, South Shore in 1926

TAKING a bath took on a new meaning for Ivor Jones in holiday town Blackpool.

At the family boardinghouse in Bairstow Street he was sometimes required to sleep in a bathtub in the cellar if his bed was needed to accomodate a guest.

The bathtub in question was for the use of the Jones family – not the visitors they accomodated in their 10-bedroom home.

Ivor said: "Grandad had a bed in the cellar too, but I never thought anything about sleeping there. It was all part of the life in a boardinghouse in those days."

By the time he was seven Ivor had mastered the art of ironing sheets and pillowcases.

Saturday was the busiest day when one lot of holidaymakers went home and another arrived.

And if Uncle Jack, an old soldier and a bit of a character, had been for a pint or three in the Princess pub he had to be kept out of the way as the rest of the family sorted out the guests.

Ivor recalls: "They bundled him into the cellar and he slept it off down there."

There was no bathroom and only one toilet for the guests to use. Each room was provided with a jug of cold water and a basin for washing and a chamber pot that lived under the bed.

Ivor remembers: "I used to empty them each morning. It seems like another world now but it was all part of the sheer hard work of running a place like that. There were no vast profits in it. If anyone made a few bob they certainly earned it."

Ivor's grandparents had come from Derbyshire to run the place. His mother, Edith, came from Wigan to work for them and married their son.

Also working in the guesthouse was Ivor's Auntie Dorothy and Auntie Vi who was in showbusiness appearing with the Tower Ballet and in pantomimes.

In the winter, Jack's parents went door to door selling to boost the family income.

They ran the house on the apartment system.

"The visitors bought their food from local shops and my mother cooked it for them. They paid cover charge which was describ as: 'For the use of the cruet'!

"Goodness knows how she ke track of what they wanted. She h the orders written down on bits greaseproof paper in the kitch and early one morni when he'd had a f Uncle Jack mixed the all up . . ."

Ivor's father was fine pianist and one his pupils was Jimn Armfield, now organist at St Peter

Uncle Jack had played drums the army and it was that instrume which attracted Ivor. He and h father were good friends and oft played music together.

Ivor recalls: " People used to st outside the front window to listen

He became a profession musician and still plays the drun today at his home in Abbey Roa South Shore.

He said: "I had a happy chil hood – good parents and oth

relatives. We worked hard but it wasn't all work. We certainly did not have a lot of money but we had a lot of fun playing on the beach and in Stanley Park and we used to go to the Ritz cinema. It cost three old pence on a Saturday afternoon."

The dark days of wartime saw changes at Bairstow Street.

Ivor recalls: "I remember men coming who were survivors of the retreat from Dunkirk. They had ferried them back to England on the famous armada of little ships then loaded them into trains. When they got to us some of them had hardly any clothing on. They were in a terrible state.

"They soon got sorted out. I remember them lining up in the street to receive pay from a table set up there."

Then Blackpool became a giant RAF training camp. And Bairstow Street became a billet.

Ivor says: "Some people ripped the airmen off because they got their food ration coupons but did not give them the food they were entitled to. On the other hand you could not vet the men who stayed with you. We had a Polish airman stop and he gave me a flying jacket and a watch. Someone stole them from my room."

Ivor enjoyed the comradeship of his own army service and today acts as a military standard bearer. But he was invalided out of the army after being blown up by a mine on a training exercise. Several men were killed.

He remembers the Glasgow Fair visitors.

"They really did not care where they slept but we never had any trouble with them in Bairstow Street and Yorkshire Street and all round there. They had brooms on their shoulders and they went off marching on the Prom with a piper to play for them. It was a tradition.

"*They were great days.*"

# Death of a soccer hero

BLACKPOOL was in mourning in January, 1938 for Blackpool soccer star Jimmy Hampson who scored 252 goals in 373 League and FA Cup appearances – a club record never likely to be beaten.

The 31-year-old England and Blackpool centre forward went out fishing in a yacht from Fleetwood which was in collision with an outward-bound trawler in darkness in the Wyre channel.

The body of the hugely-popular sporting hero was never recovered.

The other victim of the tragedy was keen angler Harry Newsome of Kenwyn Avenue.

Jimmy Hampson lived in Woodfield Road. At the time, his wife was recovering in hospital. She was seriuously ill after their child had been stillborn.

Tributes poured in from all over the country and huge crowds turned out to pay tribute at special services.

A misadventure verdict was recorded at the inquest.

On his 32nd birthday his wife placed a wreath on the water where Jimmy was last seen.

12 FLEETWOOD CHRONICLE, FYLDE NEWS AND ADVERTISER FRIDAY, January 14th, 1938

SEARCH FOR BODIES OF TWO VICTIMS OF YACHT CRASH

LEFT, a happier picture from an earlier fishing trip. In front, left to right, are Messrs. T. Hoyle, "Jimmy" Hampson, and Newsome, and behind Messrs. Louis Cardwell and E. Clegg.

CENTRE, the small boat bearing the body of Mr. Newsome approaches the lifeboat slipway.

ABOVE, the body reaches the shore.

One Recovered By Police

"Jimmy" Hampson and Mr. H. V. Newsome Lost

MAYOR'S TRIBUTE

The Mayor of Fleetwood (Ald. C. Baer, T.D.) spoke of the fine spirit of the men who had conducted the search for the missing yachtsmen, and said they had earned the ...

VICTIMS' BIOGRAPHIES IN BRIEF

—MR. HAMPSON—

JIMMY HAMPSON was born at Little Hulton, near Bolton, and worked in the pit before ...

BODY HIGH AND DRY

—MR. NEWSOME—

**Champions of the Second Division in 1929-30, Blackpool, back row (players only) left to right Watson, Grant, Wolf, Ramsey, Benton. Front row: Quinn, Ritchie, Jimmy Hampson, Upton, Downes, Tremelling.**

# The key

A GOLDEN KEY unlocked the door of Blackpool Victoria Hospital on the day of its official opening in October, 1937.

Doing the honours was a Royal visitor, the Duke of Kent, who impressed everyone with his kind and friendly manner.

In a brief speech he commented that medical science was advancing quickly. Equipment that had been up to the minute 20 years before was now out of date.

And, in a comment that might have been made today, he said: " I am sure you will agree that it is our duty to see that all the advantages of this greater knowledge in matters of medicine should be passed on to the patients."

The hospital had been four years in the building and was up and running when the Duke carried out the openi ceremony.

The area where he used the gold key has now been demolished to ma way for a new chapter in the Victo story with state of the art faciliti under construction.

The Royal visitor was keen to chat patients.

He made a fuss of 16-year-old Eliz beth Ingham of Haig Road, Blackpo who was fighting back to fitness afte prank went tragically wrong.

She had jumped about 12 feet fr part of the promenade and suffer severe spinal injuries.

Her recovery was described as medical miracle and she proud moved her feet and bent her knees show the Duke how she w progressing.

The original Victoria hospital in Whitegate Drive. It was built and maintained by charity cash

The first Matron, Miss Annie Peel, and her staff in 1894

# Laying the first foundations

MORE than 40 years ago a piece of Blackpool history turned up on land in Bloomfield Road, South Shore.

It was a foundation stone which had been laid in 1887 at a site on Adelaide Street near South King Street.

This was planned as the home of Blackpool's first hospital and the Lord Mayor of London, Sir Reginald Hanson, was invited to the resort to do the honours.

But the project collapsed and it was not until 1894 that the town's first hospital opened in Whitegate Drive where the health department offices now stand.

Before that seriously ill or injured patients from Blackpool and the Fylde either had to be treated at home, in the care of local doctors, or be taken by train to Preston's Royal Infirmary.

The ever-generous people of Blackpool stumped up £500 to pay for the site in Whitegate Drive and there were just eight beds available.

Queen Victoria gave permission for her name to be used.

On opening day the first patient arrived – a child from Oldham who had been badly hurt in an accident on a fairground ride at Uncle Tom's Cabin.

She made a full recovery.

In those days Blackpool had a population of less than 30,000.

But in just over 10 years this grew to 100,000 and was swollen many times over by summer holiday visitors.

The Whitegate Drive premises were enlarged three times during that period.

Soon after World War One began in 1914 wounded soldiers evacuated from Belgium were treated there.

By the 1920s there was talk of a brand-new hospital on land at Whinney Heys.

But not everyone thought it a good idea.

Blackpool Trades Council was strongly opposed. Members argued that the average person could not afford a cab fare and would be faced with a long walk to see relatives – especially late at nig They argued for more extension Whitegate Drive which was th much more central and on a tr route.

But Leonard Franceys, chairm of the hospital management boa told journalists: " It is the patie we are considering. Their recov depends a great deal on th environment."

Blackpool Corporation dona the land at Whinney Heys on one the few bits of the Fylde which i few feet above sea level. Th

# to good health

The Duke chatted to patients in
arious wards but seemed to enjoy
eing with the children best.

One youngster screamed so loud
hen the VIPs arrived that she had to
e taken outside but smiles greeted
im from other children including 11-
ear-old Sheila Conroy of Peter Street,
lackpool.

The Duke said he liked the way the
ospital had got away from the old idea
f Nightingale wards in which beds
ere arranged in long straight rows
though 40 years later these were still
be found in other Fylde hospitals.

It was a busy day for the Duke. He
egan by opening what he described as
rinces Way – the stretch of
romenade near the Norbreck Castle
hich was the last link in the chain of
even miles of sea defences and promenade and seafront improvements in the resort.

Then he went to the hospital and the Town Hall.

Thousands lined the streets to cheer him.

The Duke left the comfort of the Mayor's Parlour to meet veterans of World War One who were lined up outside.

A crowd of 20,000 people in Talbot Square were silent as he spoke to almost every man and then they cheered as he went to talk to disabled veterans.

Finally, the Duke switched on the Illuminations.

And, before he left town on a train from North Station, he toured the lights in an open tram decorated as a lifeboat.

**The Duke of Kent arrives to open Blackpool Victoria Hospital with a golden key in October 1937**

**Whinney Heys Hall stood on the site of today's Blackpool Victoria Hospital. Built around 1570 it was home to the Veale family remembered by brasses in Bispham Parish Church**

**Local doctors (left) on a visit to the new Blackpool Victoria in 1933. The same area is now being rebuilt**

ould be lots of fresh air and
unshine.

Prophetically, Mr Franceys
dded: "Apart from that, there will
e every opportunity for future
xpansion at Whinney Heys, which,
view of the town's progress, is so
ssential. We must have vision for
he future."

*Then the project hit a legal snag.*

A covenant was discovered which
aid only residential development
hould go on the site.

Blackpool went to the
Chancery Court and it was eventually decided this was no bar to a hospital. The first sod was cut on November 27, 1932 and the 17th Earl of Derby laid the foundation stone on June 9, 1933.

A time capsule was buried beneath it containing a copy of The Gazette in a brass cylinder.

There was a crowd of 2,000 at the ceremony and the exposed site was lashed by wind and rain.

Nurses in their blue capes and white uniforms formed a guard of honour for Lord Derby and other VIPs.

Mr Franceys told of all the voluntary work that had been done over a 40-year period and how the demand for medical treatment had grown.

During 1932 there had been 5,600 in-patients and more than 1,800 operations.

OnSeptember 29, 1936 a project planned like a military operation swung into action.

A fleet of vans transferred equipment and stores from Whitegate Drive to Whinney Heys and a fleet of ambulances, some manned by doctors, transferred the patients.

An hour after the move was completed the operating theatre was in use for the first time and an hour after that accident and emergency received its first casualty.

She was 14-year-old Violet Jarvis of Cunliffe Road, Blackpool, who had been hurt in a road accident.

A patient on a sun veranda told the press: " It's wonderful -- marvellous. It's almost a pleasure to be ill."

During World War Two Whinney Heys coped with sick evacuees, war workers, service personel and prisoners of war as well as local patients.

After the invasion of Europe wounded Normandy veterans were treated there.

In 1948 the National Health Service took over the running of Blackpool Victoria and the old hospital board was disbanded.

The City Fathers who worked on that committee had every reason to be proud of the foundations they had lain for today's hospital service.

ROYAL ARTILLERY
OLD
TOJO

Chapter Four

# The Forties

# The WAR

A NEW KIND of visitor came rolling into Blackpool as the resort switched to a wartime role.

Because the town was full of guesthouse and hotel accommodation it was a Number One target for government officials who needed to find a home in a hurry for thousands of people.

First arrivals were civilian evacuees from industrial towns and cities which were obvious targets for bombing raids.

Numbers of RAF personel in the area soon built up and were swelled by even more from giant camps at Kirkham and Weeton and from Warton.

The area was used to train RAF personnel in many skills ranging from basic square bashing on the Promenade to air navigation, radio work and many mechanical and technical skills.

Polish airmen who had escaped when their country was invaded made Blackpool their headquarters and forces from other occupied countries were also in the resort.

Civil servants from London moved in – and sometimes grumbled about their new lifestyle.

In 1943 they staged a sitdown protest on the tramlines complaining about problems in getting to work. The result? More trams!

Blackpool became a major centre of aircraft production and many workers were drafted in from other towns.

Then came an American invasion as the Warton airfield was developed.

With their natty uniforms and pockets full of cash they were a big hit with local girls.

Blackpool entertained even though there was a war on and there was criticism that the party atmosphere was making some people forget that men and women were dying out there.

But although Blackpool and the Fylde escaped the ravages that Hitler's bombers ballrooms of the Tower and the Winter Gardens.

Civilians died when bombs fell and othe were killed when wartime planes crashed.

Fleetwood fishermen helped to keep th nation fed and many paid for their wartim catch with their lives.

Hundreds of volunteer soldiers fro Blackpool found themselves prisoners of th Japanese on the notorious Railway of Deat in Burma.

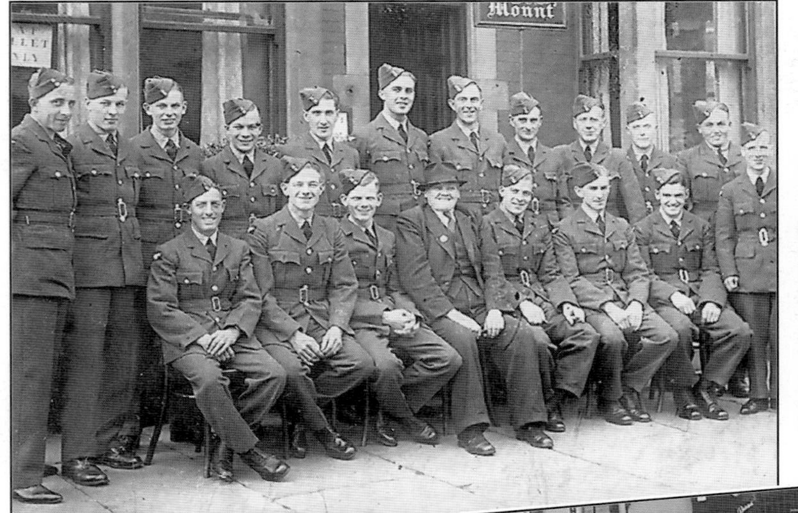

RAF men at their wartime billet. But where was The Mount?

The Stars & Stripes flutters proudly as America troops march in Talbot Square

This Messerschmitt fighter was exhibited in Blackpool to raise money for the Spitfire Fund in 1940

Pots and pans become aircraft parts in wartime Blackpool

Civil servants from London arrive in Blackpool

This picture of evacuee children was taken by the Gazette's chief photographer of the day, Frank Bain

# . . . but once peace returned, the Fylde recaptured its bright and breezy image

AFTER the big party that greeted the end of the war, Blackpool and the Fylde had to face years of austerity.

Everything seemed to be in short supply and many a serviceman returning home after giving years of his life to the conflict must have wondered what it was all about.

But spirits were cheered as Blackpool recalled the inspirational leadership Sir Winston Churchill had provided during the war.

He became the 21st Freeman of Blackpool and crowds turned out to cheer him as he was driven from the Hotel Majestic at St Annes to Blackpool for the ceremony.

Later, Field Marshall Viscount Montgomery of Alamein was given the same honour. The victory he masterminded in the deserts of North Africa had been a vital turning point in the conflict and he had gone on to play a major role in the invasion of Europe as the Nazi empire crumbled. When a new high school was built in Bispham, it was named after him.

Misery was acute in 1947 with big fuel shortages and electricity rationing. Thousands were made jobless as the former bomber factory at Squires Gate closed down.

It was bitterly cold – and even the sports scene was grim.

Blackpool lost 4-2 to Manchester United in the Cup Final.

But slowly the resort clawed back towards the old bright and breezy image.

Actress Anna Neagle switched on the Illuminations again in 1949. And they have been shining ever since.

Fleetwood got lit up too with strings of coloured lights on buildings like the Mount Pavilion and the Marine Hall. The island in the seafront boating lake was the centrepiece of a live show.

Beauty queen Sydney June Walker, aged 17 of Chaucer Road became a mermaid on a desert island!

The crowds flocked in on opening night but attendances soon waned.

People wanted holidays after the hardships of the war and tourism in Blackpool was boosted when the huge Royal Lancashire agricultural show made its home in the resort on land near Stanley Park.

## LANDLADIES ROLL OF HONOUR

**They made a home for:**

**Evacuees: 100,000 of them arrived from grey-faced expectatnt mothers to tearful children with their pathetic labels which made them look like lost parcels. Special trains brought 37,000 within four days.**

**Civil Servants: Thousands were shipped in to local hotels as their work was transfered out of London. This laid the foundations for today's major civil service presence in the area which has become such a valuable source of jobs.**

**War Workers: Although many local men and women worked on aircraft production in Blackpool, the 10,000 strong workforce included many drafted in from other towns who lodged in the resort.**

**Boys in Blue: Blackpool was a huge training area for the RAF. Space was so short that some slept in tents on the Pleasure Beach site. But thousands stayed in boardinghouses.**

**Allied Forces: Blackpool was the headquarters for the Polish air force in exile and also played host to men from Holland, France and Norway who had escaped the Nazis.**

# Target

Blackpool
Flugrüstungswerk
Genst. 5. Abt. Oktober 1940
Karte 1:100 000
GB/E 8
GB 74 65 b
Nur für den Dienstgebrauch
Bild Nr. F 888 b/40 707 (Lfl. 3)
Aufnahme vom 25. 9. 40
Länge (westl. Greenw.): 3° 01' 33'' Breite: 53° 46' 45''
Mißweisung: —12° 26' (Mitte 1940) Zielhöhe über NN 10 m
Maßstab etwa 1 : 11 500
10 830

A German military photograph which could have been used in any Blackpool Blitzkreig

THE war came home to Blackpool one nigh in September 1940. Bombs rained down o the resort and local folk woke to see jus what Hitler's aieforce could do.

Eight people died.

But, in general, the Fylde coast had a luck escape from the ravages of Hitler's Blitzkrei bombing campaign.

Sometimes the grateful residents o Blackpool saw the dull red glow in the sky a Merseyside blazed under a hail of hig explosive.

Local firemen were among those who riske their lives in the inferno there.

When it was all over the Alled force discovered that the Luftwaffe had a detaile map showing the Squires Gate area but neve gave it the pasting they might have.

Some locals thought the only bombs tha were dropped on the Fylde had bee jettisoned by pilots who had lost their wa on raids to Merseyside or Barrow.

But it is a fact that the Fylde had its shar of terror from the air.

The bombers claimed 11 dead and 3 injured.

They demolished 13 houses an damaged another 300.

Nearly 1,200 incendiary bombs fell o the Fylde along with 163 high explosiv and two parachute mines.

In addition, there were several time when mines were washed ashore on th beach at Blackpool and blown up.

Even so, Kirkham took a pasting from the Luftwaffe

Rescue workers trying to salvage a badly-damaged house in Church Road, St Annes

Youngsters from Lawrence House School, St Annes, play in a bomb crater on the school playing fields behind Church Road, St Annes

# Fylde coast!

Seed Street, near North Station, bore the brunt of local air attacks

Havoc from the air in Lindale Gardens, South Shore. But no one was hurt

**The catalogue of carnage from enemy attacks in the Fylde:**

## BLACKPOOL

First bombs of the war fell on North Shore golf course in August 1940.

The most serious incident of the whole war came on 11 September when a stick of bombs fell near North Station.

One was a 500-pounder and Seed Street off Talbot Road took the brunt.

In scenes that mirrored the worst of the carnage in big cities eight people were killed and 14 injured.

The street of little terraced houses was decimated. It was 11pm at night and in those days that meant that most people were in bed and asleep when the raiders struck.

The casualties included a couple aged 70 and a girl of six.

The bombers came to Blackpool again in October when houses in Lindale Gardens and Faringdon Avenue, South Shore, were damaged.

And two young children in a shelter nearby escaped unhurt as the gable end of a house crashed down.

There was further damage in South Shore and Marton in 1941.

## ST ANNES

A house in Church Road was demolished by a direct hit and others badly damaged in October 1940..

Nine people were badly hurt and one, a man of 72, an Oldham evacuee William Fox, died the following day. Others were refugees from the London blitz.

A lone plane flew in low from the sea to drop incendiary and high explosive bombs.

In April 1941, 200 incendiary bombs hit the government offices at heyhouses and a Special Constable was badly burned.

## KIRKHAM

Two died and 133 houses were damaged when eight high explosive bombs fell in Kirkham, in September, 1941.

The blasts were around Mellor Road, Moor Street and Orders Lane.

A man was killed and a three-year-old boy died from his injuries.

Seven others were hurt.

## POULTON

In May, 1941, 600 incendiary bombs fell at Poulton. One man was slightly hurt but there was little damage.

Other bombs fell in: Fleetwood, Greenhalgh, Lytham, Newton, Peel, Thornton, Warton, Weeton, Westby and Freeckleton
There were many lucky escapes.
Youngsters of the Blackpool Air Defence Corps survived a hit on their headquarters.
And when a fire bomb came through the roof of a house at Lytham it landed on a bed and was put out using a tin helmet.

# Banding

The legendary Glenn Miller orchestra playing at the Warton US base in 1944

The Oscar Rabin Band in Blackpool in 1944

BY 1940 Blackpool had become a vast training camp. It was the RAF's biggest centre, along with other major training establishments at Kirkham, Weeton and Warton.

Some of the RAF newcomers were professional musicians who sat in with local bands.

Men from the No1 Balloon Squadron – riggers who looked after barrage balloons – formed the Skyrockets Dance Orchestra which later became the Palladium theatre orchestra in London. It broke up in 1955 and the musical director, Paul Fenhoulet, became the conductor of the BBC Variety orchestra.

Live music in Blackpool wasn't just for dancing. Audiences loved to listen to music of all kinds. A big favourite was Toni and his 14-piece concert orchestra on North Pier. The wild-haire conductor, otherwise known as S Hopkins, led his men through the worl of Gershwin, Ravel and many others.

Among the guests at the Palace w the band led by Charlie Kunz whic scotched a story that he had bee arrested for sending coded messages the Germans by playing certain music items on radio.

Also visiting was Joe Loss – a ma who started his professional career as 16-year-old violinist in the Tower Ro Gardens band.

There was no shortage of fema partners on the dance floors Blackpool as hundreds of civil servan arrived from London and soon the ban leaders were announcing numbers: " arranged in London."

Charlie Barlow from Freckleton became one of Blackpool's best-loved band leaders. He is on the left in this saxophone section with band leader Norman Newman (right)

# Allied invasion of the Fylde

American forces in the Fylde marching through Blackpool

THE invasion of Blackpool came in 1942 when American forces arrived in the Fylde.

It was a re-run of 1917 when some had passed through.

Back then one wrote of Blackpool: " In the teeming life by the sea, the war seems a fantasy – it was very jolly."

It seemed that every Yank was called Hank ... and they found no shortage of partners.

An RAF recruit received just 20p a day but the lowest paid American was on nearly £3.50 a week. But it wasn't just about money.

Jack Greenwood recalls: "Their fancy uniforms appeared to have come straight from Saville Row and some used Spam medals and false rank badges to enhance their reputation."

GI Joe liked exciting music such as American Patrol or Woody Herman's Woodchoppers Ball. He liked jitterbug dancing but the authorities frowned on that.

And he liked romance. Some said there was more activity under the piers than up on the boardwalk.

A woman wrote to the Gazette: "Can nothing be done to stop the disgusting behaviour on the sands below Central Pier. I have never seen such behaviour in public both at night and in broad daylight."

Many Blackpool people did not like the sight of armed American military police with pistols at their sides patrolling the dance halls, or the way the black American forces were shunned by their white colleagues.

Some local girls who danced with black Americans were shunned by whites.

Blackpool entertained the trooops and the Fylde coast played host to weary workers taking break from the mills, mines an factories.

But the heartbreak of th battlefield came home to eve street in the land.

Maybe that was what prompte a letter in the Gazette from woman who said Blackpool atmosphere was just like one b party and people seemed to ha forgotten there was a war on an men and women were dying o there.

Four of Blackpool's mo famous musicians were all servi in the RAF – organists Reg Dixo Reg Holland and Horace Finc along with Freckleton-bor saxophone star Charlie Barlo one of the best loved musicia ever to play at the Tower and band leader there in his own rig for many years

Jack points out that some son

# together

Everything had to shutdown at 10pm each night but the crowds went out early.

Young couples who met on the dance floors of Blackpool didn't worry about the blackout which shrouded the resort in darkness and the songwriters wrote a song about it – You Can't Black Out the Moon.

At Feldman's Theatre the attraction was nude showgirls on stage.

At just sixpence a time the youthful airmen crowded in. But, as at The Windmill in London, the girls had to stand still or the censor stopped the show.

George Formby let in the New Year of 1941 at the Opera House starring in the pantomime Dick Whittington.

A great entertainer of troops overseas during World War Two George knew the barrack-room lyrics for many famous songs but never sang them on stage in Blackpool.

Music of a classical kind was provided by Sir Henry Wood and the Halle Orchestra with a concert at the Tower which was also visited by the London Philharmonic Orchestra with the famous tenor Richard Tauber.

Wartime may have been a great leveller but those with the cash could still find the perks.

An example was the dinner dance at the Baronial Hall in the Winter Gardens.

Freckleton lad Charlie Barlow was the band leader and it cost less three shillings and six pence for the meal and his music.

Time for a chat at South Shore open air pool as an American GI meets a local girl

The Skyrockets were formed by RAF personnel serving in the Fylde

*For thousands of people wartime Blackpool meant happy hours in the Tower ballroom where they could forget the cares of the day. And it was there that many found romance including those who became GI brides and began a new life in America.*

*The late Jack Greenwood did not see a lot of wartime Blackpool. He started the war serving in the merchant navy and after surviving double pneumonia joined the RAF and saw plenty of action in the siege island of Malta.*

*But Jack, of Bedford Avenue, Cleveleys, loved the world of the big bands and many years later wrote a lively book called Blackpool Entertains The Troops.*

Organist Reginald Dixon was Mr Blackpool Entertainment to generations of visitors with his signature tune Beside The Seaside. He spent most of World War Two in the RAF but still found time to play the Wurlitzer in the Tower Ballroom

crossed the demarcation line between Friend and Foe.

"We loved the haunting German number Lilli Marlene first heard over tank radios in Egypt's Western Desert and the Germans liked the Beer Barrel Polka or Roll Out The Barrel if you prefer. That had sold half a million sheet music copies in Britain by 1939."

But most wartime songs were sentimental and none more so than Goodnight Sweetheart from which lines were often quoted in the millions of letters written in those years between people forced apart by war.

*Goodnight Sweetheart all my prayers are for you*
*My dreams enfold you, in them dear I'll hold you*
*Goodnight Sweetheart, Goodnight.*

Sadly, there were many Dear John letters too as romance broke up relationships between the girls at home and the men overseas.

# Horror on the Home Front as the Fylde coast tastes

THE worst horrors of war in the Fylde were caused not by enemy action but by two accidents involving allied planes.

The most horrific was in Freckleton on the morning of August 23, 1944.

A terrible thunder storm had sprung up with little warning and torrential rain and low cloud set the scene for the nightmare.

A pair of B-24 Liberator bombers had taken off on a routine test flight from the American base at Warton, now the British Aerospace site.

Fighting terrible turbulence in the air they had been recalled for an emergency landing. But that was impossible so they decided to fly north and try to get clear of the storm.

Then came a radio message from one of the pilots, First Lieutenant John Bloemendal.

He said: " My altimeter and air speed have gone crazy! My compasses are spinning. I have no control at all!"

Opinion is divided about whether the plane had been hit by lightning but there was no doubt about the result.

The bomber crashed into the centre of the village of Freckleton.

It flattened part of St John's school and 35 children were killed. The Sad Sack snack bar across the street went too and 11 adults perished, including the three men in the plane.

The Liberator's fuel tanks ruptured and rivers of blazing high-octane fuel streamed down the streets and engulfed the shattered buildings.

Some of the children who survived were badly burned and when the singer Bing Crosby went to see them in hospital he was so moved that he could not sing a note for a while. Later he managed a rendering of White Christmas.

There were 10,000 men at Warton and the Americans were praised for their rescue efforts. Men tore at red hot bricks with their hands. Some children escaped without a scratch while others close by were killed.

Later, the men of Base Air Depot 2 helped to create a memorial park for the children of Freckleton.

**The scene of carnage after a B-24 Liberator bomber from the US Air Force base at Warton crashed on Freckleton village school**

# The price

## A joy ride to terror

EARLIER, in August 1941, air crash horror came to Blackpool.

It started when the CO at RAF Squires Gate was off station on a course and some of his men took off for a flying exercise of their own.

Boulton Paul Defiant planes carried out a mock diving attack on a Blackburn Botha aircraft but this should never have happened over a built-up area.

A Defiant hit the Botha at 3.10 in the afternoon when the streets of the resort were packed. People dived for cover in doorways as a hail of metal fragments fell .

The tail section of the Botha just missed the crowded Prom but a chunk fell through the roof of a guest house and into a bedroom. A RAF man, off duty on sick parade, recovered instantly to dash downstairs.

Most of the Botha went through the glass roof of Central Station – near today's Coral Island. It blew up in a fire storm of blazing petr causing horrific casualties in t station crowds.

**Plane wreckage in the street near Central Station after the horrific air crash of August 1941**

The Defiant crashed on 97 Rea Avenue, a property which w never re-built.

Mr and Mrs L.H. Franceys w were at home at the time, escap uninjured. The pilot's body w found in the wreck and the gunn who had jumped or fallen out, l the ground in Regent Road. F parachute was unopened.

There were two servicemen each plane plus a civilian mechar taking a joy ride in the Botha. I swapped at the last minute wi another man who was given a j to do by a foreman.

The tragedy cost the lives of people and 35 were injured, ma of them badly.

# tragedy of its own

Servicemen carried the small coffins to their last resting place

Survivors from the school

Grim-faced rescuers remove a body from the ruined Freckleton school

The Sad Sack snack bar in Lytham Road was owned by the Whittle Family and destroyed in the crash

Children watch (left) as American soldiers put the finishing touches to Freckleton Memorial Park

# to pay

## Drama in the skies above

SOME of the young Polish airmen who flew from Blackpool were killed in accidents.

Two died at Wrea Green when they crashed in a field after unofficial low-level aerobatics.

They were replaced at Squires Gate by 256 Squadron of the RAF.

And, in April 1941 Flt Lt Donal Rock West and air gunner Sgt R T Adams, both aged 20, shot down a German bomber over the Ribble estuary.

An eyewitness said the aircraft came down on fire like a blazing cross.

It crashed on the marshes at Banks on the Southport side of the river.

Cries of help were heard in the darkness by Home Guard soldiers on the beach at Lytham.

They found a German flier with a badly smashed arm lying helpless in the mud with his parachute.

Some of the crowd which quickly gathered by Lytham Green shouted to the soldiers to shoot the flyer dead.

He was taken to hospital and later repatriated by the Red Cross in exchange for an injured British serviceman.

Aircraft historian Russell Brown of St Annes traced his son and learned that the Luftwaffe crewman had recovered to fly again against the Allies.

## 400 perish on 'Pepperpot'

BLACKPOOL'S adopted warship was HMS Penelope –known as HMS Pepperpot because she was filled with holes from enemy attacks in Malta.

After plenty of action during the war Penelope was sent to Italy to give covering fire for troops who had landed at Anzio.

At 7am on February 18, 1944 the ship was 35 miles from Naples when U-boat 410 got a direct hit with a torpedo.

This caused a massive explosion, probably in the ammunition stores, and the ship sank in 40 seconds.

Penelope had 600 men onboard. Less than 200 survived.

More than 400 have no known grave but the sea and they included Stoker Alfred Brook from Blackpool and Coder Edwin Lawrence of Fleetwood who had just gone off watch when the torpedo hit.

Over at last. A soldier home on leave joins the party

Happy crowds in Talbot Square, Blackpool

The flags are out in Vance Road, Blackpool, to mark the end of the war in Europe

# Party

Even Adolf Hitler (bottom right) came to this party in Larbreck Avenue, Layton

Children from Trafalgar Street, Alexandra Road and Holmefield Road, St Annes, enjoy their VE Day Party

Housew celebrati

# VE Day signals the start of celebrations as World War Two draws to a close

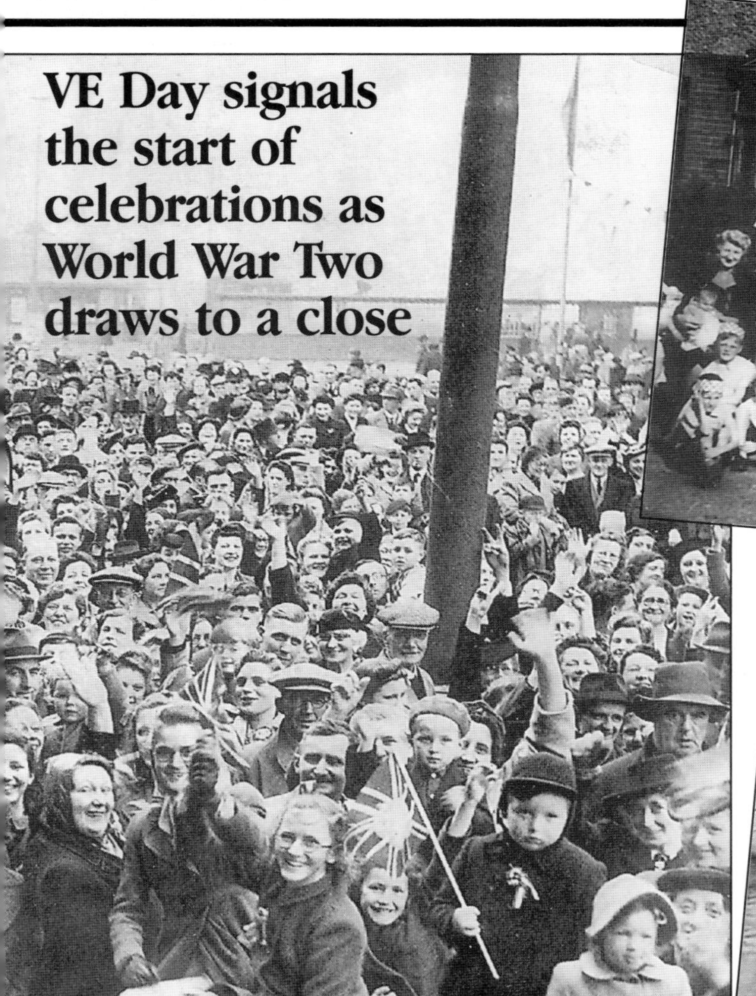

Everyone got on the picture in Winton Avenue, Marton

Young and old celebrate in this Fylde Street. Note the shelters in the background. Below: Another typical VE Day street party gets into full swing

mouflage a street air raid shelter with a Union Jack for their

Celebrating VE Day in Marton when the children were treated to a party in the Crossland Road park

# Party in the Park

PARTY time on the recreation ground in Crossland Road as grateful local residents celebrate the end of World War Two in Europe.

The photograph belongs to Mrs Eileen Adam of Poulton Old Road, Blackpool.

Also pictured is her older sister Mavis and their mother Mrs May Clarke.

Eileen has many memories of life in the area around Crossland Road and neighbouring Brook Street in Marton in those far-off days.

She was born in 1937 so grew up as a child during the war.

Her four brothers all went into the forces – three in the årmy and one in the RAF.

She said: " That meant there was a bit more room for me and Mavis because those houses in Crossland Road weren't big.

" People talk about the good old days and they were good for the fact that people were neighbourly and tried to help one another – especially during the war.

" But they were not good in many other ways. Money was in short supply. We were better placed than some others in the street but often on pay day we had to wait until my Dad came home with his wages so that Mum could buy something for tea."

Her father Joe, was a landscape gardener. And, if he called in the pub on the way home for a pint on pay night, tea would be delayed and cash might be in shorter supply.

She said: " That was the just the way they lived then. When money was short we got food on credit from Mrs Nutbrown's shop at the corner of Hawes Side Lane. They called it getting stuff on the strap and getting that credit was an important part of life for people round there."

Eileen has happy memories of her childhood. Wartime food rationing was relieved by food parcels containing sweets from a family friend in Australia. As conditions improved schoolchildren took jam jars to school for a free cocoa allowance.

She said: " It's true people didn't lock their doors but no one had anything worth pinching anyway!"

Some families filled their already crowded houses with refugees and evacuees because they needed the pittance paid for their keep.

Eileen recalls: " Some of those children were so unhappy. They must have suffered a lot. We had a little boy from London and he was always crying. But then we found out where his sister was and he went to stay with her."

Kindly Mrs Clarke was often consulted for advice and practical help by younger mums when babies were fractious or other problems arose.

Youngsters found adventure as they played around the district.

Eileen remembers a factory in Vicarage Lane making shiny metal tubes which would float in a dyke near the works.

"We found you could sit on them and paddle like a boat. Luckily no one got drowned."

The big treat was a two penny visit to the Saturday afternoon show at the Empire cinema, now a bingo hall.

Apart from the films there was a childrens talent show and the kids cheered and booed the various young hopefuls prepared to have a go.

One favourite was Peter Calvert from Brook Street who mimed to records.

A local character was John Cokin who spent most of his adult life in the same area and collected scrap and rags with a pram.

# The Blackpool Regiment

HUNDREDS of young men from Blackpool and the Fylde joined the territorial army as a result of a big recruiting drive in April, 1939.

Known as the Blackpool Regiment they were part of the Royal Artillery and were shipped out to Singapore at the tip of the Malay peninsula.

There they fought the Japanese and many of the 600 members of the Blackpool Regiment were killed or wounded at the battle of Slim River.

Soon the survivors found themselves prisoners of the Japanese army who despised any soldier who allowed himself to be a captive.

At first the Brits were locked up in Changi jail where conditions were appalling. Then came the news that they were going to a rest camp at Ban Pong in Siam – now Thailand.

It turned out to be a terrible joke. There were 25 men to a cattle truck. The metal sides were too hot to touch by day and too cold to lean on at night. There were no lavatories and little water.

The journey took four days.

Then the Blackpool lads joined 60,000 Allied prisoners building the Railway of Death linking Siam and Burma.

More than 16,000 died from sickness, exhaustion and malnutrition.

Beatings were common from guards with nicknames like Dr Death and The Undertaker.

Only the heroic efforts of medical staff kept hundreds barely alive.

Reg Dunne, of Mere Road, Blackpool, a prominent member of the Far Eastern Prisoners of War Association recalls how he and his pals clung to life in the camps.

He said: " Men hung on to the hope that one day they would go home. They had the thought in their mind that just by staying alive they could defeat their captors."

Religious faith, dogged courage, hatred of their jailers, a sense of humour despite all the horror –these were factors that helped men hold out.

The lucky ones did come home and were able to pick up the threads of normal life again.

But the trauma of the experience lives with them yet.

A frequent nightmare with FEPOWs is to see Japanese soldiers marching up their own familiar street to take them back to the camps again.

For some the effects on mind and body have been extremely severe and led to marriage break up and other family problems as well as serious ill health in later life.

The young volunteers of The Blackpool Regiment paid dearly for the day they answered their country's call.

**Off to war. Members of the Blackpool Regiment, who were all volunteers, shortly before they sailed to defend Singapore**

**Home again. Six-year-old Jack Sutter wears his dad's cap to welcome him home at Blackpool Town Hall**

**Some of those who left Blackpool for the Far East found their last resting place at Kanchanburi cemetery**

# On the march 'in a north west town'

SQUIRES GATE was chosen as the site for a huge Vickers Armstrong aircraft factory. Some of the buildings survive today alongside Squires Gate Lane.

The aircraft building operation locally was vast. There was also major activity at the Stanley Park aerodrome and engineering work went on in many locations which included some in St Annes as well as the Marton tramsheds near the Saddle pub on Whitegate Drive; Talbot Road bus station car park; and the Harrowside underground car park.

On August 6, 1940, during the building of the main factory, part of the building collapsed. Six men were killed and 16 injured.

But, by September 30 that year the first three Wellington bombers built at Blackpool took to the skies for their maiden test flights.

More than 10,000 people worked on wartime aircraft production in the Fylde and 3,406 Wellingtons were built. The last one was a Mark 10 which flew on October 13, 1945.

Aircraft production did not always go smoothly.

One worker appeared before Blackpool Magistrates on sabotage charges.

Most of the hearing was in secret because details were given of aircraft construction but it emerged the man had been careless, rather than cunning. He hoped his slipshod work would get him transferred out of Blackpool and back to his home town, after he had been sent to the resort under wartime employment regulations.

He was fined £100 with costs of almost £30 – a hefty penalty in those days.

Then there was an angry exchange of letters in the Press about the behaviour of workers at the factory.

They were accused of being absent without leave, refusing to do overtime and 'skiving' to prolong meal breaks.

The men worked from 8am to 7pm on six days a week with alternate Saturdays and Sundays off. They had an hour at lunch and two tea breaks. Overtime began after 5.30pm with double time on Sunday.

It was said that weekly flat rate earnings ranged from £3 to £8.

*But none of the letters mentioned the army of women who were also part of the giant team!*

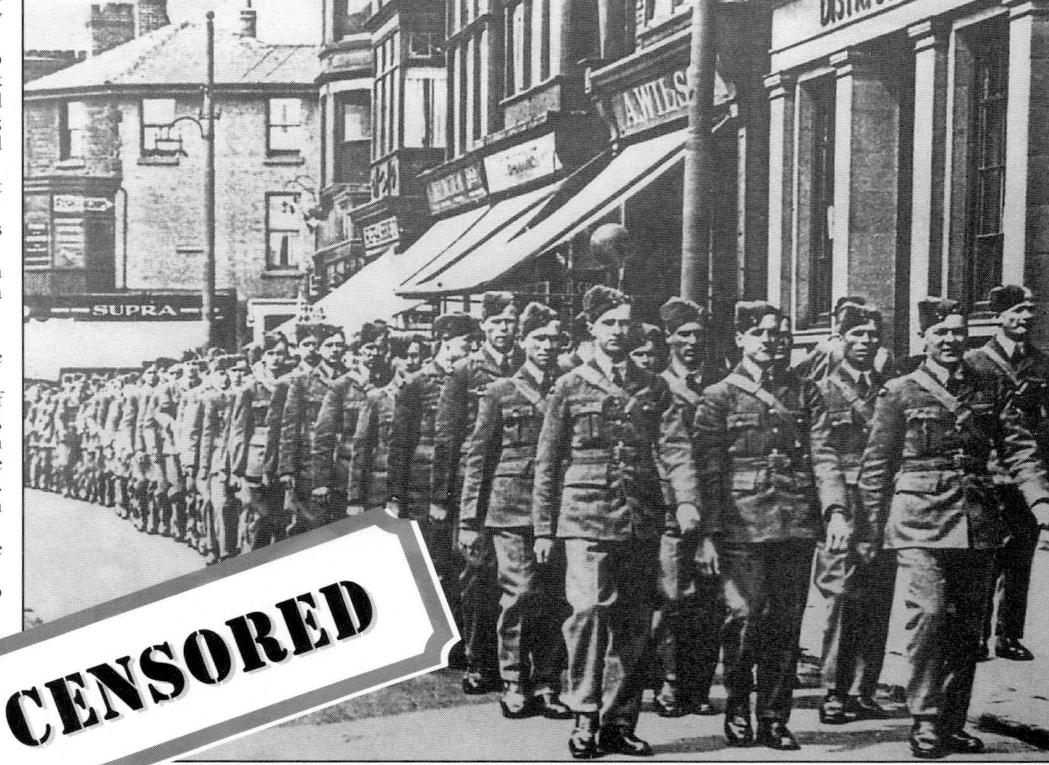


**Trainee airmen marching in Central Drive. Wartime censorship removed the Tower from this Gazette picture so it became just "a northwest town" in the caption**

**Armourers handle a 1,000 bomb at RAF Kirkham – now an open prison**

**Thousands of women (right) helped to build planes at locations all over Blackpool and Fylde. These are turret lathe operators**

**Some airmen camped out on the Pleasure Beach but complained it was too noisy to sleep!**

# Departure Gate

IN December ,1940, the historic airfield at Squires Gate became operational as RAF Squires Gate.

Before that, Fairey Battle and Wellington bombers had been moved there in a dispersal system to protect them from enemy bombing at other, more-well-known RAF sites.

And, as war clouds gathered in the '30s, Blackpool had played an important roll in teaching young men to fly for the combat many realised was inevitable.

The Civil Air Guard provided training at Stanley Park, the council-owned airfield where the zoo now stands.

In November 1938, the Air Ministry took over Squires Gate and unleashed a storm of protest from St Annes residents who feared their suburban peace would be shattered by the increased activity.

Squires Gate became the home of the No 42 Elementary and Reserve Flying Training School who took to the air in Tiger Moth aircraft.

The No9 Civil Air Navigation School used Avro Anson planes. Navigation and reconnaisance training went on right through the war and thousands of men learned these skills at Blackpool. Work was linked in with an air sea rescue unit which had launches based at Fleetwood.

On the ground, 'ack ack' gunners learned to fire at targets towed over the Squires Gate field.

It was in World War Two that the solid runways were laid at Squires Gate while Middle Lane – which connected south Blackpool with St Annes starting opposite the Halfway House – simply disappeared.

Division Farm was requisitioned and the old Blackpool Golf Club also vanished. Part went into the airfield and part was added to St Annes Old Links turning it from a nine-hole to an 18-hole course.

The former Blackpool clubhouse was re-built at Lytham Green Drive golf club.

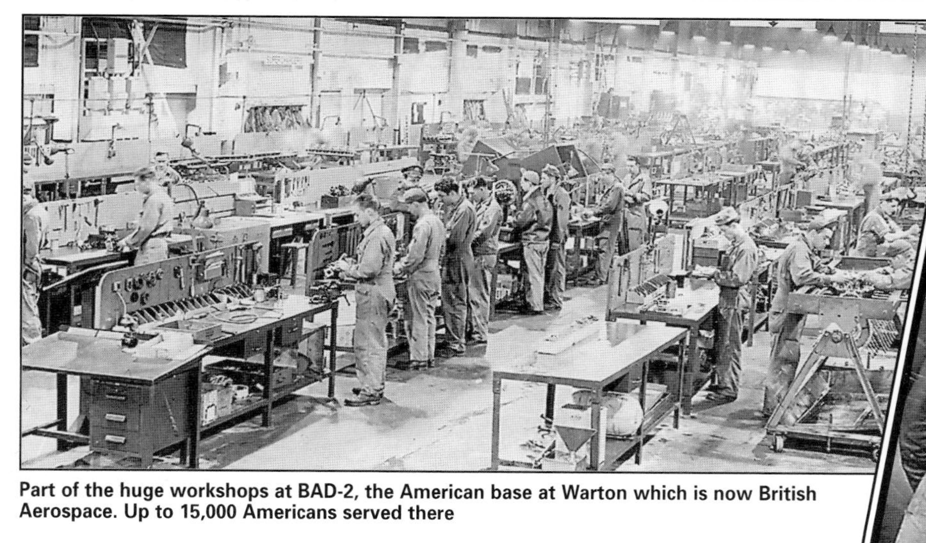

Part of the huge workshops at BAD-2, the American base at Warton which is now British Aerospace. Up to 15,000 Americans served there

# 'Accidental' air base

WARTON aerodrome started life as an RAF site, and contractors Wimpey Construction began work in 1940.

It is said that the Air Ministry were thinking of abandoning the project but instead it was chosen as a Base Air Depot for the US 8th Army Air Force.

It was No2 of four sites where US combat planes underwent major maintenance, overhaul and repair.

Choosing Warton was almost an accident. The top brass wanted Squires Gate but were told that was out of the question. Then someone mentioned Warton where construction work had earlier come to a mysterious halt.

It started again in 1942 and involved an army of 7,000 construction men with an office staff of more than 300.

The site was handed over to the Americans in 1943.

At one time there were 10,000 American servicemen at Warton and when they were off duty they caught the 'Passion Wagon' bus to Blackpool for a night out.

Other American forces spent time in Fleetwood and the smallest detachment of all, including black members of the Transport Corps, were stationed in the isolated Over Wyre village of Pilling where they guarded a giant fuel dump.

It was in 1947 that the organisation now called British Aerospace first linked up with Warton.

In those days it was the English Electric engineering company of Preston.

Back in 1938 they had been selected by the government to build Handley Page Hampden bombers at their Strand Road factory. They needed an airfield and Samlesbury was built near Blackburn.

In 1947 test flights began at Warton using a Gloster Meteor jet fighter to gather high altitude information for the building of the Canberra bomber.

Pictured centre with his two air gunners is second lieutenant Norman Zuber. Flying on A-26 Invader he collided with another Invader on November 29, 1944. Both pilots and another crewman were killed when the machines crashed on Warton Marsh

Working on a C47 Dakota (left) at the American base at Warton

American servicemen in their fur-lined jackets pose on the wings of a B24 Liberator

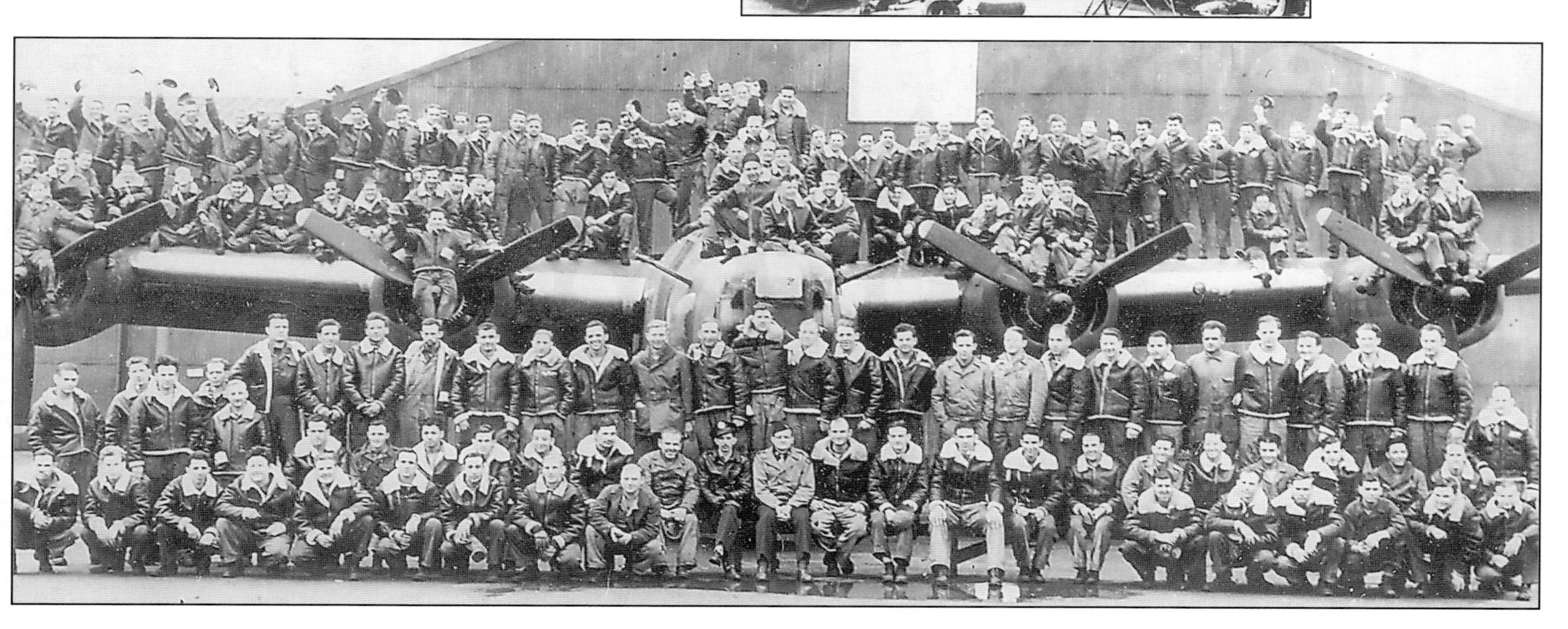

# Like it or lump it, the Yanks lend a hand

AMERICAN troops in wartime Fleetwood never forgot the day they volunteered to lend a hand on the docks.

The men were living in the pier complex and were members of the 100th Evacuation Hospital – a big medical team waiting to join the invasion of Europe to care for the wounded.

There was a labour shortage among the 'lumpers' – the dockers who worked through the night to unload fish from the trawlers and set it out in boxes and barrels or 'kits' ready for the auction sales each morning.

Some years later, in 1949, the Fleetwood Chronicle published memories of the time from the Americans.

**Workers pictured outside a traditional Fleetwood fish house or processing factory**

One wrote: "When we neared the docks the stench of the fish reached our noses and the breakfasts of a few bounced around in their bellies."

The men were divided up for the different jobs of unloading a trawler.

Some were winchmen to lift baskets of fish from the hold while others were draggers to haul the baskets of fish – around 90lbs a time – along slippery gangplanks poised on trestles called horses above the ship's deck.

Others were linemen to guide the baskets on to the planks and some were packers sorting the catch out on the fish market.

Others were sent down into the fishroom to dig out tons of ice and fish from giant storage bins called pounds.

Ankle deep in water and ice they had the toughest job.

But the Americans could not resist a bit of a boast.

" Despite the ridicule heaped upon us by the dockers by the second day we unloaded more fish with fewer men in less time than they did."

He recalled: "Our clothes smelled of fish, our hands smelled of fish and the barracks at the Pier reeked of fish."

Most of the Americans decided they preferred meat and two veg to seafood after a few sessions and volunteer numbers slumped. But there was a handsome donation to company funds which meant a cash handout for the erstwhile lumpers.

# Fleetwood's finest hour

FLEETWOOD'S finest hour came in the 1940s when the port helped to keep the nation fed.

Fish was one of the few items not subject to rationing, but distribution of the highly-nutritious food was controlled under a government scheme designed to make sure people all over the country could get their hands on some fish.

Within weeks of the war starting U-boats were attacking Fleetwood trawlers among the Hebridean islands off Scotland's west coast.

Some crews died, others were taken prisoner.

Many fishermen and their ships served in the Royal Navy on dangerous tasks such as minesweeping and convoy escort work.

Many more risked the mines and U-boats to fish in UK waters and at Iceland.

The port played host to refugee fishermen from Poland, France, Belgium and Holland and boats from Iceland and the Faroe Islands landed catches in Fleetwood.

One, the Faroese schooner Stella Marie, was wrecked on the Shell Wharf sanbanks and local lifeboatmen won gallantry medals for rescuing the crew at the height of a terrible storm.

The Humber ports of Hull and Grimsby were all but closed down during the war and businessmen in the fish processing trade based themselves in Fleetwood.

The port was a boom town and a hive of activity.

At the giant Robertson engineering complex workers toiled round the clock making equipment for the Royal Navy.

Local inshore fishermen were praised for their bravery in making safe mines found floating in Morecambe Bay.

And crowds turned out to see foreign

Fishing smacks like these laid the foundation for Fleetwood's deep sea trawler trade

nationals and prisoners of war being shipped off for internment in the Isle of Man.

Cargo had been king in the port of Fleetwood until the turn of the century when the town was in a slump because other northwest docks like Liverpool, Manchester and Preston had turned the Wyre into a backwater.

But fishing saved the day when trawler owners from Hull and Grimsby decided to exploit the rich grounds off Britain's western seaboard. And the railway network took the catch of the day to the chip shops and fishmongers of northern towns – and further afield to customers and wholesale markets throughout the land.

Money was made in wartime Fleetwood but a terrible price was paid in human life. For a small town of less than 30,000 people the port made a big manpower contribution to the war effort and many did not return.

Steam trawlers tied up on the fish dock. Catches were unloaded there. The fish was sold and some processed under the sheds around the dockside where wintertime conditions resembled the Arctic

Wartime rules forbade photography on the docks. But below is how Wyre Dock looked then. On the far side is the site of today's Freeport shopping complex

# The sea gives back its secret

IN December 1948, the Fleetwood trawler Goth sailed to the fishing grounds off Iceland's north west coast. The ship disapeared in a hurricane storm and all 21 crewmen vanished with her.

It was nearly 50 years later that the wreck was discovered by chance when the nets of an Icelandic trawler tangled on it and the funnel was brought to the surface.

The Gazette helped to foot the bill to bring the funnel back to Fleetwood. Relatives hope to preserve it as a memorial to their loved ones.

The dredger Fylde had an endless chain of buckets to scoop up the mud and produced strange grinding sounds which could be heard through the old part of town by day and night

The weather proved an enemy in 1940 and 1947. This 1940 picture shows workmen clearing snow drifts outside the Halfway House hotel where St Annes Road meets Squires Gate Lane in Blackpool

Always a popular star in Blackpool George Formby lived in the Fylde. He spent much of the war entertaining troops on the battlefield and made comedy films including locations in Fleetwood

# Turned out

Fuel was in short supply in 1947 and most people had open fires. Crowds queued at the gasworks (above) for a ration of coke. They pushed it home in carts and prams – even a wheelchair!

One of Blackpool's most famous meeting places (above) got a new frontage in 1940. The venue, in Talbot Square, is now the home of Rumours

Here's how the promenade looked in wartime. The concrete blocks were to stop invading tanks. Bathing huts and pleasure boats were still in use

IT wasn't all doom and gloo in Blackpool and the Fyld coast of the 1940s.

Even in the darkest days of th war Blackpool found time t remember those maids of all wor on the sands – the donkeys.

They got their own charter t protect them from overwork!

After the anguish of the wa years came the joy of celebration but the returning heroes foun Britain a harsh land to live in.

Everything was in short suppl but as the decade drew to an en councils like Blackpool were able to ease the housing shortage a littl by building more council homes The first residents moved on t Mereside estate.

And the resort saluted a pair o national heroes.

Sir Winston Churchill and th military leader Montgomery o Alamein became Freemen o Blackpool.

Councillors set war aside to pass local laws designed to protect donkeys from cruelty on the beach – The Donkey Charter. Here's Gracie Fields taking a trip

# ice again!

Montgomery of Alamein (above) greets the crowds at Blackpool Town Hall when he became a Freeman

Hats off to Winnie! Sir Winston Churchill (left) was also made a Freeman of the resort

AGULL
IT COSTS LESS BY
LET US PLAN YOUR ROUTE

*Chapter Five*

# *The Fifties*

# Naughty

A TRADITIONAL part of leaving inhibitions at home on a trip to the seaside is to send a cheeky postcard to the folks you leave behind.

But back in The 1950s the City Fathers were getting twitchy about this part of the Blackpool scene – as familiar as rock, candyfloss, and Kiss Me Quick hats.

Blackpool had set up a censorship panel back in 1913 but that was overtaken by World War One.

After World War Two there were some obscenity prosecutions about postcards and the Gazette suggested: "The only solution seem to be a broad-minded and experienced panel of censors."

A year later, in 1951, The Blackpool Postcard Censorship Board was formed. It included a Vicar, landlady, solicitor and retire bank manager. At the first meeting

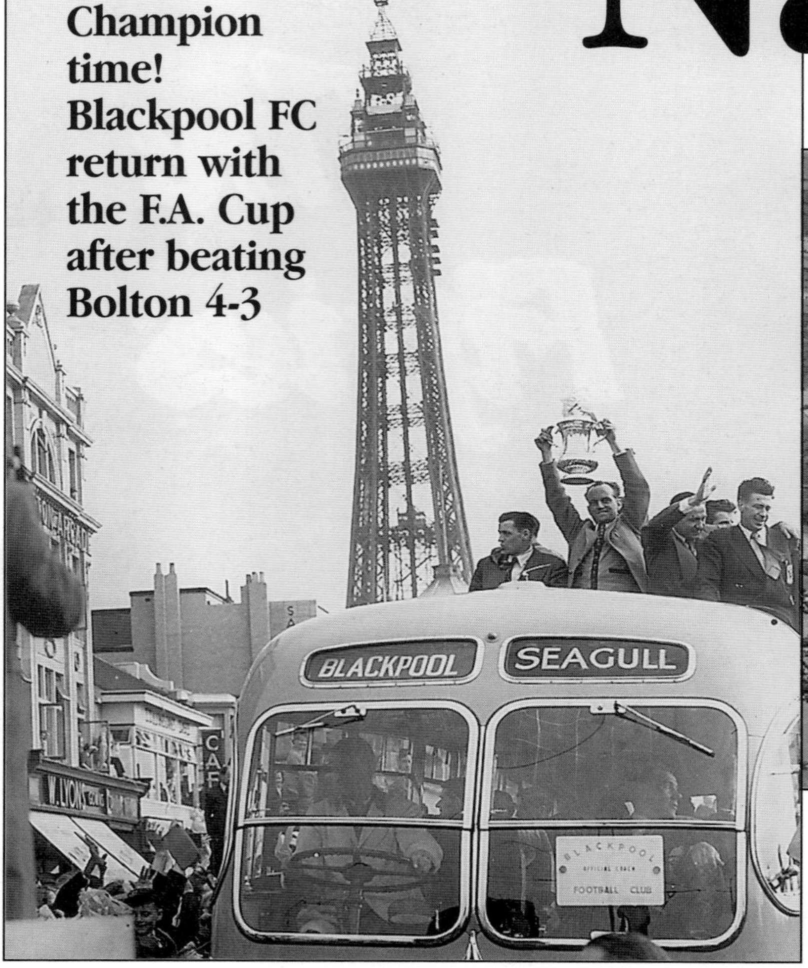


**Champion time! Blackpool FC return with the F.A. Cup after beating Bolton 4-3**

**Released in 1952 this was the first official photograph of a Hawker Hunter fighter which first broke the sound barrier over the Fylde**

# Fylde flies into history

**A youthful Princess Margaret meets Mrs Ogden, Mayoress of Blackpool, at the Squires Gate Hawker factory in 1954**

FLYING history was made at Blackpool in 1953 when test pilot Neville Duke flew faster than the speed of sound over Blackpool for the first time.

He was at the controls of aircraft B1 – the first Hunter jet fighter built in the 50s at Squires Gate by Hawker Aircraft – and a crowd of 100,000 people lined the promenade.

They heard the characteristic bang as Duke dived the plane from 40,000 feet to get up the speed.

Previous supersonic flights had been from Hawker's base at Kingston

The former wartime RAF Squadron Leader who had shot down 28 enemy planes became a local folk hero for his peacetime achievements and the risks he took. He had the charisma later accorded to astronauts.

Princess Margaret added her seal of approval to the Fylde's growing reputation for aeronautical success when she visited the factory in July, 1954 and met the tall, lean aviator.

But the sonic booms from test flying locally were not always popular. They sometimes shattered the glass in commercial greenhouses across the Fylde and Blackpool MP Sir Toby Low complained about it in the House of Commons.

And Neville Duke was forced to quit flying because of problems with his back. He injured it crashlanding a Hunter at Thorney Island airfield on the south coast. Some of the Squire Gate factory survives today as a industrial estate beside Squires Ga Lane.

It was built to produce wartim Wellington bombers and then mad prefabricated houses.

There was a major protest by loc trades unionists when the place wa closed in 1947 but it re-opened t make Hawker Hunter jets in the 50

When Princess Margaret visite there it had 3,000 workers.

Later there was a major strike ove differences in pay between Blackpo and Kingston on Thames, th company headquarters.

After the strike Hawkers shu Blackpool down.

they spent two hours thumbing through 400 cards and stamped DISAPPROVED on 20 per cent of them.

As Britain became more broadminded, complaints dwindled and the Board had its last meeting in 1969.

In 1993 the European Union tried to ban the cards as offensive to women but Blackpool still sells a million every year.

The work of artist Donald McGill who designed hundreds for Bamforth Cards was honoured in the design of Blackpool Illuminations features in the Eighties.

# but nice

IN the Fifties Blackpool was busy getting back to business as usual after the hardships of the Forties.

The end of the war had brought a holiday boom because people wanted to get away from it all and let their hair down at the seaside.

Traditional holidays were still very much the order of the day.

The textile towns ran their annual Wakes Week breaks and for many families the holiday decision was simple – it was Blackpool every summer. Often it was the same boardinghouse where many guests liked to have the same rooms and the same table in the diningroom.

Others walked the streets looking for an address that took their eye where the bedding was aired and the furniture well polished.

The shortages that had followed the end of war were easing and Blackpool guesthouses were busy. The hardworking landlady was up early to make breakfast and lunch was a substantial affair followed by high tea later in the day.

Few small hotels had a bar though so after the pubs closed at 10.30pm it was home to bed – or maybe for a bit of a party in "the digs".

Against this traditional Blackpool backdrop the resort's soccer club had a golden age fielding international stars like Matthews and Mortensen and treading the road to Wembley victory.

But this was also a decade of disasters on the Fylde coast.

Blackpool's most famous landmark was ravaged by fire which gutted the world-famous Tower ballroom.

There was a major train crash, a woman was killed when a building collapsed in Blackpool and, in the final weeks of the decade, Fleetwood was a town in mourning for the 19 men of the trawler Red Falcon who had paid for their catch with their lives in a storm off western Scotland.

Holiday town Blackpool in the Fifties. This is the Golden Mile looking south from a point near present day Coral Island

Statuesque film star Jayne Mansfield switched on the Illuminations in 1959

The Queen at Blackpool Opera House for the first-ever Royal Command Performance outside London in 1955. Among the northern stars were Charlie Cairoli, Arthur Askey, Jimmy Jewell, Ben Warriss, George Formby, Albert Modley and Al Read. Also taking part was Lancashire comedian Bill Waddington who later played Percy Sugden in Coronation Street

Carnage in the cafe area

The dance floor (right) was completely wrecked. It stands on a girder frame. Ceilings below collapsed or were broken through to let water out

# Fire in the

AT 6.50 on a Friday morning in December, 1956 the alarm bells rang at the Blackpool fire station in Albert Road.

The message was simple: " The Tower is blazing!"

And that was the start of one of the biggest fire fighting operations the Fylde has ever seen.

It was almost six hours before the fire came under control and when it was finally put out that afternoon the world famous Tower Ballroom was just a charred wreck.

Experts said only a miracle had saved the Tower itself.

There was a fresh breeze that day but it blew from the south and so it drove the flames away from the centre of the building.

When the firefighters reached the Tower that morning smoke was pouring from windows at the north end of the complex and inside they had to fight their way through dense smoke and fumes towards the ballroom area.

The Blackpool Tower Company's own firemen and many other members of staff le a hand.

Some used spotlights high in the ballroo which were normally used to illuminate t dancers to try and aid the firemen toiling the heat and smoke far below.

A journalist allowed in to see the fi fighting operations underway described it as scene from hell.

The fire had started in an area just off t ballroom and was probably caused by carelessly discarded cigarette end.

Tower house manager Bill McGinty (far left) watches as thousands of gallons of water pour out to the promenade

Firemen damping down in the ruined ballroom

# Tower!

It spread under the polished wooden floor of the ballroom and the firemen used pickaxes to rip up the blocks to get at the fire in the space under the floor.

The heat buckled other sections of the ballroom floor like a switchback and flames leaped up through the holes.

They tore up the floorboards surrounding the dance floor and pumped thousands of gallons of water into the ballroom area .

They smashed a hole through the floor so it could drain away into the gutted rooms below.

From there it poured out down the steps and onto the promenade aided by a gang of Tower staff with brooms and mops.

And while everyone fought the flames or generally tried to help, the Tower Company catering department kept the tea urns boiling and came round with cups of char.

In those days the Tower complex included a zoo up in the roof garden area.

When staff arrived they could hardly see a foot in front of them for smoke and they talked to the animals so that familiar voices soothed the frightened creatures while ventilators were opened so they could breathe.

The fumes cost the lives of 21 exotic birds from a collection of 100.

Once the fire was out the company immediately started making plans to get back into business.

The company chairman, Douglas Bickerstaffe, said the directors would start meeting everyday to plan the restoration of the fire-ravaged ballroom.

He said: " It is a great tragedy – a personal tragedy to me because the ballroom was my particular pet having known it since I was a boy."

At the time damage was put at £500,000.

Mr Bickerstaffe said it would all be returned to its former glory.

But he warned: " I do not know if we can get the craftsmen to restore it."

However, his pledge was fulfilled and the blackened, sodden ballroom was reborn in all its splendour of red plush and gold decor.

It reopened in May, 1958 for the Whitsuntide Bank holiday.

At the reopening party Mr Bickerstaffe cut a giant cake weighing 84lbs.

A a previous ceremony pensioners who remembered the opening of the Tower in 1894 were invited for a look round.

*Far left:* **The painted ceiling (left) was restored to its former glory**

*Centre:* **On the right a craftsman fits the new ballroom floor**

*Right:* **A Tower company fireman (left) using a portable search light to cut through the smoke**

# Tragedy comes to the town centre on a Friday teatime

It was a miracle that only one person was killed when Redman's cafe & shop in Bank Hey Street collapsed in June, 1956

Teatime crowds soon gathered as rescuers worked in the rubble. Behind the hoardings in Market Street beyond, the British Home Stores complex is taking shape. It opened in May, 1957

IT WAS tea time on a Friday afternoon in June, 1956 and shoppers, holiday-makers and town centre workers were on their way home.

In Bank Hey Street a team of builders were still busy at Redman's, a three-story building including a cafe. This part was closed for alterations but the ground floor shop that sold groceries was open. The company had a chain of sites across the country.

Mr Alf Millership was the foreman builder and he suddenly realised something was terribly wrong.

He raced round warning his men and staff in the shop that the building was about to collapse.

Without him, the casualty list would have been much higher.

To an eye witness it seemed as though the cellar buckled first and then the front of the structure bulged outwards before hundreds of tons of rubble crashed down into t[he] street.

Minutes before, 100 wome[n] had left the nearby Owe[n] Owen store after a day's wor[k].

Miss Amy Hardwick [of] Windermere Road, Sout[h] Shore had also just finishe[d] work at Wilcock's drape[r] shop in Abingdon Street.

She had missed her b[us] outside the Winter Garde[ns] and when that happened s[he] often walked down to t[he] Promenade for a breath [of] fresh air.

She died beneath the rubbl[e].

Seven people were treated [at] Blackpool Victoria Hospit[al] and two of them were detaine[d] overnight.

And eight women sho[p] assistants were treated f[or] shock.

Workmen building th[e] British Home Stores on th[e] site of the old open a[ir] market raced over to he[lp] police and firemen dig in th[e] wreckage.

Workmen, and the emergency services begin to sift through the rubble and clear up as best they can

# The winning start of the Tangerine dream

THE history books show that the first football club in Blackpool was linked to the Victoria Street chapel in 1877.

When it was disbanded soon after, former students of St John's CE school formed a side.

Some of them took part in the historic meeting at the Stanley Arms Hotel in Church Street in July 1887 which gave the resort a soccer side named Blackpool.

And Blackpool FC got off to a good start. In September they won their first game, 2-1 at Chorley and finished the season by winning the Fylde Cup and Lancashire Junior Cup.

They were founder members of the Lancashire League. In 1892-3 they ended the season with an identical record to Liverpool. But, despite defeats at home and away by Blackpool, the Merseysiders won the championship on goal average.

In May, 1896, Blackpool FC became a limited company and played in the Football League for the first time.

Players received a win bonus of 50p at a time when many workers were on wages of £1.50 or £2 for more than 50 hours a week.

In the early years of this century Blackpool FC fought a constant battle against financial problems and established a tradition – some of the directors ploughed money into the club.

The Seed and Parkinson families were the most prominent.

Many players were part time. But some of the directors who dug deep to keep the club afloat lived to see them star in the First Division.

Among the firsts of which Blackpool FC can be proud are the fact that they were the first club to offer to lend players to Manchester United after their side was decimated in the Munich air crash of February, 1958.

And, in 1961, they became the first Football League club to be complimented by the Football Association for not having a caution administered to any of its players during the season.

Fans call Blackpool The Seasiders, The Pool or The Tangerines and for years the orange colour of their strip was unique. It was first spotted by Albert Hargreves, a Blackpool director, when he was refereeing an international match in Amsterdam in the early 20s.

The days when coaches brought local fans from all over the Fylde to join crowds of 30,000 at Bloomfield Road are long gone.

But wherever the future leads the Bloomfield Road club, memories of the glory days in the 50s will stay bright.

# Up

Inspired by Stanley Matthews (left) the Seasiders fought back to win a remarkable 1953 Cup Final 4-3

FROM LEFT: Sta Mortensen scores the second goal. From free kick he complete an historic hat trick t make it 3-3. In injur time Bill Perry drive the ball into the net t clinch victor

The young Queen Elizabeth and Duke of Edinburgh present the trophy

# for the Cup

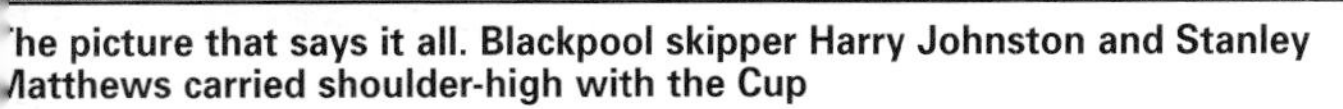

**The picture that says it all. Blackpool skipper Harry Johnston and Stanley Matthews carried shoulder-high with the Cup**

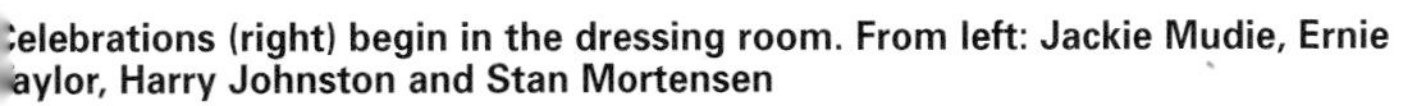

**Celebrations (right) begin in the dressing room. From left: Jackie Mudie, Ernie Taylor, Harry Johnston and Stan Mortensen**

Crowds packed Central Station on the way to Wembley

# We were the

SIR Stanley Matthews and triumphant Tangerines skipper Harry Johnston lifting the FA Cup aloft as they were carried shoulder high around Wembley in 1953 will be Fylde sports fans' abiding memory of the Millennium.

Blackpool's win is still today one of the greatest sporting comebacks of all-time. At 3-1 down to North West rivals Bolton, the Tangerines cup dream looked to be in tatters.

But, inspired by Matthews, the Seasiders fought back to win a remarkable final 4-3, with Stan Mortensen still to this day the only player ever to have scored a hat-trick in an FA Cup final at Wembley.

Blackpool's fans, who had packed special trains down to London, were ecstatic in scenes which more than made up their two previous final def – 4-2 to Manchester Unite 1948, and 2-0 to Newca United in 1951.

And when the winn squad returned to Blackpoo parade football's most fam trophy, more than 15,000 packed Talbot Square welcome home their heroes

Huge crowds greeted the return of the triumphant Blackpool team. Here is the scene in Talbot Square

Back in Blackpool the team went on a Victory Parade along the Fylde coast. Crowds not seen since the end of World War Two turned out to welcome them home

ioccer fans ooked lifferent in 953. These Vembley-ound upporters ave sashes aying: lackpool or the Cup and happy olidays

# champions!

Blackpool Captain Harry Johnston shows off the cup as the train leaves London Euston

Below: wearing a victor's garland, Stanley Matthews stands with Harry Johnston outside Blackpool Town Hall

On his last visit back to ckpool, Sir Stanley, who died May 2000, said mag-imously that it should never n nicknamed The Matthews al. "In my view it will always Morty's final," he said.

And Blackpool's cup-win-g boss Joe Smith was Mat-ws' favourite manager of -time. "He was a great nager. He always wanted us get two goals in the first f, so he could enjoy his ar!" he said.

Although home city Stoke had always been Matthews' first love, he had fond memories of his time beside the seaside, where he was known for training on the sands.

"I had a wonderful 15 years at Blackpool. I was very fortunate to play with the really great players. Wonderful people, wonderful times," he said.

But as soccer prepared to enter the new Millennium, Matthews wasn't a fan of the over-hyped modern game, where television exposure has reached saturation point.

"Football is in your living room. And the more you talk about football, the more tactics, the more difficult it is. It is overkill," he said.

But here on the Fylde Coast, it doesn't matter how many times fans replay their videos they will never tire of the sights and sounds of Wembley 1953.

In St Annes

. . . and along the Fylde coast, the crowds went wild . . .

In Cleveleys

. . . and back home in Blackpool

# London

Training is the foundation for all top athletes. Brian London, who had served in the RAF, often used the sports facilities at Weeton camp, then run by the RAF. He is seen here running with his brother Jack. Brian says: "This was set up for the photograph. I never run in boxing shoes".

BOXING legend Brian London was one of Blackpool's biggest hits of the Millennium when he won the British Heavyweight title in 1958.

London knocked out Joe Erskine in the eighth round of their British championship clash in the capital on June 3, 1958.

It was the second time he had been in the ring with Erskine.

Brian recalls: "When I was doing National Service in the RAF I fought him in an amateur bout over three rounds.

"I had seen him in the ring and I thought to myself 'I would beat him easy because he couldn't punch'. But he was so clever as a boxer that when I faced him I never laid a glove on him. As a boxer he was better than any of us was Joe Erskine, but I managed to get to him in the championship and I knocked him out."

It was a proud night for Blackpool and Brian's family who came to the resort from West Hartlepool when the youngster was 15.

His father Jack had won the championship himself in 1944 when he defeated Freddie Mills.

The British heavyweight crown was to be Brian London's only success in six title tilts – two of them world heavyweight fights against Floyd Patterson and, most famously, Muhammad Ali.

Against Patterson, London took the fight to the 11th round before he was counted out of the bout held at Indianapolis on March 1, 1959.

He recalls: "I went out to America on my own and I had none of the sparring partners and management arrangements that Patterson had. Otherwise, the result could have been different."

Ali was to be London's last title fight. The big bout was staged in London on August 6 1966. But even riding on an emotional tide of England's footballers having just won the World Cup, London was well beaten, counted out in the third round.

Aside from his British title win against Erskine, perhaps his finest hour came in his two clashes with fellow British boxing great Henry Cooper.

On both occasions – in 1959 in London and five years later in Manchester – London took Cooper the distance before twice losing on points.

Overall, in his 15-year pro career which ended in 1970, London won 37 of his 58 contests, lost 20, and drew one – the latter being his 1969 encounter with Henry Clark.

He then became a successful Blackpool businessman.

Encouraged by his father he had been a championship amateur fighter and when he turned professional he won his first 13 fights.

Tough and tenacious, Brian London was a brave boxer who brought sporting honour to Blackpool.

Today, he's still up at 5.30am six days a week at his home overlooking Stanley Park for a workout that includes a session on the punchbags in his garage.

He never smoked or drank alcohol and prides himself on his fitness.

One of Fylde's other major sporting memories of the 50s was the 1958 Open Championship held at Royal Lytham and St Annes Golf Club

Australian Peter Thomson lifted the famous Claret Jug at Lytham with a score of 278. It was Thomson's fourth title in five years after his hat-trick at Birkdale, St Andrews and Hoylake.

Lytham was the scene for Thomson's last Open triumph.

The next year at Muirfield it was South African Gary Player who was crowned champion, 15 years before Player's own Lytham triumph in 1974.

A proud moment for Brian London in 1958 when he became British Heavyweight Champion. And a proud moment for his father Jack (left) who had held the title himself

# Pride

**The winner! After turning professional Brian London won his first 13 fights**

# The loss of the Red Falcon

IT had been a tough three-week trip to the Icelandic fishing grounds and the results had not been good.

But every one of the 19 men and boys onboard the trawler Red Falcon was looking forward to getting back to Fleetwood and celebrating Christmas, 1959.

Skipper Alex Hardy was thinking about retirement from the sea and had plans to buy a post office.

Two of his crew were just 15 years old and the others had 25 children between them. If the auction prices were good they might just come out with a few pounds to treat the youngsters at Christmas.

As the ship travelled south off western Scotland the weather grew worse and worse.

Skipper Hardy, a vastly experienced and highly-respected seaman, could see the image of the Skerryvore lighthouse on his radar screen but there was no sign of the lighthouse that morning as the wind gusted to hurricane force and filled the air with a dense mist of salt spray and rain.

He talked to fellow skipper Jim McKernan steaming home ahead of him in the Red Sabre – another trawler from the Iago fishing company.

He was beginning to find shelter from the coast of Northern Ireland but Skipper Hardy and his men were out in the exposed Atlantic swells in an area known for conflicting tidal races and treacherous conditions.

And it was there that the Red Falcon was overwhelmed by what the experts call stress of weather and where the crew found their last resting place in the sea that had been their home 10 months of the year.

At first the fishing community of Fleetwood clung to the hope that the Falcon had broken down and drifted out into the western ocean.

But they had seen this kind of tragedy too many times before and when the trawler owners said the Falcon was overdue everyone knew she had gone to the bottom.

The Red Falcon was a steam-powered ship and one of the last in the fleet still burning coal. Such vessels were designed to survive terrible weather and survive they did. Even the fishermen wondered how sometimes.

Looking back on the heyday of Britain's distant water fishing industry it is amazing more men and ships were not lost although the human toll was heavy in the most dangerous job in the world.

A pall of sadness fell upon the town of Fleetwood and tarnished the tinsel image of Christmas.

In those days the port was a much more tightly-knit community than it is now and everyone seemed to have some link with the docks and the fish trade or the many businesses linked to it.

The Red Falcon disaster hit the headlines and touched the national heart. Thousands of pounds were sent in by young and old throughout the land.

More men were to die in the fishing industry before the big ships sailed away more than 20 years later.

But the Red Falcon was the last time a ship disappeared with all her crew to leave a great, sad silence when the storm had blown itself out.

CHRONICLE

FLEETWOOD EXPRESS, PREESALL, PILLING AND STALMINE JOURNAL



*Feared lost on way home from Iceland*

THE RED FALCON

THE RED FALCON'S CREW

*Previous disasters*

RED FALCON OVERDUE

*Owners say "afraid there is no hope"*

IT IS FEARED THAT THE FLEETWOOD TRAWLER RED FALCON (419 TONS) HAS BEEN LOST OFF THE WEST SCOTTISH COAST WHILE RETURNING FROM ICELAND ON MONDAY. YESTERDAY, HER OWNERS, THE IAGO STEAM TRAWLER CO LTD, SAID NOTHING HAD BEEN HEARD FROM THE SHIP SINCE HER SKIPPER WAS SPEAKING BY RADIO WITH OTHER SKIPPERS OF THE FIRM AT 7 AM ON MONDAY.

Mayor to start fund

Relatives waited

Only hope

First trip

Experienced

SCOTLAND



How the Gazette's sister paper The Fleetwood Chronicle reported the loss of the Falcon and her crew. The ill-fated vessel was lost in December 1959 with 19 men on board

# Ernie settles down on the Fylde coast

Prime Minister Harold Macmillan put St Annes on the national map when he switched on ERNIE, the Premium Bond machine in 1957

THEY call him ERNIE and he draws the winning prizes in the west.

But the Electronic Random Number Indicating Equipment does not just select the successful Premium Bond numbers. It is also at the centre of a major civil service operation which means jobs on the Fylde coast.

Wartime saw many civil servants moved out from London to safer locations like Blackpool and the Fylde where there was plenty of accommodation. And they stayed to become major local employers.

National Savings set up on a large site off Moorland Road, St Annes and it was there, on June 1, 1957, that 96 people won the princely sum of £1,000.

Prime Minister Harold Macmillan threw the switch which first breathed life into the ERNIE machinery.

He was famous for saying the people of Britain had never had it so good, with the standard of living they enjoyed more than 40 years ago.

Certainly ERNIE – and the other large government sites along the Fylde coast – have been major winners as far as local jobseekers are concerned.

Now, Ernie Mark IV is based in Marton where 1,000 people work for National Savings.

More than 40 years old he has handed out more than 55 million prizes and he can make you millionaire.

In the early days there was a 6 seater theatre at Moorland Ro where the public could watch Ern in action.

People send him greetings car and someone once enclosed a bot of castor oil to speed up his digesti process.

Yet many prizes rema unclaimed.

Which might bring a wry smile satisfaction to some local chur members.

They campaigned against t establishment of Premium Bonds St Annes because they disapproved gambling and urged local parents n to allow young people to work the

# The stars come out along the coast

**A youthful Frank Sinatra pictured above with his wife Ava Gardner in 1952. He sang at the Opera House in 1950 and returned in '53**

THE '50s were the pop years – with one revolutionary pushing open the resort's door to make ay for a hit parade of stars.

Young Blue Eyes.

Frank Sinatra's two concerts at ıe Opera House in July 1950 ıowed the way forward.

Entertainments historian Barry and explains: "It proved there as an entirely new market that ould consist of squealing enage girls who adopted their ıusical heroes not from ıddyduddy BBC radio programmes but from Mr Herman Vurlitzer's juke boxes."

Prices came down accordingly. anny promoter Harry Fielding ıade sure the 3,000-seater Opera louse had affordable seats for enagers.

Sinatra, who returned in '53, onfirmed Blackpool's pioneering op role in producing the only big rovincial venue available for a unday night show during his London Palladium residency – most towns and cities prohibited shows under Sunday Observance laws.

Gazette editor Harold Grime proved a prophet when he mused that, in 1980, greying mothers would tell adolescent daughters: "I don't know what you see in these wretched singers – I can remember Frank Sinatra in 1950."

Other American stars soon followed. The '53 Opera House season featured Johnnie Ray, Eddie Fisher, Al Martino, Guy Mitchell, Billy Daniels and Frankie Laine.

Connie Francis, Vic Damone, Tony Bennett, Nat King Cole, Billy Eckstine, Slim Whitman and Harry Belafonte later sang here.

The Brits fought back. Clean-cut balladiers like David Whitfield and Dickie Valentine and high kicking Frankie Vaughan. The girls included Alma Cogan, Eve Boswell, Joan Regan and Vera Lynn.

Then, in 1956, Bill Haley and the Comets rocked around the clock in Hollywood teen drama Blackboard Jungle.

Rock exploitation Don't Knock The Rock soon followed. Local teddy boys were escorted off premises after jiving on stage at the old Hippodrome, now the ABC, but the dancing stopped traffic on Church Street when the audiences spilled out.

This was the moment, reckons historian Band, when pop music became a way of life for Blackpool and Fylde teenagers.

Tommy Steele, Britain's first rock idol, played the Palace Theatre in '57, accompanied by the John Barry Seven – who was to drop the Seven and achieve Oscar-winning fame as composer of the Bond movie music.

A sulky young man,in white tux and black slacks, with lashings of Brylcreem visited Blackpool Odeon in '58 – as a support act. Police dog handlers stood by in case of a riot. More than 40 years on Sir Cliff Richard claims the British charts record.

Home grown competition to the likes of Brenda Lee, Gene Vincent and the Everley Brothers, came from Adam Faith, Billy Fury, Joe Brown and Helen Shapiro. There were also 'busload' tours featuring up to eight acts compered by Jimmy Tarbuck, Norman Vaughan, Ted Rogers and Des O'Connor.

But the biggest-selling British recording artist of the period was skiffle king Lonnie Donegan who burst on the scene in '56 and had 12 Top Ten hits in five years.

Barry Band concludes: "This tidal wave of teen music had the devastating effect of killing off the dozens of touring dance bands that had been the main source of popular music until 1956."

## While Eric and Ernie take a break on the beach

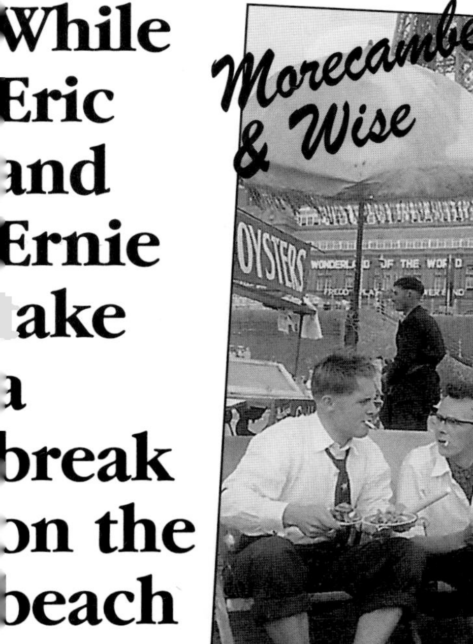

**Back in the days when sitting on the sands was still fashionable the season show stars of the day were often to be found down on Blackpool beach. Here are Eric Morecambe and Ernie Wise in 1953, shoes and socks emoved, trousers rolled up to the knee, with sticks of rock and plates f oysters in their palms – and cigarettes in their mouths.**

**The picture comes from the Morecambe family archives and ppears in a new book Memories of Eric, written by his son Gary lorecambe and broadcaster Martin Sterling and published by Andre eutsch.**

# Street life in

## An adventure playground for a young lad like Rod Park

GROWING up in the heart of holidaytown Blackpool, more than 40 years ago, was like living in the middle of an adventure playground for a youngster like Rod Park.

His boyhood home was in Dale Street at the corner of Princess Street in the Foxhall Square area.

Part of the property was occupied by doctors Wood, Baird and Page who also had a surgery on Hornby Road.

And next door the family owned a small cottage-style house let to an elderly lady at a peppercorn rent.

The Park family home had one room on the ground floor and three upstairs and Rod remembers the black lead grate and coal fires.

It was home to him and his sister Georgina, who now lives with her American husband in the USA.

Also in the family was Uncle Charlie Park, a bachelor who worked on the trams and became an inspector.

Incredibly, there was always room for a 'sleeper' or two in the season.

Rod remembers: "It may seem amazing now but lots of people did it then. Holidaymakers would turn up at a guest house to be told: "You're sleeping at Mrs Park's round the corner or down the street. They spent each night with us and trudged off through the rain for their breakfast, lunch and tea at the guesthouse.

"Lots of the kids I knew whose parents took in visitors spent many a night sleeping in a bath or on a couch or in a wooden hut in the yard to make space for the paying guests."

Saturday was no day for play for Rod and his mates.

He said: "We used to go 'bagging' at Central Station. We formed an orderly queue – there was always one lad who kept us in order – and took the visitor's cases to their digs in our carts with them walking alongside us. They could not afford taxis."

Every day saw Rod up early delivering milk to hotels and cafes around Foxhall for the Windmill Dairy in Dale Street kept by the Reynolds family. Later he delivered meat and eggs from a carrier bike.

He said: "Every youngster had a job. Saturday was a very busy day as the visitors changed over. No lunch was cooked that day. They either got salad or something from the fish and chip shop. I was often sent with a big basin to get 14 portions of fish and chips or steak puddings when I also had a jug for the gravy."

Cafes made their own meat and potato pies and had a few tricks of the trade to sell their wares.

Rod recalls: "One always displayed this fantastic pie in the window with a fancy crust but it wasn't real. The same place had a stock pot in the cellar kitchen with a fan to blow the steam into the street through a grille. The smell was fantastic and it brought the customers in all right."

But it wasn't all work for the youngsters around Foxhall Square.

They were told to keep out of the arcades.

Rod said: "There were some strange characters in there. Of course we went in. We liked [to] drop a penny in those autom[atic] machines where someone rose [out] of a grave. They were always at [the] back in the shadows. But if [the] showmen saw you and knew y[ou] were under 16 they chased y[ou] out."

Down on the sands whe[re] thousands of holidaymakers dra[nk] tea from jugs they hired at near[by] cafes, the boys met up with Ro[d's] Uncle Charlie and his mates w[ho] ran pleasure boats. Someti[mes] they got a free sail.

Rod's father Reggie had co[me] out of the Guards and went [to] work at Loxham's Garage [in] Rawcliffe Street.

The boys spent a lot of time [on] the beach. They set night lines [with] baited hooks to catch fish and to[ok] buckets of mussels home from [the] girders of Central Pier.

"It was like having your o[wn] adventure playground. Of cou[rse] we did plenty of swimming.

# The wicked woman who was trapped by a handbag clue...

**Mrs Louisa Merrifield, the Blackpool poisoner, with her husband Alfred. She was one of the last women in England to be hanged for murder**

IN 1953 Blackpool was rocked by a notorious murder case in which the killer almost escaped justice.

But she gave the wrong answer to a simple question. And that started a chain of events which signed her death warrant.

It started when 79-year-old widow Mrs Sarah Ann Ricketts hired a housekeeper.

She had lived alone for 10 years in a bungalow on Devonshire Road, North Shore, since the death of her second husband. And, apart from a touch of bronchitis, she was healthy – until she met Mrs Louisa Merrifield.

She got the housekeeper job and moved in with her husband Alfred.

Within a month the widow had changed her will in favour of the Merrifields. So when she died two weeks later they stood to inherit the bungalow and all her worldly goods.

But the doctor refused to issue a death certificate and the Coroner's office started an investigation . . . while a Salvation Army band, organised by Mrs M, played Abide With Me outside the bungalow.

Detective Sergeant Norman Steadman was a vastly experienced policeman and when he met the short, thickset Mrs Merrifield who usually wore a close-fitting hat and rimless glasses, he asked if he could take a look at Mrs Ricketts' handbag.

He was astonished when she replied: "Mrs Ricketts didn't have one."

Det Sgt Steadman pondered that she was the only woman he had ever heard of who did not have a handbag and he reported his suspicions to the Chief Constable.

Amazingly, Mrs Merrifield had placed the tin of phosphorous-based rat poison – and the spoon she used to mix it into the widow's food – in the handbag.

When she was arrested, Mrs Merrifield rang her solicitor, the leading defence lawyer John Budd.

With classic understatement she told him: "I am having a little bit of trouble with the police."

Crowds flocked to court when she appeared and later her husband was also charged with murder.

But he walked from the dock at Manchester Assizes a free man after the jury couldn't agree if he knew about the murder plot.

His wife was found guilty and Mr Justice Glyn-Jones donned the traditional black cap to tell her she must hang.

He said: "You have been convicted, upon plain evidence, of as wicked and cruel murder as I ever heard tell of."

On September 18 Mrs Merrifield was hanged at Strangeways Prison.

Her husband returned to live in the bungalow and died, at the age of 80, in 1962.

# the Fifties

course it was in the sea. We knew It contained sewage but no one worried about pollution."

In the winter there was acres of space in the diningrooms of the guest houses.

"Out came the model trains and you could sleep in a different bedroom every night. We had a lot of fun."

The Foxhall lads were careful not to trespass on the turf of the Ibbison Street boys but they liked to wander round the little streets around Bonny Street behind Central Station where fishermen boiled shrimps in the backyards.

Where the employment office now stands in Tyldesley Road was a school with the playground on the flat roof two storeys up.

" We climbed up the fire escape to play on there and were always getting told off for it."

Tucked away behind the cafes, guest houses, and shops around Foxhall Square were a variety of small workshops – anything from sign writing to sheet metal work and light engineering.

Squeezed in among them was a traditional gypsy caravan in which lived the aged Gertie.

Rod admits now: "I am afraid we made her life a misery at times by our pranks."

The Foxhall folk were well known for their charity fund raising. They contributed a lot to help build the Princess Alexandra home for the blind.

Says Rod: " The place was like a village. All the business people belonged to some kind of organisation or association and they all had a dinner dance every year."

Some of the landmarks of the area are still there today like the Philharmonic Club.

Others included:

■ An arcade kept by the Aspinall family. It later became a cafe and one of the first to sell soft icecream to the delight of local youngsters.

■ The Fisher brothers who sold meat, fish and greengrocery.

■ Court's shop where children were sent to buy cigarettes for adults and the tobacco would be wrapped up in a paper parcel.

■ Henderson's fish and chips.

■ The sweet shop kept by Mrs Morris. Her husband was deputy head of a local school.

■ Ex-Blackpool soccer star Allan Brown had a fancy goods shop on Princess Street.

■ Nearby was Turner's Gymnasium where Blackpool boxing star Ronnie Clayton trained. Rod later married his daughter Veronica.

■ The ambulance station provided a first aid dressing station for visitors who had often cut their feet on the sands.

■ Trams came and went to the Blundell Street sheds.

■ Probably the first Chinese restaurant in Blackpool. The Ping Pong.

■ Sid Beavers: "He was a tremendous character. Every morning he came out of his newsagents shop and blew a bugle. No one knew why. Had a big sign that said Durex in the days when that side of life was not talked about openly."

Jimmy Armfield's parents had a grocers and the brothers Norman and Ronnie Cook ran a grocery.

Even large hotels bought their produce from small traders.

Youds of Station Road were the first firm Rod recalls to start visiting the caterers selling labour-saving products like soup and bakery mixes.

A food exhibition in the resort led to many caterers buying potato rumblers and food mixers.

In the winter hoteliers attended courses at Courtfield, part of Blackpool and the Fylde College, to study the latest catering ideas and methods.

In the summer, many of the hotelier families held down other jobs outside the guesthouse to help make ends meet.

Rod attended Revoe Infants school, Thames Road and Palatine schools. A drama course at the college led to backstage work at South Pier where duties ranged from helping to stage Cal McCord's Cowboy Show to acting as a second for wrestler Dominic Pye.

Rod's father Reggie had done part time work at the Foxhall hotel and became bars manager at the Squires Gate holiday camp – later Pontin's.

His Mum Betty also worked there.

Later the couple went into the pub trade and so did Rod.

But he swopped the life of a bars manager in Scotland for a beat on the streets of Blackpool as a Lancashire policeman for 24 years.

He said: "I had seen the Golden Mile from one angle as a youngster now I saw it from another as a policeman. But it was still a great place with some great characters."

Workmen (above) taking the new runway at Blackpool Airport across Leach Lane in August, 1953. It meant new road links between St Annes and Marton

Mountaineer Alfred Gregory (right) gets a hero's welcome outside the Town Hall

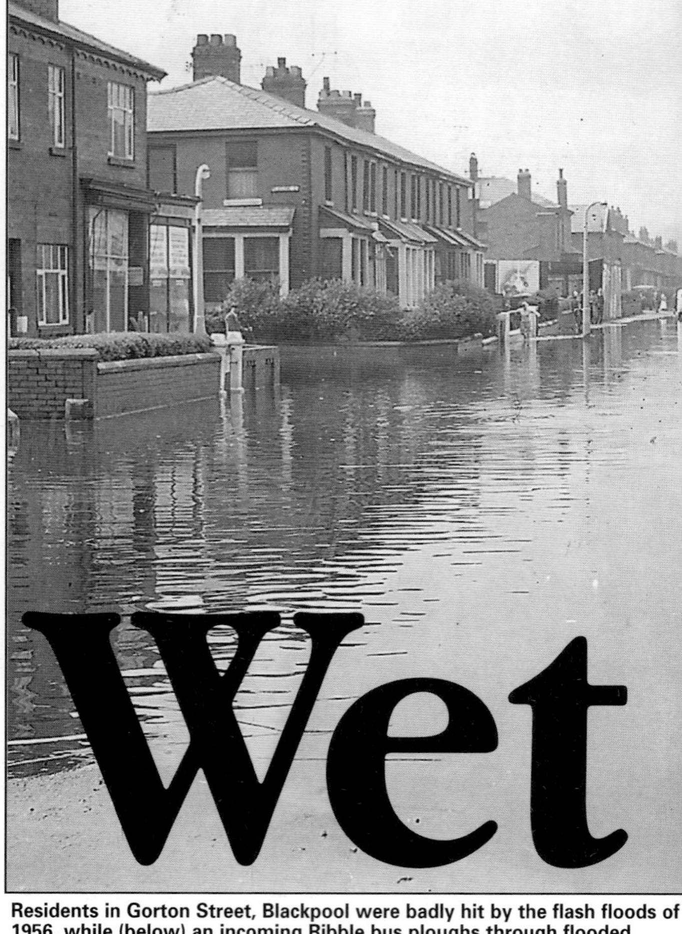

# Wet

Residents in Gorton Street, Blackpool were badly hit by the flash floods of 1956, while (below) an incoming Ribble bus ploughs through flooded Whitegate Drive overtaking a tram on the Marton route near the junction with St Ives Avenue

A TROPICAL-STYLE storm hi Blackpool on the afternoon of July 18, 1956. There was dramati thunder and lightning and tw houses were hit as a deluge of rain began t fall at 2pm.

Within 15 minutes there were reports o flooding and the rain continued for 9( minutes.

By that time there were serious problems

Homes in Queen Victoria Road, South Shore were three feet deep.

It was calculated that one and a hal inches of rain fell in 45 minutes.

But, in general, the 50s had a much sunnier face than the previous decade.

The Coronation and the ascent of Everes lifted the nation's spirits and there was ar optimistic mood in the air.

Blackpool had a link with the Everes success. Mountaineer Alfred Gregory, a Blackpool travel agent, was a member of the team and responsible for stills photography

He took many memorable pictures anc got a VIP welcome home.

Mr Gregory's photographic skills anc love of travel and adventure led him into a whole new career.

But Blackpool itself looked much the same as it had done for years.

And, down on the raunchy old Golden Mile, the trippers were still digging deep ir their pockets to sample the salacious shows

The Queen and Prince Philip with Lord and Lady Derby at Blackpool Opera House in 1955. The royal party were in the resort for a special variety performance

On the right the Queen salutes the audience from the Royal Box

# & wild!

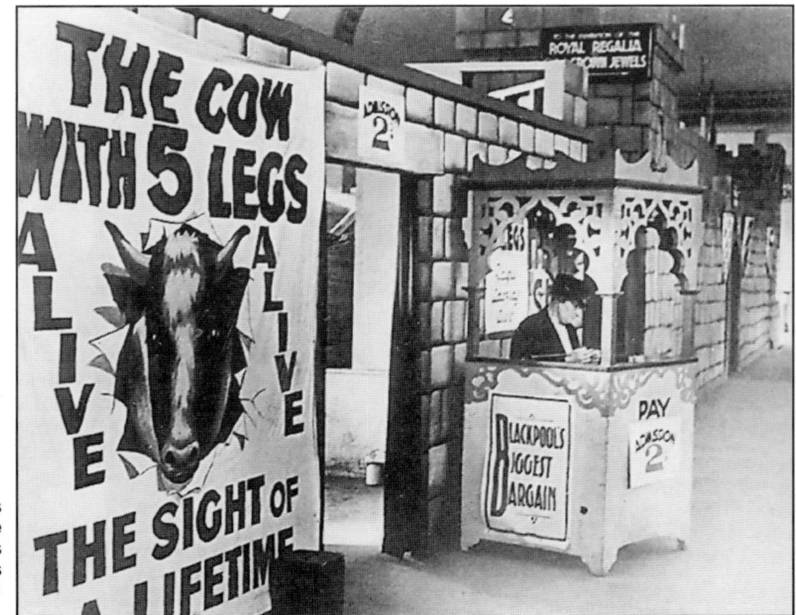


The 1950s Golden Mile was as scandalous as ever!

When Princess Margaret flew in to Blackpool in 1954, half a million people lined the route to Fleetwood. She is pictured with VIPs on the North End quay off Queens Terrace before sailing to Barrow and back in HMS Coquette

DOUBLE
DIAMOND

Chapter Six

# *The Sixties*

# Swinging

**Rock and rollers! Young women didn't mind what they looked like, by day, so long as those curls were bouncing by night**

**The Golden Mile was a seedy delight of sideshows, from the Palace of "Strange Girls" to tattoo booths for men**

**The '60s also (below) marked the arrival of the head-turning mini-skirt**

*All pictures taken from Alfred Gregory's Photographic Portrait: Blackpool, a Celebration of the 60s. Published by Constable*

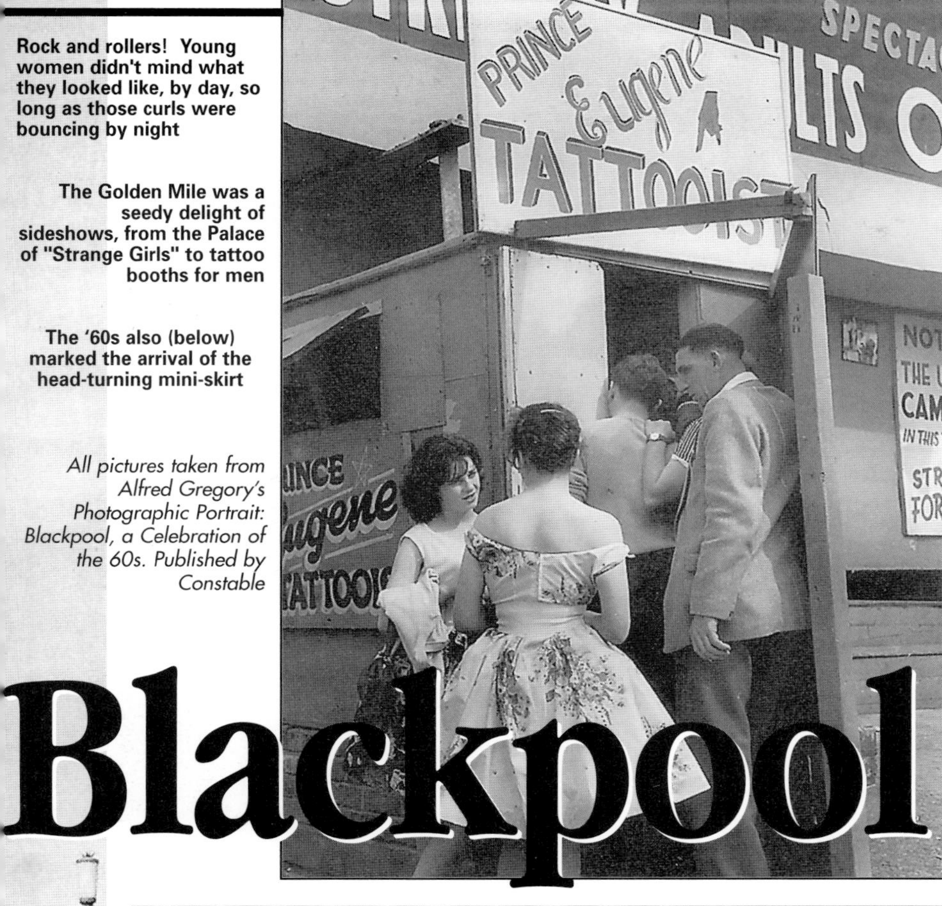


# Blackpool

IT WAS the age of Mary Quant, the beehive hairdo, the miniskirt, rock – and rollers! Beat music had arrived – the Beatles and the Rolling Stones both played Blackpool – and although competition was emerging from continental holidays the cheap charter summons to sunnier climes had yet to blight Britain's premier resort.

Blue collar Blackpool was big in the swinging '60s, a boomtown. There was still a mass of humanity on the sands and a mess of fag ends – smoking now equally popular with both sexes – and chip papers on the promenade.

The town was about to go bingo barmy and Blackpool Tower Company was losing ground to EMI as the wind of change swept through entertainment. It also heralded the arrival of the first nightclubs proper.

Between them, British Rail and the Ribble/Standerwick coach company brought more than four million visitors in '64.

Holiday trade was starting to shift from summer to the Illuminations – and conferences were beginning to prop up off-season trade too.

Perhaps the greatest change was to be seen in the emergence of a younger visitor. The much-vaunted permissive society had also officially arrived.

The spirit of liberation, which had grown through the 50s, flourished in the 60s. Romance was almost tangibly in the air. Nights were feverish. Visitors knew their priorities.

And girls left rollers in their hair ALL DAY LONG under a headscarf – just to look their best for night. Skirts were full – or mini. The lads looked pretty good too. The Mods and Rockers of the mid-60s took over from where the Teddy Boys left off.

The Golden Mile had yet to be sanitised by local authorities – the clean-up came in the '70s – and remained gloriously decadent and downright dodgy . . . an assault on all the senses and superlatives!

The seaside was a sideshow of non-stop striptease – "It makes the old feelyoung", D'etranges Demoiselles (the so-called Palace of Strange Girls or Des Filles Bizarres), Tarantula "part woman, part beast", Tanya the Tattooed Girl brought to Blackpool at "enormous expense" – continuing the fun and freak show tradition established decades before and which exists to this day in the form of Ripleys Believe it Or Not! Auditorium and other attractions.

The teenager had officially arrived too. One Golden Mile show featured The Fattest Teenager You Have Ever Seen – When She Walks She Wobbles.

Down the prom an elderly lady in a booth "patronised by royalty" offered to guess your age for 6d. Or buy fish, chips, tea, bread and butter for 2s 6d – half a crown: 12 and a half pence today – along with jugs of tea for the sands.

There were four cinemas, including the showcase Odeon, three major ballrooms, three swimming pools – Miss Blackpool still held sway at one; the ill-fated department store RHO Hills, which would ultimately perish in fire; a casino; the Tower; UCP tripe; and more gipsy fortune tellers than you could count using the fingers on both hands – crossed with silver or not!.

Former Blackpool-based photographer Alfred Gregory captured the spirit of the age in a series of pictures Blackpool: Celebration of the 60s (Constable,'93) with a foreword by another fan – Dame Thora Hird.

Alf had gone a long way from his boyhood haunt – towards the top of Everest with Sir Edmund Hillary and Sherpa Tenzing in 1953 as photographer to the first successful assault of Everest.

Blackpool had already celebrated his achievement by naming a street after him – and Everest got a look in too.

But the pull of Blackpool of the '60s – resort retreat of the "Dreaded Yette That Haunts the Himalayas" – a species Alf had eluded in its homeland – proved too strong.

Alf pictured it time and again – and even returned at The Gazette's invitation to revisit the Golden Mile, Tower and Pleasure Beach in the '90s to coincide with publication of his book.

The veteran mountaineer took time out to enjoy the Avalanche ride at the fun park adding: "I've spent all my life avoiding avalanches – look at me now!"

*And he applauded the enduring essence of Blackpool – the unashamed pursuit of unadulterated fun in all its forms.*

The Beatles on the stag[e] of the ABC Theatre which opened in May 1963. They playe[d] live Sunday night TV concerts there including th[e] debut of Yesterday b[y] Paul McCartney. The world's most recorded song was sung solo t[o] the backing of his own acoustic guitar

# Blackpool rock

WE loved them, yeah, yeah, yeah! Beatlemania swept Blackpool in the swinging '60s after the fab four's first chart topper From Me To You.

The enterprising ABC chain had booked a package of shows for the Blackpool ABC – former Hippodrome – where a fresh-faced Cliff Richard was starring with the Shadows for the summer.

The deal included FIVE Beatles concerts.

The mop-haired Merseysiders had two vacant Sundays – snapped up by the Queen's Theatre.

Local entertainments historian and author Barry Band recalls: "For seven Sundays in the peak season of 1963 the Beatles were top of the pops in Blackpool."

It could have been longer. Central Pier producer Peter Webster had seen the lads play at the Marine Hall in Fleetwood in the summer of '62 and had been offered the band for the summer '63 season. He turned them down. "I didn't think much of them."

The Beatles returned in '64 after conquering America. John, Paul, George and Ringo did a live telecast for ITV's Blackpool Night Out at the ABC on Sunday, July 19.

"What a scream," the Gazette headline reported. All police leave was cancelled to cope with the crowds.

They headlined two Sundays at the Opera House – for promoter Harold Fielding. The first saw them mobbed as news leaked of their arrival and thousands of fans crowded the airport and town centre. The second was a softly-softly affair as the Beatles' arrival was kept a closely-guarded secret.

A Gazette writer noted they sang 10 songs that were barely heard for the screaming which was said to reach its pitch when Ringo was featured singing I Want To Be Your Man on a darkened stage – while Paul's invitation to "sort of clap your hands and sort of stamp your feet" got an "ear-shattering response."

Just about every group and solo star of note in Britain and America headed here – because of the availability of large theatres.

The Beatles entered and left the Winter Gardens through the back door via the ballroom in the summer of '64 where – 48 hours earlier – the Rolling Stones had been chased from the stage.

The Stones sparked a riot, amidst 4,000 people, at the Empress Ballroom, when, according to local folklore,Keith Richards retaliated to a Scottish heckler.

At the time Richards told the Gazette: "A group of youths kept spitting at us while we were playing. I lost my temper and tried to kick him. He just went too far."

Mick Jagger added: "These lads wouldn't stop it and Keith lost his temper. I suppose he shouldn't have done it." Emotions ran high. Tables, chairs and mirrors were smashed. The Stones fled . . . smuggled out of the building by a rooftop exit.

Comedian Ken Dodd , already a legend for long-running shows, was given his dream order by management to "stay on" in order to avoid the Opera House audience being caught up in the Floral Hall fracas!

Police retreated under the onslaught of bottles, and other missiles, while the mob smashed the Stones' drums and amplifiers to pieces and even threw a grand piano off the stage.

Blackpool band , the Executives, who had earlier appeared as a support act also suffered: equipment was damaged, the organist finished up with a black eye, the Latin American drummer was hit over the shoulder with a chair and another drummer was hit by a cymbal.

And Blackpool chief constable Stan Parr darkly warned: "Sever[al] other groups are booked to visit th[e] town during the remainder of th[e] season – and such unruly condu[ct] will not be tolerated."

Sixties shows featured the Da[ve] Clark Five, Joe Brown and th[e] Bruvvers , Gerry and th[e] Pacemakers, Billy J Kramer and th[e] Dakotas, and comedy showgrou[p] Freddie and the Dreamers, th[e] Rockin' Berries and the Barr[on] Knights.

Gerry Marsden even had th[e] dubious privilege of being ouste[d] from a May, 1963, show after bei[ng] booked as a supporting act in a[n] annual charity concert at the Ope[ra] House.

It starred Sammy Davis Junior but the bill was too crowded [to] allow the American singer his 8[0] minute act.

Gerry and co, with just o[ne] Number One hit to their cred[it] How Do You Do It?, were paid [off] and given tickets for the show.

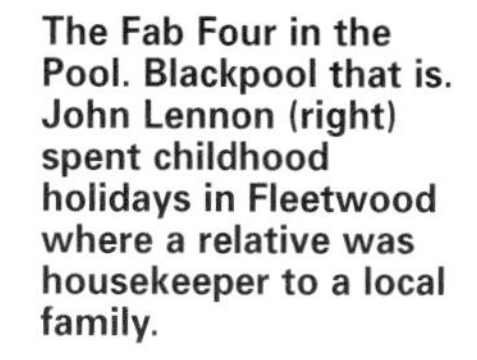

The Fab Four in the Pool. Blackpool that is. John Lennon (right) spent childhood holidays in Fleetwood where a relative was housekeeper to a local family.

Below: fans await their arrival while (below left) Louis Tussaud's waxworks welcomed the Beatles to the Golden Mile

# and rolling

Winter Gardens staff clear up in the aftermath of the Rolling Stones riot. Earlier fans had crushed forward (below)

The bad boys of Rock and Roll ran into a storm at the Empress Ballroom. Minutes after this picture was taken fans invaded the stage

# Fall of a people's

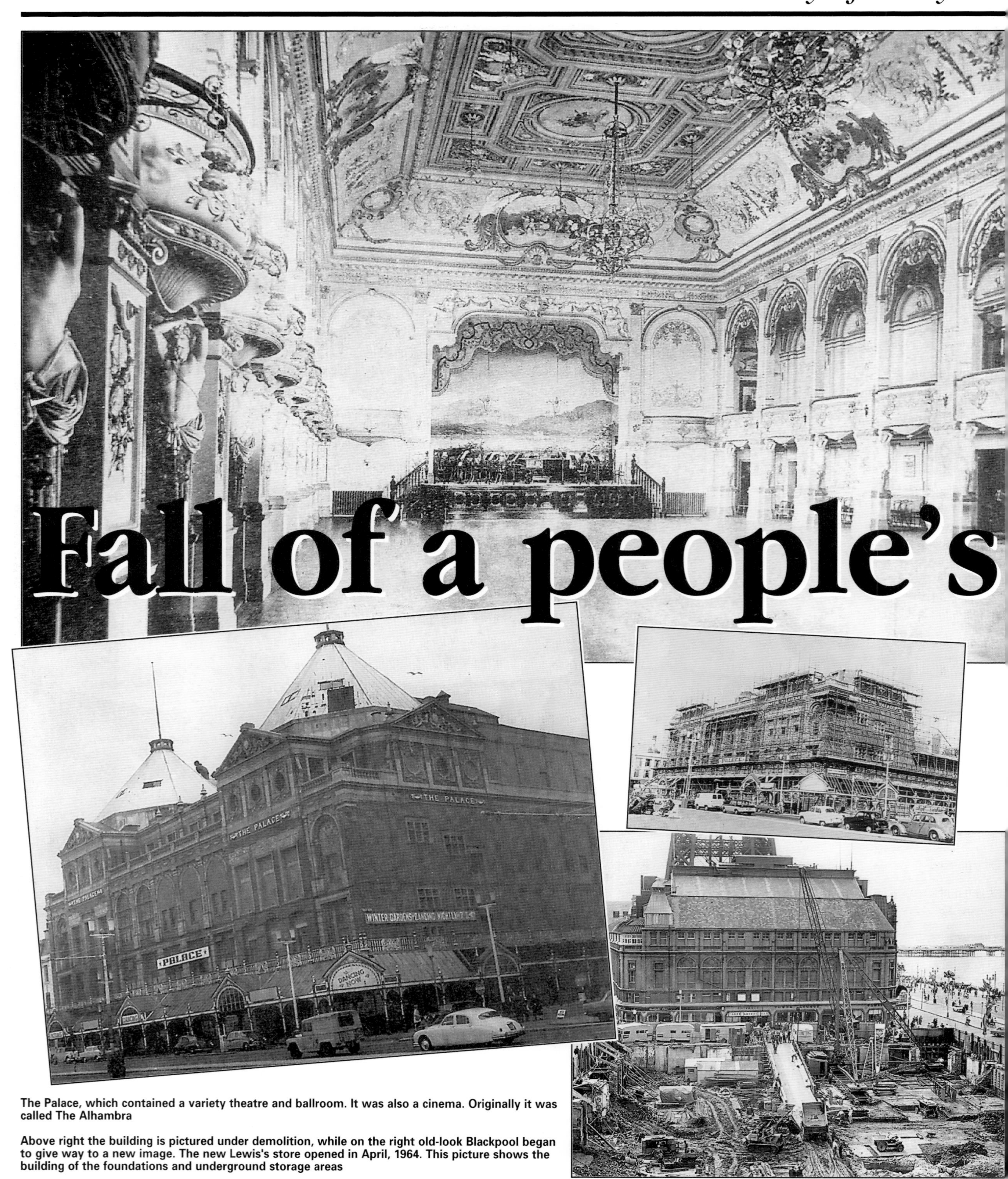


The Palace, which contained a variety theatre and ballroom. It was also a cinema. Originally it was called The Alhambra

Above right the building is pictured under demolition, while on the right old-look Blackpool began to give way to a new image. The new Lewis's store opened in April, 1964. This picture shows the building of the foundations and underground storage areas

Almost as ornate as The Tower ballroom the Palace dance floor (left) was an impressive venue

The completed Lewis's building. Now changed again it is home to Woolworths, Harry Ramsden & Mecca Bingo along with other shops and stores

# palace

The old Palace Band early this century

IT was the end of an era. The seafront Palace was demolished in the '60s to make way for another form of entertainment – shopping.

The short stretch of Central Promenade which it occupied had long been Blackpool's most desirable building site.

Hotels, houses, even bath houses were developed there over the 18th and 19th centuries, but the area came into its own with the advent of theatre.

First the Prince of Wales Theatre. Then the sumptuously ornate Alhambra, out to rival the Tower. Later, under a Tower Company buyout, the Palace Varieties – known as the People's Popular Palace of Pleasure.

The Palace, variety hall, theatre, ballroom, erstwhile circus, skating rink and picture house, was demolished, along with the neighbouring County Hotel, in 1961.

Its loss signalled the end of one way of life – and the start of another. The retail renaissance.

It went to make way for Lewis's, Blackpool's last, and now, alas, lost "proper" department store. The wind of change swept through town.

The spectacular store opened amid a fanfare of publicity, and before a crowd of 1,500 shoppers, on April 2, 1964 .

The flagship store, with its distinctive modernist architecture, and sea-green honeycomb panelling frontage, soon became a landmark.

The town was delighted to have the full-line department store which established itself as an anchor of town centre shopping and built a loyal customer base both here and in the surrounding areas.

It remained part of the Sears Group until '88 , one of 10 Lewis's throughout the country. When the business met difficult times it was rescued by finance director James Fyffe who arranged the purchase of all of the stores apart from Selfridges.

The Blackpool lease was purchased a year later as part of a £15m move to give bosses full control of the empire but in the same year entertainments giant First Leisure informed Lewis's of its "possible interest" in acquiring the store as an extension of its seafront neighbour, the Tower.

The one-time showcase store sailed into stormier waters in early '91 when the business went into receivership, largely because of the general economic climate and recession.

A rescue package was put together with the help of Lancashire Enterprises and Blackpool Council ' seemingly saving 300 jobs in a management buyout.

But it was to all end in tears, after months of speculation, in January '93 – tempered with some optimism as Woolworth's unveiled a £3 million plan for a new store just a block away from its old site.

Although the building was transformed to accommodate new outlets including the showcase Harry Ramsden's fish and chips "with chandeliers" restaurant the loss of a major department store pushed Blackpool, once rated the region's third shopping centre after Manchester and Liverpool, further down the retail league.

The site had a troubled history as the Palace Variety Theatre . At one point, in 1960, Douglas Bickerstaffe, chairman of the Blackpool Tower Company, which owned the site, insisted the owners had no intention of selling the Palace and County island site "to anyone".

It was, he said, the most valuable site in Blackpool, and there had been numerous inquiries.

The denial came as Billy Smart's New World Circus made a bid to purchase the freehold – in the hope of opening a circus "and other features" in 1961.

Yet the demolition gangs moved in at the end of the '61 season ending a chapter in Blackpool entertainment history which is still lamented today.

# Shot down: Fylde's

THE TSR2. It was the Warton-developed bomber 20 years ahead of its time – a hi-tech child of the cold war.

But it wasn't enemy fire that brought it down in 1965.

It was grounded by then-Defence Minister Denis Healey's cutbacks in a defence review.

It was an early lesson to local planemakers on the vagaries of the industry – and the whims of politicians.

There were two prototypes of the Tactical Strike Reconnaissance Aircraft – the pride and joy of the then-British Aircraft Corporation.

It completed preliminary trials at Boscombe Down before arriving at Warton for more work.

Flying the revolutionary new bomber called for the very best pilot skills.

One of the two BAC flight test teams was headed by Wing Commander Roland "Roly" Beamont – a man accustomed to flying at high speeds at low levels and withstanding strong G forces.

A former Lytham St Annes man, and a frequent visitor to the showcase Warton base, the wing commander was the most experienced high speed test pilot in Britain – capable of pulling seven and a half G compared with the then-average RAF Lightning pilot's five and half or six .

He made his very first flight , aged seven, in an Avro 504 biplane , but his flying career started in the '30s. He flew 109 different types of aeroplanes in war and peace including Battle of Britain Hurricanes, enemy train-busting Typhoons, Gloster Meteors, the North American Sabre and Canberras. He piloted the latter's first flight from Warton in 1949 and also became the first man to make a "there and back" flight to America in less than a day. He also piloted the English Electric Lightning, pride of joy of Warton in the '50s and '60s.

The wartime fighter ace, although a seasoned aviator, was thrilled to become the designated pilot for the first flight of the British Aircraft Corporation's TSR2 a top secret tactical supersonic aircraft designed to replace the RAF's Canberras.

In addition to its tactical reconnaissance role the TSR2 was capable of a strike with a conventional or nuclear weapon – and was also seen as reinforcing Britain's nuclea defences until the Polaris submarines were fully deployed.

But after all the high hopes, the TSR2 was to turn into one of the biggest disappointments of the Warton work force and the test pilot himself – when Healey's axe fell on the programme.

It was the aircraft closest to Beamont's heart, representing the then-pinnacle o planemakers' achievement.

"We knew just after one circuit of the airfield that it was a winner," he recalled.

The ill-fated warplane has since been restored by the Imperial War Museum and i now on display at the historic airfield a Duxford, Cambridgeshire.

It's already been seen there by Mr Beamon

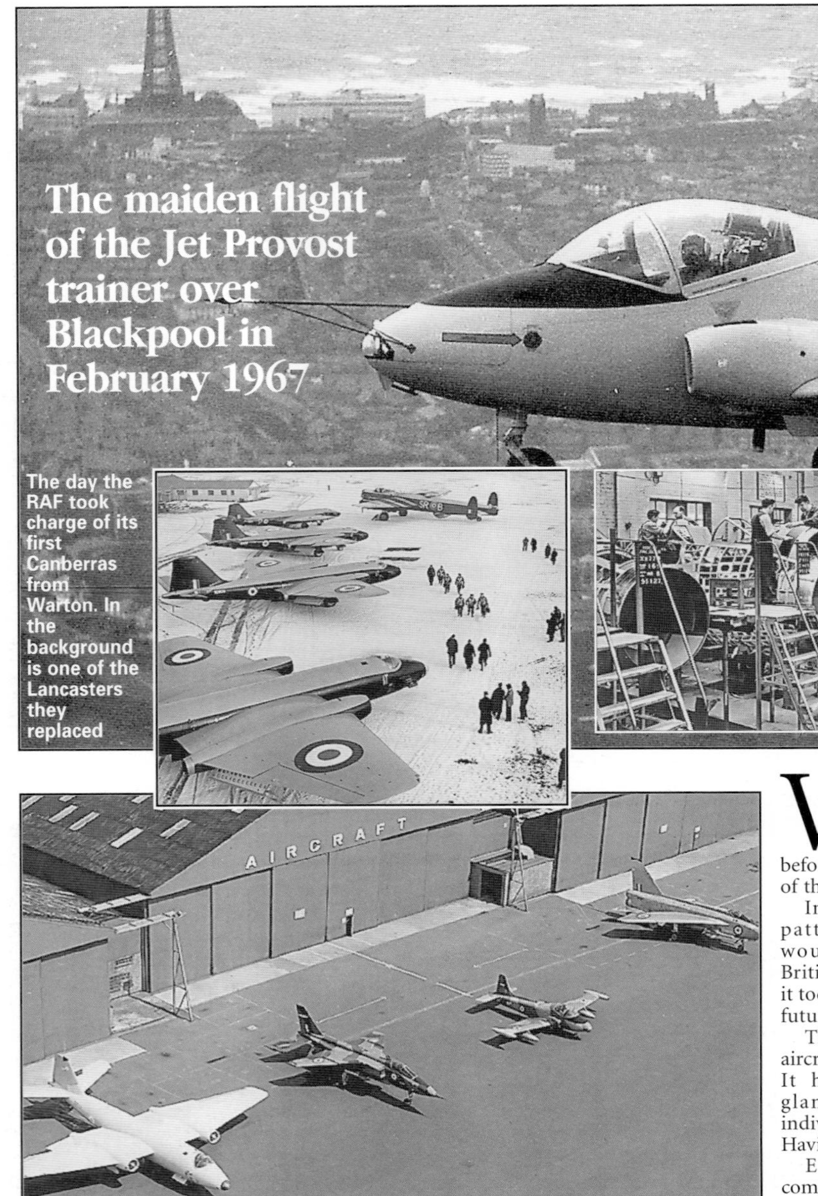


The maiden flight of the Jet Provost trainer over Blackpool in February 1967

The day the RAF took charge of its first Canberras from Warton. In the background is one of the Lancasters they replaced

Lightning under construction

Long before the computer age – one of the drawing rooms at BAC Warton in 1962

A line up of Warton's most famous jets of the late-sixties. (from left) the Canberra bomber, Jaguar fighter-bomber, Strikemaster trainer and Lightning fighter

WARTON – home of Britain's best planemakers – was flying high in the '60s before the boom Tornado years of the '70s.

Insiders, having seen the pattern of mergers which would ultimately lead to British Aerospace as we know it today, were less certain of the future.

The Government wanted the aircraft industry "rationalised". It had already ended the glamour associated with individual names such as De Havilland and Hawker.

English Electric – the company which had ruled the roost for Preston, Warton and Samlesbury – had merged with Bristol Aircraft and Vickers Armstrong to form the British Air Corporation.

A government white paper in the '50s had suggested that all future wars would be fought with missiles. In '65 a defence review scrapped the Warton workers' pride and joy – the prototype Tactical Strike Reconnaissance Aircraft (TSR2) the then-epitome of aviation excellence.

Ian Lawrenson, a member of the North West Heritage Group, made up of British Aerospace workers past and present, reckons: "The writing was on the wall in the '60s. The rot had set in. Great things were still happening but some of the heart was going out of it. The loss of the TSR2 in particular was a huge blow."

Shortly after the cancellatio of the TSR2 project a new dea was struck between the UK an France to develop the Jagua combat aircraft.

The initial prototype, French version, first flew i September '68 with the firs UK-built example flying fror Warton in September '69. I paved the way for anothe international accord in '69 this time involving Germany when the UK signed a agreement to develop the Multi Role Combat Aircraft bette known today as the Tornado.

Warton was also th birthplace of the Provost je trainer which made its maide flight in 1967 and was later t evolve into the Strikemaster, big overseas order winner.

# plane of the future

who flew the TSR2 on its maiden flight before the big warplane was scrapped.

He said: "It was a complete technical success at the point of cancellation and as a defence system its continuation would have been justified."

Not that the aerospace and aviation technology developed for the TSR2 was lost – much of it was incorporated into subsequent aeroplanes such as the Tornado.

Meet Roly Beamont
HE DEALS IN DANGER FOR PERFECTION


**TSR2, escorted by a Lightning, takes off from Warton**

**Warton aircraft workers (above) take a look at the finished plane before flight testing began**

**This prototype TSR2 was dumped on a testing ground at Foulness in Essex. A second prototype was restored and is now on display at the Imperil War Museum**

## The last hand of happy families

THE year is 1966 – and members of an entertainments dynasty are circling Blackpool Tower like basking sharks.

The days of local control for the town's major entertainments assets – bar the Thompson family-run Pleasure Beach – are numbered.

Share prices pick up as news of a sale gains momentum – just days after Blackpool Tower Company announces a drop in profit and dividend.

It had once been very successful. In 1948 the Tower Company made a profit of £500,000 and declared a staggering 35 per cent dividend to shareholders.

Now City pundits predict a pre-Christmas sale: "Mr Lew Grade's Associated Television is interested in the Blackpool set-up."

The report is quickly denied by cigar-smoking Lew: "I don't know where they get these rumours."

If anything it's brother Bernard Delfont who ultimately gets in on the act. He's already staged shows at North Pier and put acts into other theatres. Blackpool's been in his blood since his professional hoofer days back in the 20s – when he performed here – and he's already helped Charles Forte buy the three piers in town.

Bernard was to later recall how he got an "open cheque" from EMI in 1967 to build their leisure interests – and how the-then-chairman of the Tower Company Dr Ted Badman "was as far removed from the world of popular entertainment as it was possible to imagine. When I called him to mention the possibility of a bid he was immediately interested – almost too interested."

They agreed to meet on neutral ground where neither man would be recognised . . . and struck the £4.6m deal in the tea room of Crewe station shaking hands over the Formica table top.

Blackpool's major assets passed out of local hands . . . and have stayed that way ever since passing from EMI, to Thorn EMI ('79), Charles Forte ('81), First Leisure ('83) – a company created after Lord Delfont masterminded a management buyout of Forte's leisure assets – and now Leisure Parcs ('98).

The Delfont and Grade dynasty's links with Blackpool ended when media mogul Michael Grade took over First Leisure in the '90s.

He was less convinced of the value of what his late uncle Bernard described as the "jewel in First Leisure's crown".

Faced with the challenge of reinventing "an institution with a great history and real potential" Mr Grade decided to "offload" the seaside pleasure concerns.

It was the end of an era.

Blackpool historian and archivist Brian Crompton, who now works for new Tower owners, Leisure Parcs, recalls: "In many ways the '60s was the time of greatest change because until then Blackpool had been dominated by smallish local companies run by businessmen who also lived locally. The '60s marked the move towards takeovers and mergers by larger organisations and people who were not part and parcel of the culture of the town. For the record, Blackpool Tower Company, which was formed in 1891 to build the Tower, still exists within EMI, but as a trading name has been dormant since the '80s."

# Tears of a clown

Charlie (below) in his heyday at the Tower Circus with sidekick Paul

Charlie Cairoli with his family in 1960. Charlie junior, fooling around with a watering can, became a clown in his own right

CLOWN PRINCE Charlie Cairoli bowed of Blackpool Tower Circus – on docto orders.

Three months later his wife Violet, now found her husband sobbing at their North Sh home.

"Are you in pain, my love?" she asked.

Charlie's reply broke Violet's heart.

He was crying because he would never hear children laughing again.

The tears of the clown were genuine. His wid recalls: "He loved children – and did it all for the

Three months after quitting the w he loved in 1979 – Charlie Cairoli, father-of-three, was dead.

It's a tribute to the man's comic leg that – almost two decades after death – he is still remembered w love, affection and a great deal respect.

Charlie Cairoli was the greatest the great clowns: an internatio figurehead of fun. And in the ' Charlie was at the peak of his pow – a man who had truly come into own.

Blackpool Tower archivist Br Crompton recalls the '60s as Cairoli years for the Tower Circus

Italian-born Cairoli, wh parents were in fact French clow learned his trade the hard way. the time he reached his teens he l appeared as an acrobat, horse rid conjurer and musician. His fam starred in the world-famo Circus Medrano in Paris in the l 1920s. He never performed Italy.

Charlie's father Jean, once top the European circus bills, ended years of sawdust duty in 1947 the Tower Circus, returning to dressing room to tell his s Charlie: "Eh bien, Charlie, it finished. Continuez."

Charlie first came Blackpool for the season 1939 and got stranded h because of the war – and briefly interned as an ali He had to have a work permit and report to t police station – but he soon found he liked it he

Members of the Yokoi Troupe

Captain Sidney Howes presents his African Lioness in 1965

nd Blackpool liked m here, too.

Violet recalls it as ne of the worst years of er life. "It rained for the hole summer and I didn't now a word of English."

For some time he worked in e shadows of Doodles the clown it after his death in the '40s began establish a tremendous following his own right through the '50s and 0s. At his side for 31 years was his wn familiar stooge and sidekick, ttle Jimmy Buchanan, and, for any years, white-faced clown Paul. 1970 Charlie was featured in This Your Life.

Mr Crompton explains: "Charlie lped make Blackpool Tower a ust-go place for the masses. People ite literally got off the train and ent to book a circus ticket before ey even got to the boarding house. ccommodation wasn't their first iority – the circus was."

And in those days the circus turned the compliment with three ll performances a day – morning, ternoon and evening.

Mr Crompton concludes: "Charlie iroli had a very special magic, an peal that spanned generations. He as very different to other circus owns. In a sense he was inimalistic, he didn't have a lot of ops or wear big clown makeup. His ain feature was his clown nose. In ery other sense he was very human not at all grotesque or frightening. endeared him to people."

Memories of the glory days are as vid as ever for Violet, a former robat with the Cairoli family's rival rcus, but who married Charlie in 34. All but two weeks of their nine- onth engagement were spent apart.

She is especially proud of her late isband's framed certificate from e Queen after he starred at the oyal Command Performance at ackpool's Opera House in 1955. Charlie himself recalled it as one of the happiest moments of his life – describing Prince Philip as "outspoken and clever."

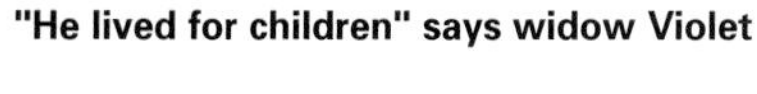
"He lived for children" says widow Violet

He also starred in another Opera House show – to mark the 100th anniversary of the resort council's Charter.

The couple would go for a drink at Yates's after each show and Violet still remembers her husband's capacity for fun.

"He was always playing gags on me – never nasty gags, but funny ones. I still miss him very much."

Charlie's legacy also lives through his son Charlie who for years was billed as Charlie Cairoli Jnr – although dad insisted he had a trade before he joined the circus. He is a qualified engineer.

"I was in the Tower Circus with my dad during his last summer there in '79," says Charlie, now a dad himself.

"He had a couple of heart attacks and his doctor told him to pack in performing so I actually took over from him."

It's a source of lasting shame for many in the resort – particularly members of the Charlie Cairoli Appreciation Society – that there is no statue in memory of the great entertainer in the town where he performed for four decades. A bid for cash to finance a memorial was rejected by the National Lottery four years ago.

# The show must go on

LORD Delfont said he felt sorry for the elephants as he bowed to pressure from activists who had campaigned loud and long against the appearance of animals in the Tower Circus.

Since 1990 the spectacular shows in the giant ring set between the four legs of the Tower itself have been without animal acts.

But the circus goes on – despite another plan to replace traditional performances with a display of robots.

It is still an accolade in the circus world to appear at Blackpool Tower and the circus continues to attract top acts from across the world.

Apart from the unusual setting – not in a tent, of course, but in a lavish indoor arena – the circus is unique because of the finale when the ring area can be flooded with thousands of gallons of seawater.

On one occasion the finale depicted the wartime battle of the River Plate but the audience never realised the real drama they were watching.

The model ships were controlled by swimmers and one nearly drowned when he became stuck inside a model of the German battleship Graf Spee. He was rescued by quick-thinking colleagues.

But the audience were happy the night the stand-in girl on the aerial rope act accidentally went topless! Her borrowed costume was too small. She descended red faced while the band played For She's A Jolly Good Fellow.

The circus ring has also been used as a boxing and wrestling venue, as a film set for a film about te silent screen star Rudolf Valentino – even as the venue for a religious service. For well over a century it has been at the heart of the resort's entertainment scene and looks much the same now as it did in Victorian times.

The Flying Marilees from Texas

# Where

# BIN

**The craze swept Blackpool and the rest of the Fylde in the '60s – as the bingo belles recall**

THE Empire bingo hall at Hawes Side Lane, Marton, celebrated its 25th anniversary in September '99 – but the success story dates back further.

Owner Elaine Bottomley , 51, recalls the '60s as the years when all eyes were down – and houses were full.

"Blackpool was buzzing. There was bingo, introduced by Billy Greenwood, at Central Station from 10am to 10pm, games all over town. Pre-68 it was a licence to print money but the act drove all the cowboys and dodgy operators out. Stanley Raymond was the hanging judge of bingo. The aim was to stop the Mafia infiltration but regulations went too far."

The Gaming Act cleaned up the game's image. The Bottomley bingo empire started with Exchange bingo, opposite Talbot Road, with other outlets at Marton, South Shore, St Annes, even Preston. They took over old cinemas, the Palladium, Rendesvouz, even an old theatre.

"We had a nice little numb going," Elaine recalls. Card gam were played upstairs in the snug the Empire. "It wasn't licensed."

Elaine explains: "My late husba John Bottomley started it back in t '60s. He was a butcher in South Sho and used to see the old ladies off play bingo at the Lido which was licensed at the time. He saw opportunity, borrowed money off h sister, got a mortgage, and boug into the Exchange. In the morning sold weighing scales to butchers – h other business – and in the afterno ran the club. The jackpots used bring 350 people in but some da there were just 10-20. It built up. the '60s anything went. You could p

Elaine Bottomley outside her 'empire' in Hawes Side Lane, Marton

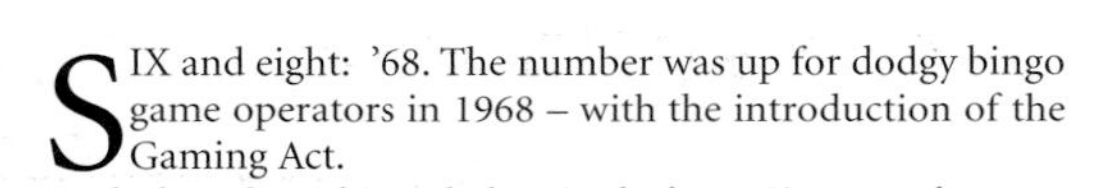

SIX and eight: '68. The number was up for dodgy bingo game operators in 1968 – with the introduction of the Gaming Act.

Blackpool was bingo balmy in the '60s. Cinemas, theatres, even Central Station had succumbed to the craze.

The '60s had taken the brakes off gambling. Bingo was even played in the Tower Circus – cancelling the '68 school sports cavalcade to the horror of locals. The game would ultimately come to architect Frank Matcham's other glorious creation, the Grand Theatre, to bridge the gap between demolition threat and salvation by the "Friends."

Bingo was big business. In '62 aldermen pleaded for a Blackpool outlet to continue to use its first floor as a bingo hall – rather than lose the town £2,000 in rates, put 33 people out of work, and end the fun for 65,000 members. Bingo was the craze that had "ousted whist", said one councillor, and the salvation of empty eyesore premises.

Tudor Bingo Club , which ran bingo at Central Station and other venues across the Fylde, was one of the giants.

Since '66 club members have raised £120,000 for charity in six years – including the police dependants' fund and mayor's charity appeal.

A surprise gift of £2,000 from Tudor boss Billy Greenwood enabled Blackpool and Fylde Civilian Disabled Society to open debt-free – to the delight of chairman and councillor Leonard Broughton. Then Lancashire deputy chief constable Stan Parr was named an honorary life member. Mr Parr, who was to later fall from grace, described Blackpool as the most generous town in the county. "If you have a worthwhile cause you will always get people to listen and put their hands in their pockets."

But with the bigger money stakes came darker links – and warnings of Mafia infiltration. Organised crime was out to exploit the nation's favourite game. Hollywood gangst George Raft who had Mafia links in "real" life tried a failed to win a gaming licence in London.

Local police went bingo busting time and again checking on membership at dens where bingo went hand hand with roulette and card games.

In a '63 raid, led by the then deputy chief constable Blackpool, names and addresses of 100 players, mos women, were taken, to ensure all had legitima membership.

The '68 Gaming Act introduced licensing and tough restr tions and drove unscrupulous operators out of business.

Blackpool and the Fylde remained a bastion of the gan Even under Lottery threat it endures in community clu seafront arcades, and big glitzy centres.

Such was the lure of bingo in '60s Blackpool that Stanley Raymond, chairman of the Gaming Board of Gr Britain – and the man who drove the Mafia out of t Bahamas gaming scene – visited the town to investigate mix of bingo and "hard gaming."

He wasn't happy with what he found on a tour of 10 bin clubs and eight gaming clubs in Blackpool and St Annes th lasted from 7pm to 6.30am.

The proportion was higher here than elsewhere, claimed. On a bleak January night he found "hundreds housewives" playing bingo and feared for their exposure the "unlimited gambling of roulette or similar games in t same club."

He called for a code of conduct and tougher inspectio and rode out of town vowing to return in the summer.

Bingo has been subject to stringent regulations ever si the Gaming Act of '68.

To bring the story up to date, the National Bingo Ga

Central Station becomes a Tudor Bingo hall – the company was run by Billy Greenwood

# 'House' can also be a home

in any game you wanted, we had roulette going, the card table."

Elaine had started working for John when she was 18. "I married the boss." By '75 the couple had opened the Grand Casino on Station Road in South Shore.

John died in 1991. Today the empire is down to the Empire. Elaine, mother-of-three, sees it as the Cinema Paradiso of the bingo business.

She admits: "It was hard to carry on. I had six months feeling as if I was in a massive hole then I realised that if I didn't lift myself out of it others would suffer. The big boys would like to wipe out places like this but it's not bingo, as we know it, in one of those aircraft hanger-like places. Here I've got a good business, super people, and a real community social scene. I'm not the Mother Teresa of bingo but I've got a nucleus of people who, if we closed tomorrow, wouldn't go to the likes of the Mecca but would stay at home. For some it's their only outing . Some, who leave here at four o'clock, won't talk to anyone until they come back here.

"That's why we opened on Christmas Day to do 35 dinners five Christmasses back, it's why we do freebies, lunches, other treats, such as a 10p paperback book club, and it's why we keep admissions at 30p, the same price for eight years. It's warm, friendly, comfortable. I couldn't close – what would happen to my ladies?"

SIX and five: in '65 Cleveleys-based entrepreneur Albert Mason realised bingo was going to be big and started promoting the game in the one-time Odeon cinema on The Crescent. It's claimed to have been the first cash bingo game on the coast.

One of the longest established clubs is at Fleetwood – Barney's Bingo Club on Poulton Road. It's managed by Norman and Bunty Gallagher and their family, one son and two daughters.

Bunty recalls that in bingo's heyday her father Barney – who went to court to prove that prize bingo was not a game of chance and won the case – had a string of bingo halls across the Fylde. It all started in an arcade where Woolworths now stands at Cleveleys. "It was affectionately referred to as the tin hut."

The family ran bingo at the Queens Theatre, Blackpool, now C & A, at a former cafe at Foxhall Road, South Pier, the Marine Hall at Fleetwood, St Margarets Church, Fleetwood, now a block of flats, and the old Victoria cinema in the port – now Barney's.

"With being a fishing town a lot of the women had spare time to play bingo," Bunty explains.

Barney's Bingo is at bottom left of this picture of the old Queens Theatre, now C&A in Blackpool

Bernadette Gallagher at Barney's Bingo, Fleetwood.

was launched in '86 to revive interest in bingo and update its image.

Strict gaming laws meant Parliamentary legislation was necessary and a new Bingo Act was passed enabling participating clubs to link up simultaneously.

It's only earlier this decade that some of the restrictions eased. Prior to deregulation in '92 bingo was the Game That Dared Not Speak Its Name.

Now licensed bingo clubs can promote themselves under three different categories: bingo clubs, social clubs and the National Bingo Game. Bingo remains big business in Britain – particularly in the North – with almost 1,000 licensed and operating bingo clubs: about half of them owned by large groups – the major players such as Mecca – while the rest are private clubs owned by independent, often family, operators.

## A runner for your money

**UNTIL the more liberal days of the 1960s, people who liked a flutter on the horses or the dogs often had to break the law to enjoy a bet. Wealthier people tended to play by the rules.**

**They could have credit with a bookmaker and telephone or even post their bets to his office.**

**On the race course anyone could deal openly with the bookmakers.**

**But the man or woman in the street had to put a wager on in a different way.**

**They might approach the bookie's runner who had a regular beat in a pub, on a street corner, outside a factory.**

**He was the illegal go-between and sometimes, like the prostitutes, rock sellers and sunglasses vendors, he was taken to court and fined.**

**Or the gambling man could visit a betting shop which was illegal and usually hidden discreetly out of the way down an alley or in some rented room.**

**Every now and again the police raided these locations. Sometimes they gave the bookie 24 hours notice.**

**In 1963 the Betting, Gaming and Lotteries Act paved the way for betting shops, bingo and casinos.**

**But there were strict regulations about the way the betting shops were run – no gaming machines, soft drinks or tea and coffee. There could be no radio or TV either and, because TV was sometimes ahead of the bookies telephone result service – The Blower – it was possible for punters to cheat and win.**

**The effect was to make more people interested in betting because the industry now had a more respectable image and was more accessible.**

**But the runners continued to operate for years. Now they had a permit and a special bag for collecting the bets with a clock that recorded the time the bet was made.**

**Blackpool had a number of illegal card playing clubs in the 1950s. There was a boom in legal cards and roulette in the '60s but a number of locations closed because there was not enough business to support them.**

# The end

Days of steam! A locomotive pulls out of Central – perhaps an express to London

Inside Central Station in 1955

# All change as Fylde tram routes

Lytham Road, South Shore, near the Lido building was once a busy tramway scene

How Devonshire Square looked when trams were running on the Marton route

Workmen demolish the Blackpool landmark at Devonshire Square in 1965

# of the line

ON a cold autumn night 35 years ago a train pulled out of Blackpool and transported a chunk of the town's history into the record books.

It was November 1964, and Blackpool Central Station had closed down.

The end of the lights that year was also the end of the line.

Many people in the town could not believe the decision to shut down a terminus more than a century old which had brought in millions of trippers and deposited them at the heart of holiday town Blackpool.

Old railwaymen used to say the takings from the toilets at Central paid the rates bill but Blackpool council didn't shed too many tears when they signed a deal with British Rail which gave them Central and a vast swathe of land reaching south and leading out through South Shore and Marton to the boundary for what was recognised as a bargain price of £950,000.

Ironically, most of that land is now devoted to the railway's arch rival, road transport.

The Central Station story began in 1863 when it opened as Hounds Hill station – little more than a shack at the end of a single track line from Lytham.

North Station was then known as Talbot Road.

By the turn of the century hordes of holidaymakers and day trippers were flooding into Blackpool by rail and the town itself was expanding fast.

In 1903 a new direct line was opened from Kirkham to South Shore and Central and it is along this rail route that Yeadon Way now runs.

The land occupied by the Central Station tracks – where hundreds of coaches used to be shoe-horned into a parking space at night – was cleared to become known as the South Shore Central Corridor and has been converted into the biggest coach and car park in Europe.

In its heyday Central Station was a hive of activity.

When visitors arrived they were wooed by touts encouraging them to find lodgings at various boardinghouses and hotels.

An army of youngsters with home-made wooden carts waited to transport luggage in return for a few pence while hundreds of departing holidaymakers scrambled for a seat on the train home.

Stations on the Fylde coast could handle two million visitors in a summer season.

On one summer Saturday 434 trains came and went and 190,000 passengers arrived and left.

The most unfortunate passenger was a circus elephant which was loaded into a specially-reinforced van but went berserk near Preston and had to be shot by soldiers.

When the iron road first came to the Fylde coast it was from Preston to Fleetwood in 1840.

On the same night Central Station closed down the last train from Fleetwood's "top station" on Queens terrace to Blackpool North made its run which ended a link of 65 years.

Less than 18 months later the quayside station was closed leaving Wyre Dock as the port's rail terminus until it, too, was closed in 1970.

When Central Station closed a long-serving railman told the Gazette: " They have cut the heart out of Blackpool."

But the deal was just part of the wind of change that was beginning to blow through Blackpool. It paved the way for the demolition of the Golden Mile and the development of attractions like Coral Island.

The police station and courts complex were developed to ex-railway land off Chapel Street.

The vast complex of Central Station (above) with Central Drive on the left

Central Station on a Saturday morning. Many new arrivals headed for the New Inn by the Golden Mile to wash away the taste of smoke and steam from the train journey

Visitors from Oldham arrive in 1963 barely a year before it closed

# are dismantled

THERE were big changes to Blackpool's tramway map in the Sixties.

At the time, trams had become unfashionable in the transport world and big cities were busy dismantling their systems.

In Blackpool, the town hall decided it was time for serious pruning.

The first victim was on the Lytham Road route which linked through to Starr Gate on the seafront via Squires Gate Lane.

The track needed to be relaid so instead of spending the money the Transport department closed most of it down in 1961.

A popular trip with visitors was to board a tram at Talbot Square and ride out to the Oxford Hotel junction at Marton via Church Street and Whitegate Drive.

Then the cars went through Spen Corner by Hawes Side Lane and down Waterloo Road to the Royal Oak pub where they joined Lytham Road.

This circular journey got the axe in 1962.

Other sections in south Blackpool were closed in 1963 and so was the line that saw Fleetwood trams plying the route along Dickson Road between the Gynn and Talbot Road where the entrance to North Station was sited.

A desire by the council's surveyor's department and the police to build the modern Gynn Square traffic system came into this although tram fans said the cars could have run through the middle of the roundabout.

The demise of Blackpool's inland routes revived memories of yesteryear when plans had been mooted for a Blackpool-Poulton-Thornton-Cleveleys tramway (1899) and a Blackpool- Garstang route in 1901.

And it recalled the days of Lytham St Annes trams.

They started in 1896 and linked with the Blackpool system. But huge losses led to a growth of bus services and the last Lytham St Annes tram ran in April, 1937.

Glasgow abandoned trams in 1962 and, with Blackpool's inland routes gone soon after that, left the Blackpool-Fleetwood system the only electric tramway left in the land . . . until Manchester and Sheffield discovered their attraction once again!

When the ABC theatre was opened on May 31, 1963, Cliff Richard and The Shadows arrived on the Showboat tram. It was the last time a tram ran in Church Street

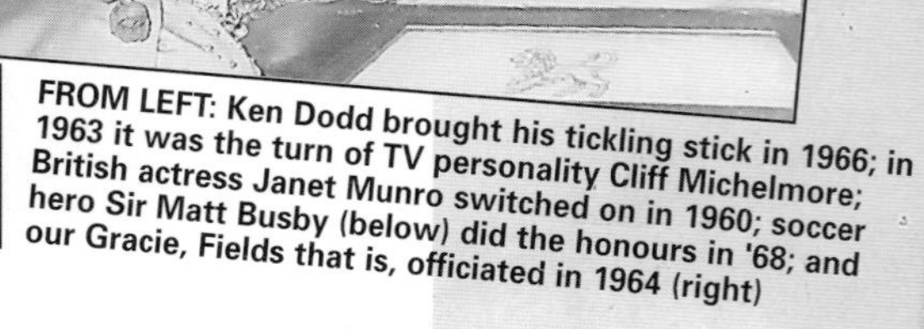

**FROM LEFT: Ken Dodd brought his tickling stick in 1966; in 1963 it was the turn of TV personality Cliff Michelmore; British actress Janet Munro switched on in 1960; soccer hero Sir Matt Busby (below) did the honours in '68; and our Gracie, Fields that is, officiated in 1964 (right)**

# Lights nights!

**George Formby, who immortalised the little stick of Blackpool rock, was an obvious choice for the 1953 switch-on; while below, Curvy Jayne Mansfield added a touch of glamour in 1959**

THE QUEST for a celebrity to trip the Lights fantastic has always had that razzle-dazzle of glamour since the decision was made to turn on the 1934 display with a special ceremony .

Janet Munro did the honours in 1960, our own Violet Carson (Coronation Street's famed battleaxe Ena Sharples) in 1961, and the lovely Shirley Ann Field in 1962.

OK, so the term glamour slipped slightly with 1963's switch-on celebrity Cliff Michelmore but Gracie Fields (1964) brought it back and '65 saw David Tomlinson, star of the hit Disney movie Mary Poppins deliver a supercalafragalistic start to the show.

Enduring comedy king Ken Dodd, who begins his new Millennium at Fleetwood Marine Hall on January 1, 2000, did the honours in '66, and – surprisingly! – vacated the platform in time for Dr Horace King, Speaker of the House of Commons, in 14s beg mp9 13/1167.

Football fans also turned out in droves to see the '68 switch-on by football legend Sir Matt Busby while the '69 ceremony was marked by a Canberra Bomber!

**Lancashire lass Gracie Fields was as popular as any modern rock star. She' pictured here in 1967 when she visited her beloved Blackpool to open the Brindle Lodge old people's centre on Mereside.**

# Five die in train crash

**Plate layers dwarfed by the wrecked carriages at Weeton**

DEATH came to the quiet countryside of the Fylde one Sunday morning when a Fylde rail wreck claimed five lives.

It happened as a diesel-powered train sped towards Fleetwood from Colne.

It was timed to link with a steamer leaving the port for the Isle of Man.

Two of the dead were territorial army officers from Bolton on their way to visit a Manx TA unit.

The train passed the Weeton railway bridge and rounded a bend on an embankment above the fields.

But parked on the line was a row of wagons used for moving the stone chipping ballast on which railway lines are bedded.

The diesel smashed into the wagons with an explosion and a blue flash. Two carriages weighing 30 tons apiece were catapulted into the sky like a grotesque archway

The driver, 61-year-old Thomas Shaw of Farrington, near Preston, was among those killed.

Police, fire and rescue crews launched a big rescue operation after the crash.

Track workers who had missed death by inches immediately joined in the rescue operation and a fleet of ambulances queued up in the nearby lanes.

A bus driver who had come to collect the railway maintenance men drove off to hospital with 50 walking wounded onboard.

There were 19 more seriously injured who were detained in hospitals in Blackpool, Preston and at Weeton RAF camp.

The train had been crowded with holiday-makers from East Lancashire, Manchester and Preston.

It was the first fatal rail accident since November 1924 when the Liverpool to Blackpool express crashed near Lytham and 16 were killed.

In 1903 a driver was killed at Blackpool North station and in 1893 three people died.

A man was decapitated the first time trains ran between Preston and the Fylde coast in 1840. The first line linked with Fleetwood.

# Blackpool store blaze

HISTORY repeated itself when a £1.5 million fire blasted through the heart of Blackpool town centre in May, 1967.

For it was the second time that the department store of RHO Hills in Bank Hey Street, just behind the Tower, had been burned out.

The previous blaze came in 1932 when the store was full of staff and customers but there was no panic and everyone got out safely.

The 1967 outbreak was discovered early in the morning and within a couple of hours the five-storey building had been reduced to a smoking ruin.

At the height of the fire the flames were leaping 100 feet into the sky and outlined firefighters on turntable ladders as they tackled the huge blaze.

Chunks of blazing material were blown on to the roofs of neighbouring buildings. Firemen poured their hoses on the Tower building just across the street to stop it catching light in the fierce heat but flames did reach canvas sheets draped on the Tower itself to shield workers from the wind.

Circus animals were taken outside and tethered to the Promenade railings.

Huge crowds gathered including scores of dancers in fancy dress who had just left a Round Table ball at the Winter Gardens.

Inside the store there was no sprinkler system and tons of inflammable stock added to the inferno which roared through the famous building.

Managing director William Cantrell heard the news at his holiday location in Somerset and drove back to Blackpool through the night.

He found that several fireproof safes had been rescued. Amongst other things they contained was £2,000 in cash and customer hire purchase records.

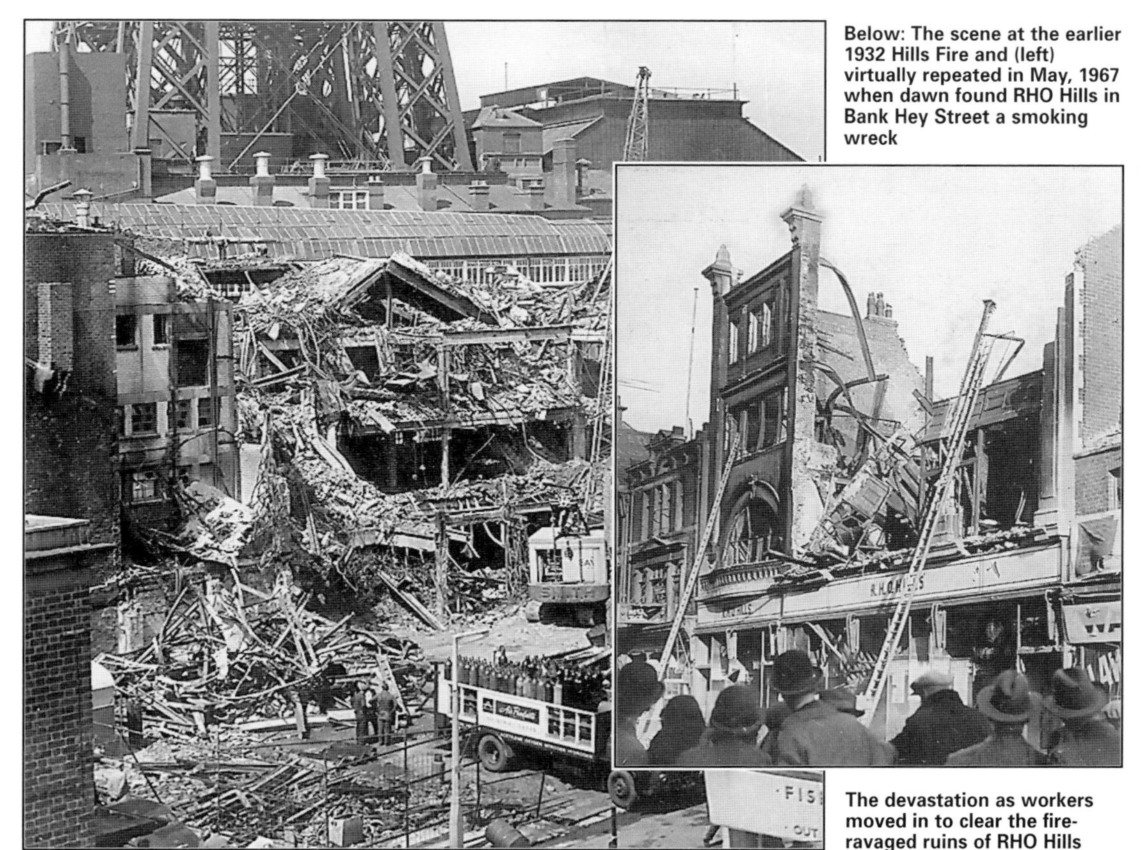

**Below: The scene at the earlier 1932 Hills Fire and (left) virtually repeated in May, 1967 when dawn found RHO Hills in Bank Hey Street a smoking wreck**

**The devastation as workers moved in to clear the fire-ravaged ruins of RHO Hills**

**Colourful character Eddie Sergeant, who was Lord of the Manor of Kirkham**

## A new town for old...

THE dawn of the Sixties found Kirkham a sleepy market town where traditional textile industries had declined.

It seemed stuck in a time warp from its historic days as a major centre of life in the Fylde.

It's most colourful local resident, Eddie Sergeant, owned the Manorial Rights and ran a strip joint called The Lower Deck Club at his home at Carr Hill.

But Coun Oswald "Ossie" Aitken had a plan to give the ancient town its biggest shot in the arm since the Romans built a fort near Dowbridge.

He wanted to turn the huge wartime RAF camp on the outskirts into a giant suburb of new homes.

Kirkham had a proud past but he wanted to give the place a bright future.

In 1967 his prayers were answered when a government body called the Land Commission said it was going to build 1,000 houses on the RAF camp and link the satellite town with the rest of Kirkham via a bridge over the busy Blackpool-Preston road.

But the Land Commission was scrapped – a decision described by a top planning official as having: "a disastrous effect on Kirkham."

The issue of Kirkham new town dragged on for 20 years. At one stage a construction firm bought the RAF site for £400,000 but then went bust. In the end, of course, the houses were never built.

The site became Kirkham open prison.

But local builders like the late William Harrison had changed Kirkham anyway. The development of new housing and a rebirth of local industry and shopping turned the town into a bustling, busy place again and gave it the future Coun Aitken had dreamed of 40 years ago.

**When Blackpool's Brian London took on American Howard King in the open air in Stanley Park, heavy rain began to fall. In the so-called Cloudburst Bout, which Brian won by a sixth-round knockout, the ring was spread with sawdust and the boxers fought in their bare feet**

**Brian London at the weigh-in at the Odeon, Leicester Square for his bout against Muhammad Ali – then known as Cassius Clay. The American successfully defended his world heavyweight title**

# England

**"Flat Jack" Simmons, who earned his big break with Lancashire when a professional for Blackpool. He is seen on the right with Blackpool team mates in 1968**

**Tony Jacklin, in 1969, became the first home-based player to win the British Open since 1951. On the left he kisses the winner's Claret Jug at Royal Lytham**

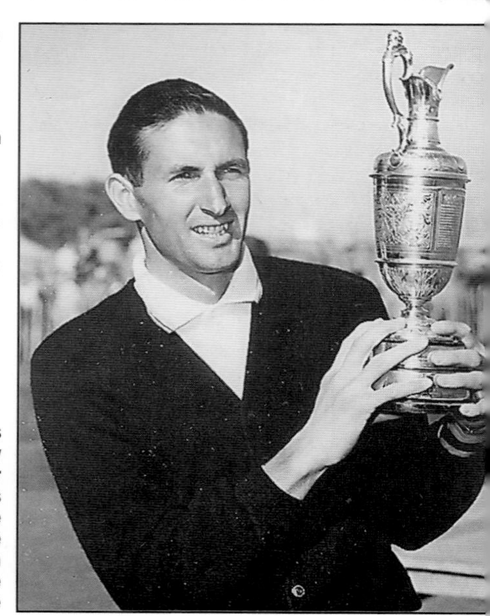

**Six years earlier New Zealander Bob Charles toasted the same success on the Fylde course**

# has a Ball!

BLACKPOOL FC legend Alan Ball was to celebrate the 1960s on top of the world as part of England's greatest sporting success of the millennium – winning football's World Cup.

Ball, then only 20, was among the England players who were the toast of the nation when they held the Jules Rimet Trophy aloft at Wembley after that famous 4-2 final victory over West Germany. Ball went on to win 72 England caps.

It was a far cry from the Farnworth-born lad's early days as an apprentice at Bloomfield Road trying to make it into football's big-time.

Blackpool gave him his big break. He signed professional forms with Pool in May 1962. Four years later, having played 116 league games for Blackpool and scored 41 goals before moving on to Everton, he had his hands on the World Cup.

Jimmy Armfield may not have got quite as close to the trophy at the final whistle. But he too was part of England's World Cup winning squad.

With 43 England caps to his name Armfield also captained his country on 15 occasions. And to the Blackpool public he remains one of their favourite sons.

A combination of his "Gentleman Jim" character and the fact that he was a one-club player who made an astonishing 568 appearances for Blackpool means that, on the eve of the new millennium, the calls are just as loud as ever for Armfield to be recognised for his services to sport in the New Year Honours.

Accolades galore were something which British golf ace Tony Jacklin had to live with after his Open win at Royal Lytham and St Annes in 1969.

Jacklin became the first British winner since Max Faulkner triumphed at Royal Portrush in Northern Ireland 18 years earlier. A four round total of 280 saw Jacklin home ahead of Bob Charles and Jack Nicklaus.

New Zealander Charles had won at Lytham only six years earlier. His 277 score earned him a play-off with American Phil Rodgers in which Charles' superior putting won the day.

In cricket Lancashire, led first by Brian Statham (1965) and then Jack Bond (1968) paved the way for the great successes of the 1970s by recruiting the likes of Clive Lloyd and Blackpool favourite Jack Simmons.

"Flat Jack" Simmons, who earned his big break with Lancashire when a professional for Blackpool, ironically also made his county debut – the first of his 429 matches for Lancashire – at Stanley Park against Northamptonshire in 1968.

Another of Blackpool's favourite sporting sons Brian London had his all-time heavyweight showdown with Muhammad Ali in 1966. But there was to be no fairytale ending. London was well beaten, counted out in the third round.

**ABOVE: England soccer players (below) share a joke at Burnden Park in 1960: From left Bryan Douglas, Bobby Smith, Jimmy Greaves, Jimmy Armfield and Ron Greenwood**

**MIDDLE PICTURE: The World Cup winning England Team pose with the Jules Rimet Trophy.**

**TOP PICTURE: In the top picture England skipper Bobby Moore holds aloft the World Cup at Wembley in 1966**

A6 Garstang Preston
caster, Blackburn
& Birmingham
anchester (M 61)
iverpool (A580)
ASHTON
THEATRE
CHARLIE GIRL
WELCOME
GRAN
GRAND THEA
Congratulations
to a

Chapter Seven

# *The Seventies*

# Hip
# and

**In 1976 Blackpool celebrated 100 years since the resort became a borough. There was a parade on the Prom and a lavish showcase of entertainment talent at the Opera House with a special five-hour Command Performance.**

ON the face of it – Blackpool was rocking. The psychedelic Seventies had arrived and Britain's top tourism town was as hip, hot and happening as an Austin Powers movie.

Circus chick Mary Chipperfield wowed the Blackpool Tower circus audiences in her striking outfits – outdoing the zebras in one of her favourite black and white striped jumpsuits.

Mirth master Les Dawson posed "provocatively" in swimming trunks after moving, with wife Meg and their young family, to Islay Road, Ansdell in 1975 – to become one of Lytham St Annes' most famous adopted sons.

There were new developments. The zoo, model village, Pembroke Hotel, Hounds Hill centre, the Palatine and Coral Island amusement centres – and the arrival of the Revolution at Blackpool Pleasure Beach – the first modern 360-degree ride in Europe.

It was a decade of hard news too. There was fire, flood , murder, even famine – when Blackpool South MP Peter Blaker feared a sugar shortage would affect traditional supplies of Blackpool rock!

Scandal too – chief constable Stan Parr fell from grace after an investigation of irregularities.

On the tourism front there was change

By 1975 a third of Blackpool's holiday accommodation was self catering.

The entertainment emphasis was shifting to couples-consciousness and swinging singles instead of just the traditional family holiday-makers of the textile town Wakes Weeks. Day visitors grew with the opening of the M55.

The Blackpool club scene had taken off and neon was beginning to turn night into day at many of the town's top after-dark hotspots.

Hair was long, flares were wide, glam rock was the style, disco was big business, and the punks were on the way.

It was fun, it was frenetic – but was it for families?

The jury was divided. For many this was the decade when the tourism rot set in – and much of the blame was down to TV.

Tourism chiefs had noticed a switch away from an evenly-spread holiday season.

Once-strong summer trade was losing out and the Illuminations – and political conferences – were becoming more important for tourism cash.

The type of visitor was changing too – and Blackpool still had aspirations for overseas trade and so-called white collar workers.

Blackpool Corporation leaders realised Britain's best and biggest seaside resort could no longer afford to rest on its laurels.

**Funny man Les Dawson striking a pose at his new luxury home**

In 1972 – four years away from the heady celebrations of Blackpool's centenary year – the town carried out its first visitor survey after the council joined forces with the English Tourist Board.

It was an eye opener.

About 10,000 adults were interviewed nationwide – forming the frankly tenuous basis for claims that Blackpool attracted almost 13 million day trippers during the season, out of a loyal bank of six million regulars, and more than three million staying visitors.

But tourism trade leaders were also interested in the social background and breakdown of those visitors.

The survey concluded that by far the greatest majority of visitors to bluecollar Blackpool were skilled and unskilled manual workers – and, as ever, elderly folk.

Nor were visitor numbers, in these and other groups, left increasingly out in the cold since peaking in the '50s and '60s, growing.

The season was shifting too with greater emphasis on t Illuminations period.

There was mounting conce at the state of the ente tainments industry with ma of the major concerns – b Blackpool Pleasure Beach – o of local control and into b business hands.

And then, as now, pund were musing where were t BIG entertainers?

Danny La Rue and Mi Yarwood were among the st names in the '72 season b Blackpool's boom days – wh the resort could comman international stars of the calib of Frank Sinatra, Nat King Co and new boys on the block T Beatles – were going.

Landladies were becomi an endangered species too – census showed numbers h halved since 1951, from 4,0 to 2,055 in '71.

Dr John Walton, professor social history at the Universi of Central Lancashire, recko the '70s survey was a turni point for what he calls t "world's first and bigge working class seaside resort".

His research for Blackpo (Edinburgh/Carnegia £12.9 charts it as the "moment alar bells rang."

**The new road to Blackpool. A VI audience watched Environment Minister Neil Carmichael open th M55 on July 3, 1975, from the Broughton end. It cost £14m for 12 miles and took 25 months to build.**

**The old A583 Preston to Blackpool road had often been choked with traffic jams and had a bad reputation for accidents. But motorway travel meant mor day-only visitors to Blackpool**

**Three months earlier in 19 British Aerospace demonstrat the versatility of their Jagu fighter by turning the almo completed motorway at Weet into a runw**

# hot Harold!

**Demolition men were busy in Blackpool town centre. Property around Hounds Hill came down in 1973. In 1974 Central Station (seen here) and the Palatine Hotel (on the right) came down to make way for Coral Island which opened in 1978. The old North Station and Cocker Street baths were also scrapped in 1974**

Blackpool was also up against increasing competition from cheap foreign package holidays – particularly Spain.

People with more income were beginning to jet away from it all – in the hope of sunshine and hotels that offered more in the way of standard facilities.

Holiday camps were doing hi-de-hi business too, extending options for families wanting value-for-money accommodation and guaranteed entertainment. So much so the local hotel and guesthouse association united against a proposed new camp in '73.

Blackpool began to dig in to halt the downmarket shift with new attractions, publicity and additional facilities.

Some hoteliers began investing in quality. Stringent fire regulations were introduced at the turn of the decade in a bid to improve safety at guesthouses.

Others converted to flats or opened retirement and rest homes.

Big conferences, out of season, began to prop up trade. And there was even talk in the mid-70s as to whether Blackpool could survive using conference facilities provided by the Tower and Winter Gardens. Wasn't it time, some farsighted individuals argued, that Blackpool had a purpose-built conference centre similar to those already seen at other resorts?

**Long before the days of iron-wall security Prime Minister Harold Wilson (left) arrives at the Imperial Hotel, complete with famous pipe, for the 1975 Labour Party Conference**

**Mary Chipperfield was as stripey as her zebras back in 1978**

**Coronation Street stars in Trader Jacks at the Imperial Hotel. Mike Baldwin (actor Johnny Briggs) later had a club of his own in the soap –The Graffiti Club. Also with Imperial manager John Herdman (left) is actor Fred Feast who played Rover's Return barman Fred Gee**

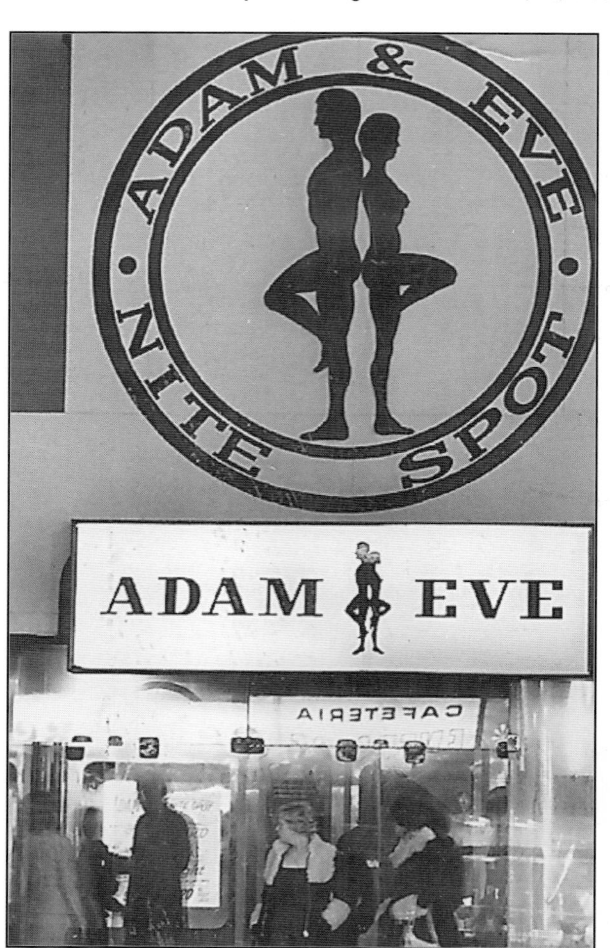


**The Adam and Eve in Chapel Street was a well-known venue**

THE '70s may have been the decade that was to give awful breath to a spoof super hero like Austin Powers . . . but it put Blackpool on the map as the disco capital of Britain.

The 007 Club, Tiffany's , Lemon Tree, Adam and Eve, Trader Jacks, Scamps, the Dixieland, the Gallopers.

The resortwas buzzing.

It may have started in the '60s with a handful of late licences but come the '70s the clubs were in full swing.

And discos could be held anywhere. One enterprising local organised a pre-rave scene Northern Soul night at his family's farm and called the venue The Scabby Donkey.

A '70s survivor who is still going strong is veteran dj Peter Schofield, now at the Waterfront after his almost nine-year-long reign at Brannigans.

It's not far from where his music career started in the late '60s with the teen and 20 nights at the Savoy Bowl club.

"It was John Barnett, now of The Wave radio station, who got me started. I went as a customer and he invited me to have a go – I was hooked," says Peter.

He recalls the decade as the key music era. Boxer Brian London and business partner Ronnie Hunter established the 007 club at Tower Street in Blackpool before its eventual move to Topping Street – and recruited Peter.

"It was the first proper nightclub," he claims. "People came from far and wide.It was the place to be. George Best was there regularly, along with other professional footballers and showbiz folk."

Rivals included the Lemon Tree at Squires Gate and ultimately the Adam and Eve and other clubs in town.

"The 70s was the disco age," says Peter. "The music was magic, James Brown, Motown, the Supremes, Santana, more, and the atmosphere was buzzing. Probably those were the best days of my life and career. It w all so new – and safe too.Life was as fragile as it is today. Blackpool w breaking the barriers down. Bri London was – is – a lovely guy t He knew how to control his emp but he was also ahead of his time – did half price drinks and oth promotions in the 70s. It w basically 85 per cent locals – we w mobbed out. We had a big cel where the beer was delivered and lift to put the stuff in – Brian refus to use the lift and would take it all and down stairs as part of h training."

Peter did a few stints at the Ada and Eve and the Dixieland showba where he lost most of his gear in fire.

"The disco age arrived in abo '75. It was the period I enjoyed be There's been a renaissance for t '70s but unless you have lived in t period you can't really experience t music – how it really felt at the ti and appreciate it as much now. It w a decade of difference too: there w disco, Motown, Northern Soul, ev punk."

Competition intensified. "Mo pubs and hotels started putting on, crossing over to make money. was lucky because with the 0 having a late licence – 10.30pm 2am – I could work other venu until 11.30pm and then nip in t back way. If I wasn't too late Bri was fine but one night he was waiti behind the door as I sneaked in!"

Schofield went on to run the pla himself – as Secrets and Schofield's and won the Disco Mirror Mo Exclusive Nightspot award in '86.

He also worked the Village, in t former King Edward cinema. "It w fabulous time for music, all the dan stuff came through, although ra was an absolute disgrace. In the '8 everything got cut throat – the wor and his wife wanted a late nig licence. Brannigans showed the way first with its 11pm licence, th midnight, then 1am. Everyo followed suit."

So what does the future hol

**The ballroom at the Mecca complex on Central Drive was a popular nightspot for many years**

# Night Fever

*Blackpool is simply the Best as disco capital of the stack-heeled 1970s . . .*

We've lost the family image and we'll ever get that back but Blackpool is still he top party place in the country – and till has a relatively safe environment. If ve all work together getting it right it an only get better."

As for the secret of his own survival n entertainment?

"I have always been a personality dj the sort that talks to people, ecognises regulars when they come in, as a joke with them.

"The irony is I'm not the only old imer around – it's like a time warp, a ot of people come up and tell me they emember me from the O07 days in the 0s! It was the best time of my life – here was Brian London in the wings nd two little gogo girls dancing in a age behind me – and me wearing dirty reat big stacks, flares, cardies down to ny ankles, button down Ben Sherman hirts. And who would have believed it vould all become fashionable again?"

The 007 Club opened at a former vorkingmen's club on Water Street, lackpool, in 1970 – teetotal licensee rian London's first business venture utside the boxing ring.

Seaside sophisticates loved the place. t had black walls with luminous aintings of Ian Fleming characters – nd an illuminated tableaux tracking he line of fire from James Bond's gun.

The dj was positioned in the prow of an 007-style speedboat – with psychadelic lights ahead and mini-skirted go-go girls in a cage behind.

Months later Brian, under his real name Harper, successfully applied for a 2am licence – and another bar as membership was growing so fast the original was becoming congested.

After another change of premises to Victoria Street Brian's new-look 007 club opened on Topping Street in 1977.

Tiffany's ballroom in Blackpool's Mecca building went up for sale in July '82 – ending an entertainment era that spanned 16 years and an earlier identity as the Locarno.

When the 007 club in Tower Street was extended in 1971 George Best was there to drum up business for Brian London. The Manchester United star had played at Bloomfield Road earlier in the day

At the height of its popularity the venue was packing thousands of revellers into its bars, disco and Highland Room.

The Central Drive entertainment centre opened in 1964 with a 36-lane J Arthur Rank bowling alley, Mecca ballroom , multi-storey car park, restaurant and coach park.

The ballroom became Tiffany's in 1974 when a modernisation programme included the first video tape machine to be used in a British disco.

In the late '70s it turned to all-dayers and daytime discos to tempt trade.

It had a brief revival in 1990 as the ill-fated Night Out cabaret restaurant but in 1991 was repossessed by Rank Leisure.

Its latest incarnation – after a brief spell as Some Place Else – is as the Rhythm Dome.

The Lemon Tree, opened at Squires Gate in 1966, was owned and run by the Levine family and became one of the most popular nightspots on the Fylde with a casino and Mexican Bar until its popularity waned in the late '70s.

It eventually closed in the '80s. The derelict club was later demolished , to make way for a retirement complex. In 1993 former dj Eddie Gee recalled the glory days of the '70s "when the car park was jam-packed every night"."

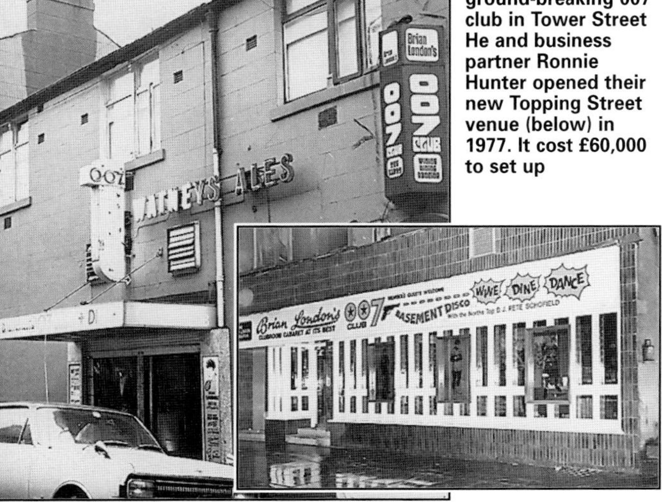


Brian London's ground-breaking 007 club in Tower Street He and business partner Ronnie Hunter opened their new Topping Street venue (below) in 1977. It cost £60,000 to set up

# Licensed to thrill

WHEN he retired as a professional boxer in 1970, Blackpool's Brian London looked for a new career based in the resort.

And his decision to get involved with the entertainment industry made local history.

His 007 Club, named after super spy James Bond was a first for Blackpool.

Nightlife was slowly changing from the days when pubs closed at 10.30pm and there was nowhere else to go except home.

Brian London was in at the start of the night time revolution and his club did well as enthusiastic party people revelled in the idea of staying out until the early hours with a drink in their hand and music in their ears.

More liberal laws on drinking and gambling which were introduced in the Sixties oiled the wheels of change .

A man who never smoked or drank alcohol, Brian soon learned the ropes in the licensed trade.

His first club was a much more basic place than today's discos with their amazing light and sound shows and sophisticated equipment. But it was not short of customers.

The 'Double Oh' was housed on the first floor of an old building in Tower Street – part of a network of little streets which were later demolished to build the Hounds Hill shopping centre and car park.

When that happened Brian operated briefly in Victoria Street but then settled in Topping Street where he still owns property today.

Brian calls his house in North Park Drive Be Lucky – a phrase often heard in the boxing world.

He said: "Everyone needs some luck in life and I got into the club business just at the right time when it was taking off and going up."

# Let there be Lights

FOR decades the Illuminations were seen as the "jam on the bread and butter" or the "icing on the cake" – depending on which cliche tourism traders favoured.

But in the late '70s the emphasis – and the sand on which Blackpool had built its tourism trade – was shifting.

By the end of the decade the Lights had come into their own – established as far more than just a late-season tourism temptation.

They were beginning to become almost as significant as the traditional main summer season.

Now the crucial period between the first Friday in September and November has become the major player in the resort's season.

Traders now look to the Lights to save the day. With every successive year since the late 1970s the Illuminations have played an even greater role in either underpinning successful summers or proving the salvation of the season.

The '70s marked a decade of innovation for the Illuminations roll call of honour too.

Disc jockey Tony Blackburn switched on the Lights in 1970 – followed by the cast o Dad's Army – a TV series which still prove enormously popular!

Other switched-on celebrities of the '70 included footballer Gordon Banks, actres Wendy Craig, Tom 'Dr Who' Baker , Miss U Carol Ann Grant, and, sandwiched betwee the beloved Grand National winner Red Ru and Kermit the Frog and The Muppets, Terr Wogan – who recalled the '70 heyday when he hosted th year's ceremony.

Switched-on celebrities: (from left) Tony Blackburn 1970; England goalkeeper Gordon Banks 1973; Actress Wendy Craig 1974; Red Rum 1977;

Tom Baker as Dr Who 1975

Danny La Rue in 1972 wit the then-Mayor of Blackp Coun Edmund Wynne

# Danny dazzles resort

ONE OF the most enduring Blackpool favourites in the seventies was Danny La Rue who switched on the Lights in 1972 with a "live" link-up to Concorde.

Dazzling Danny, now 72 years old himself, is back in Blackpool next year – 50 years after first stepping on stage and 45 since changing his name from Daniel O'Donnell to Danny La Rue (doubtless to the relief of a certain Irish singing star with a large following of ladies of a certain age).

Danny's own career shows the more things change the more they stay the same.

He's been coming to Blackpool since the late '50s and has nothing but happy memories of the town.

"I worked at The Queens – if you'll pardon the pun – even before I was Danny. I was the feed for Jimmy Clitheroe, if you can believe that!"

The showbiz legend was the first big name to be announced for Leisure Parcs 2000 summer season – confirmed as headlining Palladium Nights in the Winter Gardens Pavilion Theatre.

It was the first time a full summer season show has been staged there in more than 20 years – and Danny was delighted to be back and reopening "such a lovely theatre" given the loss of so many venues in the last three decades.

He recalled the Pavilion from its earlier incarnation – when it played host to stage spin-offs from TV comedies such as Nearest a Dearest.

"I can remember watching Hyl Baker climb a ladder to measure h billing alongside Jimmy Jewel – a make sure his name was no bigg than hers."

Danny, who's played most of t big theatres in Blackpool – a indeed Britain – loves the vulgarity the resort.

"It's the best resort in the count – that's why it's so easy for people knock it."

It's a far cry from Danny's fi Blackpool seasons when he w dubbed Danny La Blue.

"I'm about as controversial as t Singing Nun these days," confesses.

Stanley Parr, Chief Constable of Lancashire

# Fall from grace

THE sacking of Lancashire's Chief Constable, Stanley Parr of Blackpool, in 1977 was part of a scandal that rocked the Fylde.

The story began in 1962 when he became Chief Constable of Blackpool's own police force.

St Helens-born he had an excellent CV including a bravery award for saving a drowning child and his war record as skipper of a minesweeper.

Stan Parr liked the social life and the status that his job in Blackpool gave him.

In 1969, when Lancashire police was being reorganised ahead of the new-look council structure, he got the deputy Chief Constable's job.

The Gazette at the time reported he was a popular personality in the district, had a neat sense of humour and a relaxed manner.

Three years later he succeeded William Palfrey as head of Lancashire police.

But Stan Parr's links with Blackpool and the Fylde remained strong.

His downfall began when Det Sgt Harry Roby made a complaint about his boss to a government official.

It went right to the top and Sir Douglas Osmond, Chief Constable of Hampshire, headed a probing inquiry into Stan Parr's conduct as a senior policeman.

The Chief Constable was found guilty of showing favours to his friends – powerful men in Blackpool and the Fylde society – misusing police manpower and falsifying documents.

One issue involved the police treatment of a young woman whose car mounted the pavement near Kirkham late one night resulting in the deaths of two Preston women who were walking home.

Yet the disgraced Chief Constable and his wife Lillian received many cards and messages of support at their home in Holly Road, North Shore.

Officials of charity groups in the resort spoke of him in glowing terms.

A new inquiry began, headed by Peter Imbert who was then with Thames Valley police.

It looked at allegations linked to councillors in Blackpool referring to applications for planning permission.

Along the way there were libel writs, debates in the House of Commons and complaints about leaked secret documents.

The whole sorry tale painted a seedy picture of Blackpool society which did nothing for the resort's image.

Stanley Parr died in Blackpool Victoria hospital, aged 67, in 1985.

Peter Imbert (above) headed the inquiry

County Coun Frank Lofthouse

Officers in the Imbert inquiry with some of the mountain of paperwork created by the inquiry

Blackpool police headquarters and court complex came down in 1981. It stood in South King Street. The old fire station was round the corner in Albert Road.

# Bigger is beautiful

IN 1974 town halls were thrown into turmoil by the Local Government Reorganisation plan.

The idea was that small councils were not efficient and that bigger was more beautiful.

In the north, Fleetwood Borough and Garstang Rural District Council were thrown into bed with the urban councils of Thornton-Cleveleys, Poulton and Preesall to form Wyre.

In the south, Lytham St Annes borough teamed up with Fylde Rural Council and Kirkham Urban District Council to become the new authority of Fylde.

And Blackpool was stripped of its County Borough status which had given the resort the power to run its own affairs with departments like education, social services, the fire brigade and police.

Now it was to come under the control of Lancashire County.

But in the elections that ushered in the new look, Conservatives from the Fylde coast gained a strong position at County Hall and Coun Leonard Broughton of Blackpool was appointed leader of the County Council.

# Murder of the hospital innocents

A poignant floral tribute for one of the innocent victims

IT was a manhunt which was to end in what many considered to be a travesty of justice.

Just after midnight, on a chill February night in February 1972, four children were stabbed in their beds in the children's ward at Blackpool Victoria Hospital.

The savage attack was carried out by the hospital's eye specialist Dr Ahmad Alami, a Jordanian.

A girl of four, from Poulton, and two little boys, aged two, of Fleetwood, died of multiple stab wounds. The fourth child, also two, survived critical injury and revisited the resort in the '90s with his fiancee. A fifth child on the ward escaped injury.

Two nurses, a staff nurse aged 49 , and a student nurse, aged 22, were also injured in the night of horror. The staff nurse managed to raise the alarm but her assailant escaped after attacking the sleeping children.

Upon retirement in the 1990s former Blackpool chief superintendent and Queen's Medal winner Ken Mackay was to describe it as the most distressing scene he had ever witnessed.

The police manhunt and inquiry was led by Lancashire force legend Chief Supt Joe Mounsey, head of the county's CID.

It came at a time when he was also hunting the murderer of a teenage girl whose body was found in a field off a lane at Wrea Green on January 2 – in a painstaking inquiry police got their man after matching the tyres on a car about to be crushed at a scrapyard with tyretracks at the scene.

Mounsey was also involved in the Manchester Crown Court trial of criminals involving in the resort gem raid and killing of Blackpool Superintendent Gerald Richardson.

Yet Dr Alami was never tried for the Victoria Hospital crimes after being pronounced unfit to plead to a murder charge at Lancaster Crown Court. He was detained in Broadmoor mental hospital before being transferred to a secure psychiatric hospital in Bethlehem, Israel, in 1976.

Two years later he was no longer in detention but receiving treatment as an out-patient – and BBC Horizon programme makers received a 700-name protest petition from the Fylde after proposing a drama-documentary based on Alami's own writings.

The Fylde's four MPs tabled a Commons motion urging the BBC to reconsider showing the programme – which was said to examine Alami's "thought processes" in the two years prior to the attacks.

Corporation chairman Sir Michael Swann defended the documentary as a "serious investigation of the thought track of a paranoid schizophrenic."

Alami's father, Saad al-Alami, the Mufti of Jerusalem and senior Islamic cleric in the city, was believed to have been instrumental in having his son transferred. Alami senior died in 1993.

The case aroused great concern in the medical profession and led to the British Medical Associatic issuing guidelines on how to preve mentally-sick doctors fro endangering patients .

The doctor had a history psychiatric illness and had be diagnosed paranoid schizophren long before he took up his job at t local hospital.

As stricken families grieved f their lost children the Hon Secretary rejected calls for formal inquiry into the murde claiming it would serve no usef purpose.

Department of Health officia also stressed Dr Alami was a patie in a hospital, not a prisoner servi a sentence.

A fountain was later erected at t hospital in memory of the de children.

Dog handlers patrolled the hospital area after the horrific early morning killings

Det Chief Supt Joe Mounsey (third from left) head of Lancashire CID, talking to officers near Victoria Hospital

Crowds turned out when the tragic children were laid to rest in the same grave

# Five killed in trawler blaze

WHEN the Fleetwood trawler Dinas sailed for the Icelandic fishing grounds one Friday afternoon in September, 1971, some of the crew settled down to a heavy drinking session.

This so-called party was to ease the pain of parting once again from family and friends for another three weeks at sea in the harsh conditions of the Icelandic fishing grounds.

It was a time of unrest in the industry when crewmen were increasingly unwilling to accept the customs and practices that operated for generations. They wanted a better deal.

But on the Dinas the plan was force the ship to return to port so the crew could have another couple of days ashore.

In the rough, tough world of the fishing trade such campaigns often included throwing pots and pans and food supplies over the side or vandalising the ship.

This time the scheme was madness personified. Three men got together to start a fire in a small storeroom below decks. But instead of causing a little damage it generated fierce heat and deadly smoke.

In the big eight-bunk cabin next door where men had been drinking, five crewmen died on a calm, sunny afternoon in Morecambe Bay.

And it was weeks later, at a party in the port, that a young fisherman broke down in tears and told the sorry story of what had been done that fateful afternoon.

As a result, three Dinas crewmen went to prison for five years each for the manslaughter of their shipmates.

The case focused a spotlight on conditions in the fishing industry and was a factor in a strike over money aimed at recognition of the trawlerman's working lifestyle.

But all this was overtaken by the decision of the Icelandic government to extend fishing limits.

In the Autumn of 1972 the limit was extended from 12 to 50 miles and Fleetwood trawlers began a battle with the gunboats as skippers defied the new Icelandic rules and carried on fishing.

Gazette journalist David Pearce spent three weeks on the Fleetwood trawler Wyre Captain reporting life on the Cod War front line.

But one of his reports, sent back in a telegram via the offices of the Fleetwood Fishing Vessel Owne Association, never saw the light day at the Fleetwood end . . .

After gunboats risked collisio with Fleetwood ships one night ar cut away their fishing gear, a grou of skippers decided to quit the we coast grounds and steamed roun Iceland's north coast to comple their voyages on the eastern bank

This protest helped to secu naval protection for the ships Iceland but, at the time, trawl owners were worried it would le to more crew trouble and that m might refuse to sail north. Th censored the report.

WEST LANCASHIRE
EVENING GAZETTE

Special

STREAMLINE TAXIS 23535

Two policemen wounded in North Shore gun terror

BLACKPOOL POLICE CHIEF SHOT DEAD IN GEM RAID CHASE

Today: a city of

Crowds around Clifford Road and Egerton Road in North Shore where the raiders' Triumph had been rammed by police cars

# Police heroes

Car dealer Fred Sewell was jailed for 30 years for his Blackpool crimes

IN August, 1971, a gang of London villains came to Blackpool to rob Prestons jewellers shop in The Strand.

They may have had links with local crooks but that has never been proved.

The five-man mob was headed by car dealer Frederick Joseph Sewell and they booked into a guesthouse. They then changed digs because the landlady wondered why four of them wore sunglasses all the time!

On the Monday morning heist Sewell stood guard with a sawn-off shotgun while his team got to work rifling the shop. But they did not know the manager was in the repair room and had alerted the police.

The London robbers met several brave men that day and the first was firefighter Ronald Gale, a sub-officer with the Blackpool brigade.

He was held at gunpoint after he tried to tackle the gang in the shop Then he was coshed over the head with a crowbar.

In nearby Queens Square a window cleaner poked a mop into the getaway car which slowed down the gang's escape.

During a car chase through North Shore, two police constables were shot and badly injured.

Superintendent Gerald Richardson was mortally wounded by Joe Sewell as the 38-year-old policeman seized him by the throat in a back street off Sherbourne Road.

Sewell eluded police roadblocks to get out of the resort hidden in the boot of a car.

But money talked when a newspaper offered a £10,000 reward and a tip off came.

Police burst into Sewell's London love-nest where Det Chief Supt Joe Mounsey, head of Lancashire CID, snapped the cuffs on the killer as he lay on a bed.

He is now nearing the end of a 30-year jail sentence.

Four other members of the gang were also jailed.

Supt Richardswon was posthumously awarded the George Cross, the civilian equivalent of the illustrious Victoria Cross.

The same honour went to police officers Carl Walker who was shot down by Sewell as he gave chase and the George Medal to Ian Hampson who was also shot and wounded in the pursuit.

Eight other Blackpool officers received bravery awards.

The case underlined the growing threat to policemen from violence in general and guns in particular.

It resulted in a petition bearing 250,000 names calling for the return of the death penalty for murder.

Supt Richardson's widow, Maureen, handed it in at the House of Commons.

Police Superintendent Gerald Richardson

## "I was looking down the barrel of the gun. It looked as big as a cannon . . ."

Retired police inspector Carl Walker returns to The Strand in Blackpool from where the pursuit of the Sewell gang started

WHEN policeman Carl Walker got a radio call to check out the alarm at the jewellers he thought someone had probably made a mistake opening up the shop.

But this was no routine check.

He reached The Strand to find the Sewell Gang running for their getaway car and as he approached a shotgun was pointed from a window.

Carl knew how deadly that weapon could be and stayed in his Panda car patrol vehicle.

So began a chase in which Sewell's girlfriend tried to block Carl Walker's path in another car.

"Of course I didn't know it was her at the time. I just cursed her for getting in the way."

Later Carl cornered the gang in an alley off Lord Street near the old Odeon.

They reacted by driving their Triumph 2000 estate car straight at the police car at top speed like a dodgem car.

"It knocked me across Lord Street and they drove off again."

At first Carl thought the Ford Escort was too badly damaged to drive but he found it still worked and set off in pursuit again.

The gang were cornered and rammed by police vehicles so made a run for it on foot.

Carl found himself following Sewell and others down a back street.

" Sewell was at the back. He turned and fired a handgun at us two or three times. I kept going. The one thought in my mind was to catch him. I thrived on a rough and tumble. I had been a Cumberland wrestler and a rugby player and I knew if I caught hold of him I would keep hold."

Sewell had already shot and wounded PC Ian Hampson at another location.

He stopped and took better aim while the other gang members commandeered a butcher's van.

Carl recalls: "I was looking down the barrel of the gun. It looked as big as a cannon. I saw the smoke and the bullet went through my thigh and threw me to the ground."

Luckily for him it missed major blood vessels and bone.

But still Carl did not quit.

Sewell had turned away to get into the van but Carl was up and hopping towards him.

" One of the others told him and he turned to face me. I was very close and he was very angry. I thought he would probably shoot me dead. I collapsed on the ground and he didn't fire. It was a hard decision for me to make, and I didn't have long to make it"

Moments later, Fred Sewell was confronted by Supt. Gerry Richardson and killed him after the gang crashed the meat van and took to their heels again.

Meanwhile Carl recalls being carried into a house – "afterwards I was worried I'd bled all over the carpet but it was all right!"

"They put Gerry Richardson in the ambulance with me but, of course, he died in hospital. I was lucky but it was a very sad day. I got on very well with him. He treated his officers with civility and we respected him. He was very good at the job and probably would have been a chief constable one day."

Carl never suffered from the nightmares that some officers experienced after the incident. But the damage to his leg forced early retirement by which time he had become an inspector. The limb still pains him but he manages a walk sometimes on the fells of his beloved homeland in the Lakes.

Carl Walker received the George Cross for his undoubted courage and devotion to duty and is rightly proud of the award.

But he won't be drawn on the capital punishment debate.

He simply concludes: " The law said Sewell should go to prison and he did. He will come out in 2001 and he'll be an old man."

# *Three disasters struck Lytham St Annes*

Rescue workers carry a body from the scene

These were the stark scenes from Pontins Holiday Camp in Blackpool in June 1972. Seven people died when an executive jet burst into flames and ploughed into chalets.

Tyre brake marks at the end of the runway indicated the pilot had tried to stop the aircraft. Investigators believed the railway lines which the jet hit helped lessen the impact – and prevented it from ploughing through more chalets.

It skidded off the runway and left a trail of devastation. A broken landing lamp, a four-foot-high bank of churned-up earth, smashed perimete fence, twisted railway line, and 1 demolished chalets. It threw concret blocks into the air like toy bricks. Fue exploded – destroying more chalets Two staff from the camp had a narro escape when a burning fuel tan crashed past them. The jet's nose whee lay at the side of the rail line. Lumps o the "skin" of the aircraft were scattere among the debris of the chalets.

On the putting green where the je came to rest was a large mass o scorched grass, tangled wires of boxes c

A chunk o aircraft wreckage lies among th chalets. It was a miracle more people were not killed

# DEATH & dis

THE Ashton Theatre at St Annes was destroyed in a dawn blaze in September, 1977.

Four fire brigade crews fought the inferno for over an hour but were driven back by the flames and could not save the major entertainment centre.

The charred remains and the building shell were all that were left of the popular theatre on St George's Road which once hosted a galaxy of stars.

Only hours before the blaze hundreds of theatre lovers had enjoyed St Annes Parish Church Operatic and Dramatic Society's production of Charlie Girl.

The dejected drama group was left counting the "phenomenal" cost of the loss of props and costumes, most of which were destroyed.

And local thespians were left lamenting the loss of the town's only theatre as campaigns to rebuild the theatre failed on cost grounds.

The busy centre had attracted thousands of summer holidaymakers with star names and in winter staged local amateur dramatic productions.

The theatre had been developed from a bandstand which was built for £35 in 1913.

The Ashton Theatre became an inferno

Firefighters at work inside the burning theatre

A web of hosepipes snake through the gates of Ashton Park. Blackpool comic K Platt, who died in 1998, was to be the last star at Ashton Theatre

# in the seventies

instruments. The largest remaining part of the plane was the tailplane.

Holiday camp chief Fred Pontin, who flew from Bournemouth to Blackpool to visit the site, praised firefighters for keeping any blaze at bay. "There was so much petrol the whole lot could have gone up in flames."

It was also a miracle that all the camp's 2,500 holidaymakers escaped unscathed. The fatalities were confined to the twin-engined executive jet – which was bound for Munich and carrying eight people: two crew and six passengers. The only survivor was pulled clear of the wreckage by one of Pontin's young chefs assisted by Denis Neale, England's number one table tennis player, who was playing exhibition matches at the camp.

The flight was one of many between the Fylde and Munich carrying technicians working on British Aerospace's multi-role-combat-aircraft .The Germans' flight had been diverted to Blackpool but they spent the day at Warton – on the eve of a visit by the Duke of Edinburgh.

Ambulance staff wait with a trolley stretcher to recover bodies as firemen damp down the flames

# aster

Evening Gazette

ST ANNES PIER THEATRE DESTROYED BY FIRE

Night sky blaze is seen at Preston

OPERA HOUSE

THE BACHELORS

LENA ZAVARONI

NORMAN COLLIER

At the height of the St Annes Pier fire in 1974

A couple watch from the shore as St Annes Pier blazes like a torch

Not one of the birds from the St Annes Pier aviary was hurt. But bantams like this one (below) had to be rounded up later

A Save Our Pier meeting (below) at St Annes in 1975. Organiser Mrs Margaret King is on the right

IT had been one of the most glittering moments in the social history of St Annes.

In June 1974 Princess Anne attended a gala charity concert – starring world-acclaimed violinist Yehudi Menuhin – at St Annes Pier to celebrate the centenary of the St Annes Land and Building Company, headed by property millionaire Gabriel Harrison.

It was held in the magnificent Moorish Pavilion theatre which had been restored for the centenary concert.

Just one month later the pier theatre – widely considered to be one of the most distinctive in the land – had gone: destroyed by fire in just two hours.

Mr Harrison was left to lament the loss of a dream: "Lancashire and England has lost one of its most beautiful examples of architecture. It would be impossible to get craftsmen to build a similar theatre – it was unique."

No-one was hurt in the fire – including bantams, birds and various fancy fowl in the pier's aviary all captured and taken to safety by firefighters and pier staff.

St Annes Pier was built in 1885 for £18,000 and opened by Lord Derby. It was 10 years before the domed Moorish-style pavilion was added.

A year after fire destroyed the end of the pier the structure became one of 27 listed for preservation by the Department of Environment .

There was fury when the company proposed to demolish the end of the pier – more than 2,000 signed a protest petition and many attended a Save Our Pier meeting.

But in 1982 its fate was sealed when the pier suffered another major fire – which this time finished off the Floral Hall which had been saved from total destruction in '74.

In '85 the seaward end of the pier – a mangled skeletal mass of metal – was demolished using gelignite after the scheme was approved by the Secretary of State for the Environment.

Victorian-style balconies, harking back to the glory days of the Floral Hall and Moorish Pavilion, were added to the famous landmark in the '90s.

# THE GRAND

## A 1970s DRAMA IN NINE ACTS

### THE TIME

Summer '72. The Grand, opened July 23, 1894, has been made a grade two listed building two years earlier. It has not been operating as a theatre "proper" for nearly 10 years. The Tower Company has been taken over by EMI.

### THE SCENE

Notice of the Tower Company's application to demolish the Grand appears on the doors of the theatre. High drama!

Fighting to save the theatre in 1973

### ENTER

Steps of the Grand. Retired banker Burt Briggs begins 10,000-strong protest petition. The Gazette spotlights the Grand Dilemma, more people protest, and the Government announces a public inquiry. Friends of the Grand formed at a public meeting attended by 300 people, February 11, '73.

### THE PLAYERS

Burt Briggs, John Hodgson, joint chairman; Billy McGinty, treasurer; Marjorie Higham, secretary; Samuel Lee, solicitor – he's now chairman of the Grand Theatre Trust and says to this day: "It's one of the best things I ever did."

### THE PLOT

Inquiry dismisses demolition bid August '73, inspector suggests a trust forms to run theatre. Friends raise funds and awareness, professional appeal starts under chairman Geoffrey Thompson – another stalwart supporter to this day – and company stalemate leads to "eyesore" claims. Then Bingo! EMI offers compromise. Housey-housey front of house. It's a black day for the Grand – but buys time to keep the dream of the theatre alive. Realists, who include FoG leading lights newly appointed as theatre trustees, agree to bingo on condition EMI "rehabilitates" theatre. Bingo dies, building stays and improves. Friends and trustees organise events and shows to keep theatre dream alive .

### ALL LIVED HAPPILY EVER AFTER?

Three-year EMI bingo lease runs out at the end of the '70s, Lord Delfont offers freehold to trustees, cheaper deal signed quickly. Blackpool Council offers £100,000: £50,000 from civic lottery cash, the rest interest-free loan, funds from Friends , other major pledges. Exit, stage left, EMI. Enter, on the side of right, the Friends. Grand passes into Trust hands October 1 '80. Theatre reopens with Merchant of Venice starring Prunella Scales and Timothy West March 23 '81. Financial problems aren't over – but at least the pound of flesh days have gone.

### REPRISE

Prince of Wales attends gala opening May 29 '81, summer season farce returns and, to bring the story bang up to date, the Grand has just broken records and topped the million pound mark with Comedy Bonanza '99. And that's far from the end of the story . . .

### FOOT(LIGHT)NOTE

On August 15 1973 the Gazette led with this news: Grand Theatre Is Saved From The Hammer. The same issue carried a picture story reporting 10-year-old singer-pianist Jacqueline Crichton's success in a weekly Butlin's talent contest heat. As Jacqui Scott she went on to star in Evita June '90 – having appeared at the Grand's Royal gala reopening before Prince Charles in '81 and over summer '83 with then-husband Keith Harris.

### EPILOGUE:

Samuel Lee, Grand Theatre Trust chairman, and one of the key figures responsible for its salvation in the '70s, says the Grand is an extraordinary example of outstanding architectural design provided for ordinary people.

"It is a source of pride for the people of Lancashire – and it is our duty to cherish it for those who will follow us."

National experts claim the Grand's fightback in the '70s helped turn the tide of post-war destruction of theatres when umpteen Victorian , Edwardian and Art Deco venues were lost.

YOU NEED Friends, especially in th theatre – as a '70s threat to one Britain's best loved venues, the Grand underlined.

Ii is one of the most outstanding example of theatre architecture in the world – widel acknowledged to be one of Victoria designer Frank Matcham's finest creations.

Actors and actresses of internation acclaim, including some of the mos celebrated names in entertainment histor have fallen for its charms.

Yet, more than a quarter of a centur ago, we almost lost Blackpool's Gran Theatre – opened in 1894 – t demolition.

The fact that it is not only standin but doing remarkably well, thank you having just completed a recor breaking season, is testimony to th fighting spirit of Friends who unite to Save the Grand.

Today the battle is held up as national example of how to mak sure the show goes on – a rallyin cry to crusaders across the land.

Arts Council writer Judit Strong singled the story out fo praise in her guide to strategies fo theatre renewal earlier this year.

The Grand's star billing in th fightback guide Encore was hel up as a triumph by Nation Theatres Trust director Pete Longman.

He explains: "Wha happened there is truly inspi ational. It was a huge act faith."

Today the theatre command a unique place in the heart "luvvies" and locals alike.

But it could have ended i tears and curtain down fo all time – the publi hadn't rallie around.

A giant birthday card went to actors' union Equity for the Grand's 80th birthday in 1974

In 1979 Bingo was keeping the Grand Old Lady alive. On the 85th birthday, appeals director Mary Paul presented a birthday card to bingo manager Bob Parsons

Blackpool Zoo opening here Spring 1972

# ...and you can come too...

BLACKPOOL Zoo opened on the site of Stanley Park Aerodrome in 1972. The zoo opened to a mixed reception when Animal Magic presenter Johnny Morris did the honours – in pouring rain.

The viability of the proposed attraction had been questioned years before it opened, when plans for the prime site included a holiday camp and Disney-style development.

Zoo director Cyril Grace predicted a great future – with Blackpool Zoo established as one of the finest in Europe – and the scheme was applauded as a tourism boost to a town already blessed with attractions.

But in the 1970s, also the local heyday of circus animal trainer Mary Chipperfield, zoos had not attracted the adverse publicity which now surrounds the keeping of animals in captivity.

Within a few years of opening one of the zoo's biggest champions, then-attractions and leisure committee chief Councillor Raymond Jacobs, was defending zoo problems and the wisdom of pumping more cash into the centre.

Criticism has dogged the attraction, from continued concern over conditions in which animals are kept, to controversy over loss-making attendances.

Councillor Robert Wynne has since echoed his father – and fellow councillor Edmund, who originally challenged the viability of the operation – in condemnation of zoo losses.

The zoo has come under threat in recent years as a result of losses. A more commercial approach was adopted in a bid to balance the books by 2001.

The emphasis shifted to conservation and gradual improvement of the conditions in which animals are kept – the new lemur open enclosure is an example – although animal rights activists remain worried.

Critics, however, remain adamant the zoo was ill-conceived from day one, an anachronism which should be consigned to history.

**TV personality Johnny Morris (top picture) whose animal shows were watched by millions opened the zoo. He's seen here with Mayor Edmund Wynne**

**Mother Christmas, otherwise Janet Cummins (above) promoted the zoo in 1973 while visits to Bloomfield Road (left) soccer stadium were an early way of encouraging visitors**

# Clitheroe Kid has the run of toy town

IT WAS the very model of a modern major attraction ... The Model Village was officially opened at East Park Drive, Marton in June, 1972 – complete with a scaled-down celebrity comedian for the honours: Jimmy Clitheroe, clad in red blazer, grey shorts and Cub cap.

To dissuade Jimmy from taking up residence in the village's impressive castle, then-Mayor Edmund Wynne attended too.

The village, with everything built to a twelfth of life size, grew steadily in size and popularity with visitors wanting to be Gulliver for a a day.

What was once a Blackpool Corporation tip and barren plot – albeit a prime development – was transformed into a local version of Liliput by a consortium including Blackpool businessman Monty Rose.

The site, which was initially rented from Blackpool Council at a rent of £3,100 on a 21-year lease, was developed at a cost of £50,000. Owner Leonard Broughton, a local councillor, later described it as "a refuge from public life."

The estate has passed through several hands since. Fans include Blackpool's head of tourism Jane Seddon who said: "The Model Village is one of Blackpool's secret hideaways and it is an absolute delight to walk around."

**Diminutive comic Jimmy Clitheroe helped Mayor Edmund Wynne open the Model Village**

# The mall with a mucky mural!

Plenty of old property remains on the left towards Victoria Street as the multi-storey car park takes shape (right). The top right hand building is still there. It was the Tower Company maintenance headquarters

This is Water Street in the old Hounds Hill district.

# Resort is a KNOCKOUT

HERE are Blackpool's hungry It's A Knockout champions. . . waiting to be called through for a victory dinner in their honour at the Winter Gardens.

The year was 1971 and the team had won the TV game show's international final, Jeux Sans Frontieres.

The athletic lads and lasses entered Europe by being the highest losers in the UK heats and then emerged champions by taking the coveted golden trophy in Essen, West Germany.

Blackpool's link with TV's now-relaunched It's A Knockout (Channel 5 picked up the series which was dropped 15 years ago by the BBC) is something of a mini-marathon.

The town entered teams in numerous series and hosted the international finals of Jeux Sans Frontieres three times including 1976 – the resort's centenary year.

At that last final, in the South Shore open air baths where the Sandcastle now stands, persistent rain dogged the building of a Camelot-style castle set.

There were pools of water everywhere on the public walkways and when the giant spotlights were switched on just before transmission, the intense heat created a cloud of steam which engulfed everything.

When the programme ended, the German TV producer, Frau Tyler, came over to the BBC caravan, congratulated the crew for their professional approach and then asked 'How did you get the castle to rise up out of the water in that way?'

The 1971 Blackpool It's a Knockout team

*he '70s set the cene for shopping, nodern mall style, ut it was this aucy frieze that roused most omment*

BLACKPOOL put itself on the national retail map in the 1970s with a development that set out to rival the malls f the big cities – Hounds Hill.

The name recalled a long-lost istrict of town but the development as to alter the heart of the town entre for all time – paving the way r further change.

Work began in October 1977 on lackpool's £5 million covered opping complex The Hounds Hill Centre r Laing Development in partnership with lackpool Council – which paid for the site nd part of the car park.

The new shopping centre, bounded by ictoria Street, Adelaide Street, Tower reet and the rear of properties fronting ank Hey Street, was central to the ouncil's pedestrian-only proposals which ould ultimately alter the character of the wn centre – albeit at the cost of some istinctive property.

Laings hailed the centre as one of ritain's most streamlined and modern opping areas – incorporating 40 shops, staurant, coffee bar, with extensions to e existing Albert Road multi storey car ark.

Geoffrey Anderson, a director of Laings, ent so far as to describe it as the "the cus of shopping in the future".

It opened a year after schedule in 1980 ut, oddly, it was the saucy 22ft by 8ft aside sculpture, a frieze of frolicking udes, which graced the entrance and oused most comment.

Critics, including several senior onservative councillors, whose colleagues had granted it planning permission, branded it a mucky mural.

One claimed if it was in his front room he would no longer be able to invite the vicar round for tea. Another insisted it was not suitable for children to see.

Skipton artist Judith Bluck, Fellow of the Royal Society of Sculptors, who had created the frieze in the late 70s, explained it was nothing more than an affectionate look at the seaside, emphasising the family, sun and fun – and if nudity had been good enough for the Romans and Greeks it was fine for Blackpool!

The hapless frieze was frozen out during redevelopment of the centre in 1998 with a multi- coloured kite rebranding the centre in a £5 million refurbishment to take Hounds Hill into the 21st century.

Blackpool Civic Trust members urged the town to preserve it for future generations as part of the resort's 20th century.

Blackpool Pleasure Beach chief Geoffrey Thompson stepped in to save the frieze, rehoming the racy sculpture at his fun park alongside the Turnpike ride.

**As the steelwork of the roof goes in, Victoria Street looks very different than it does today. Centre stage is the old Gazette building**

# Tornado take-off

## *. . .then tragedy strikes in the sky off Blackpool*

BRITISH Aerospace was born in the Seventies – along with the Tornado aircraft.

The Multi-Role Combat Aircraft – become known as the Tornado – ad been conceived in 1969 under an nternational agreement signed etween Germany and the UK.

The Warton site was developed to ccommodate the planned final ssembly of all UK versions and a new angar was constructed by 1976 and fficially opened by Princess Anne.

The first flight of the UK prototype ornado, PO2, took place from arton on October 30, 1974. Final ssembly of production aircraft began 1978 and the first production odel, Tornado BT001, a trainer riant for the RAF, was officially lled out from 302 Hangar on June 5, 79.

**Planemakers and VIPs take a look at the first Tornado**

TRAGEDY struck the Tornado project only a week after crowds watched the aircraft in a thrilling display at Warton.

Test pilot Russ Pengelly and navigator John Gray lost their lives when the top-secret plane crashed into the sea 44 miles off Blackpool.

At the time the Tornado was being developed by Fylde planemakers under the banner of a specially-created company called Panavia. It was designed to replace the RAF's Phantoms, Lightnings and Canberras and had been ordered by the German and Italian air forces too.

A huge salvage operation was mounted to recover the wreckage of the aircraft which cost £9 million.

Russ Pengelly, who was known as a highly-skilled and courageous pilot, was married with two young sons and lived in Clifton Drive South, Fairhaven.

Mr Gray lived in Hampshire and was a Squadron Leader based at the Boscombe Down experimental station.

*In November 1977 floods struck th*

Evening Gazette

Storm havoc—4-page picture special

# BATTERED FYLDE IN GALES AND FLOODS

Floods hit Lytham homes

**From left: Firemen onboard a Land Rover in Grange Road; West View residents wade out via Grange Road; and Warrenhurst Road looking towards the Memorial Park gates. Pictures by Bill Curtis of Fleetwood**

# The Big

**Evacuating families at the junction of South Shore and Broadwa Fleetwood**

**Mopping up in Lytham at the Ribble Cruising Club building on the river bank**

**No trams were running through Anchorsholme Lane junction to Cleveleys and Fleetwood**

**Traffic beats the flood water on Beach Road. Picture by Bill Curtis of Fleetwood**

*Fylde. – and Fleetwood bore the brunt of the storm . . . just as it had 50 years before*

# Flood

KEITH Riley and his family thought they were in paradise when they moved into their new seafront home in Fleetwood.

During the long, hot summer of 1976 Keith often arrived home from work, got changed and joined his family on the beach 100 yards away.

He recalls: " I felt like a millionaire. I thought I had the biggest swimming pool in the world and then, a year later, we got the pool in the house."

The floods that devastated the coast that year changed Keith's life in a big way.

For after the trauma of seeing his family put at risk and their dream home wrecked, he pledged to try and make sure it could never happen again. And that led him into the world of local government as a councillor.

Long before then Keith and his wife Joan and their three young daughters had lived in Leyland and often had days out on the seafront at Fleetwood.

In 1976 they moved into a detached house on Marine Parade in the port and were happy in their new beachside base.

Keith said: "We were townies and we knew nothing about the ways of the sea nor the power it can unleash. But we certainly got a rude awakening that night."

On the fateful Friday, Keith and the family were watching TV blissfully unaware of what was building in the darkness just west of their home.

Then a neighbour knocked at the door.

Keith said: "He was a Fleetwood man and he told me the sea would flood us that night. I went with him in his car to the central car park near the Mount where we could fill some plastic sacks with sand."

But attempts to stave off the onslaught of the floods were totally in vain.

"Late in the evening the council came round with more sandbags and they were telling people each house could have two. You can imagine the replies they got."

Like many others the Riley family tried to block off the doors of their home with towels but then realised their fitted carpets were floating.

Keith said: "We knew there was nothing we could do.

"I went outside and I saw part of the seawall collapse. I watched a river of water pour through."

## *. . . then the Dunkirk spirit shone through*

Eventually they retired to bed and Keith admits he had a hefty nightcap of Scotch.

When he woke up in the early hours the waves were pounding the sea wall so hard the vibration was literally making his house shake. He watched a mirror on the wall moving with each new shock.

The days that followed brought new problems.

Wading out of the area and carrying the children Keith and his neighbours were angry at rubber-necking motorists who choked the flooded streets to gawp at the aftermath of the storm.

He said: "One drove on the pavement where the water was less deep and a neighbour of mine was so incensed he threw a stone to make them move out of our way. We felt like refugees in a war and they had just come to gloat."

With the children safe at a relative's home in Thornton, Keith and Joan came back to their ravaged house.

They were worried about stories of looting in abandoned homes.

It was then that the Dunkirk spirit of the floods shone through.

The couple joined a squad of neighbours and they all worked together to clean out eachother's houses.

Keith said: "The community spirit was fantastic. People really did help one another and the atmosphere was great. The Rossall Tavern pub was open all hours and people forgot themselves and thought of others. It lasted about six weeks."

In the aftermath came anger which led to public meetings and the formation of the Fleetwood Flood Association.

Keith says that although no one was killed outright in the disaster he reckons six deaths of sick and elderly people in the weeks that followed were brought on by the stress of it all.

Keith said: "Our view was that the sea defences were inadequate and that the council were ill-prepared for such an emergency."

He was one of the independent candidates put forward by the association who joined Wyre council to lobby for better sea defences which have now been installed. He is now a Labour party representative.

Keith said: "We still live in the same house and I am vigilant about the need for constant maintenance on the sea defences.

"Over the years a lot of work has been done all along the coast – south Blackpool is the latest example. But in Blackpool they seem to make the concrete ramparts look rather more attractive with landscaping than we do in Wyre."

**Keith Riley, now a councillor, recalls the floods of 1977**

**There was no let up from the storm for days. This is the old Anchorsholme pumping station**

Lancashire County Cricket Club, inspired by overseas star Clive Lloyd were crowned one-day champions, winning the Gillette Cup in 1970, 1971, 1972, and 1975

Jimmy Armfield got a tremendous reception from his team, Manchester United players and the crowd as he entered the field for his last game for Blackpool on May 1, 1971

Gary Player (right) at Royal Lytham in1974. Five years later Seve Ballesteros (left) made himself a "local' hero on the same links. Ballesteros shows his card after a second round record-equalling 65 at Royal Lytham & St Annes in 1979 when he won the British Open

# Giants among men...

Bill Beaumont: lifted England to their first rugby Grand Slam for 23 years at the end of the 1979-1980 season

FORGET flares – headbands and scrum caps were the sporting fashion of the 1970s as rugby giants came to the re on the Fylde Coast.

Head and shoulders above the rest as Fylde's own favourite rugby nion son Bill Beaumont who rose om playing in the shadow of St seph's Church at Ansdell's intimate oodlands ground to tower above e world's greats at Twickenham and yond.

Beaumont won his first England p against Ireland at Lansdowne oad on January 18, 1975, coming in lock after Roger Uttley pulled out jured.

It was to be a bittersweet perience for Beaumont whose but was to be tainted by him being the losing side as England were nt back across the Irish Sea beaten -9.

Even so, it was the start of an ustrious England career for Beaumont which led to the ultimate honr – named captain of his country.

Again his reign as skipper was to rt with defeat – 15-6 against France Paris on January 21, 1978. But ain there was to be a silver lining.

Beaumont went on to be an spirational skipper lifting England their first Grand Slam for 23 years the end of the 1979-1980 season.

It wasn't just Beaumont and the nion code which dominated the lde sporting landscape during the 0s – because down the road at ackpool Borough a Rugby League rytale was unfolding.

Blackpool Borough – who were to d up being forced to leave town – ve the resort its Rugby League ghlight by shocking the wider orting world with their heroics in e 1976-77 season.

Against all the odds, Borough arched all the way to the final in the estigious John Player Trophy urnament before falling at the final rdle.

Unfortunately for all sporting mantics, big-name Castleford oved just too strong for brave orough with the Yorkshire side nning out 25-15 winners in a atch screened live on national evision.

Blackpool FC suffered a far more miliating public fall from grace at e start of the decade when they opped out of top flight football – ver to return.

The Blackpool Borough team who set off on a 1976 season that was to end at Wembley.

Pool finished bottom of the old First Division pile at the end of the 1970-71 season with just four wins and 15 draws from their 42 matches leaving them with just 23 points.

The last match of the season was a doubly sad day for the Seasiders as it saw all-time one-club favourite Jimmy Armfield bow out after 568 league appearances.

By contrast Lancashire County Cricket Club, inspired by overseas star Clive Lloyd were crowned one-day champions, winning the Gillette Cup in 1970, 1971, 1972, and 1975 as well as being Sunday League champions in 1970.

Down the road at Lytham St Annes there were two sportsmen enjoying that champion feeling as the Open came to town twice in the '70s.

South African Gary Player triumphed in 1974 with his four-round 282 enough to see him home by four strokes, ending with a memorable shot at the 18th from just by the clubhouse wall.

Borough's Jimmy Molyneux in action during the 1976-77 season

Five years later a Fylde sporting star was born – even if he did come all the way from Spain! – with a similarly memorable finale.

Seve Ballesteros wooed sports fans throughout the world with his spectacular 1979 win at Royal Lytham which included some trademark great escapes in his 283 total.

And what's more he would come back to Lytham and win it again in an even more gripping finish. But that's for the 1980s . . . and next week's Story of the Fylde!

CHLORIDE The Capacity
To Keep Things Moving
4

Chapter Eight

# The Eighties

# The march of

A giant champagne cork pops as Mayor Collin Hanson opened Hounds Hill

Hoteliers (below) wait to look round Coral Island which had risen from the ruins of old Blackpool (bottom picture) looking from the Palatine across to Central Station and the New Inn

BLACKPOOL in the Eighties tried to live up to its motto of Progress. But not all the moves found favour with local people.

There was criticism of the long-standing Conservative administration when they shut down Derby Baths and more grumbles about an expensive beer festival called Karneval which the town hall organised to reinforce links with twin-town Bottrop in Germany.

This criticism helped the Labour party to victory later at both County Council and Blackpool town hall level.

However, the '80s saw the launch of a 20-year programme of sea defence works; Hounds Hill shopping centre was opened; and so was the Tower Shopping Centre in Bank Hey Street, the former Binns Store.

Yeadon Way was unveiled creating a road link from the M55 to the giant car parks on old railway land which can hold up to 6,000 vehicles.

Sports facilities at Stanley Park and a £1 million indoor bowling centre were created.

The Pembroke (now Stakis) hotel was opened in 1982, built alongside the existing Derby Pool.

The First Leisure Corporation spent £4 million on the Winter Gardens complex and £2 million on the piers.

# Progress

**Trawlers in Wyre Docks Fleetwood below. The last big ships sailed away in 1982.**

**Picture:** Bill Curtis of Fleetwood

## *and a monster attraction . . .*

BLACKPOOL of the 1980s was big, brash, buzzing – and full of hot air. But even seasoned locals went ape at the oversized monkey business which promoted Blackpool Tower's £1.3m acelift in the summer of '84.

King Kong came to town – to be suspended more than 200ft up he 90-year-old listed building. The giant inflatable gorilla was all of 5ft tall with an 80ft waist, 30ft wrists – and three-foot-long fangs.

Pressmen and VIPs gathered to meet the monster – fortified by a ingle-style breakfast and special screening of the original 1933 lassic.

The zany marketing stunt was the larger-than-life brainchild of lackpool-based public relations supremo Brian Cartmell .

His £20,000 publicity bonanza captured the imagination of the vorld's press as Kong was brought to Blackpool from San Diego in California.

The ape , all 18,700 sq ft of flame resistant nylon, weighing ,500lb, was inflated with hot air via a fan blower through its right eel . . .

The success of the scheme confounded expectations of all nvolved – including Clive Preston, then northern operations irector of Tower owners, First Leisure.

"It's a mad idea and one first seen in America," said Mr Preston nonths before the off-the-wall idea became reality. "It is probably npossible and impractical."

Kong's arrival in a giant packing case proved an event in itself. ower staff had to use a forklift truck to get the crate into the Tower and removed part of the glass roof of the ballroom in order to nflate the big ape.

He held court at the side of the Tower for 17 days until the wind vas knocked out of him by 20 men who took three hours to deflate, ower and box the genial giant.

It was a wet day in May but crowds braved the rain at Garstang Cross to cheer the monarch

John Riley, then the mayor's attendant in Fylde, chatted with the Queen. She had recognised hi[m] as a former member of the Royal Household sta[ff]

# Landlady's

The Queen saw the Ayrshire bull Myerscough Cavalier and talked with tenant Richard Barton about her own Ayrshire herd which grazes at Windsor. Mr Barton's son Henry is now tenant at Lee farm. Below: the Queen chats to Lancashire farmers wives

At Salwick, Lucy Burrows aged seven and her sister Debbie, 10, made an unscheduled gift of roses to the Queen

Mayor of Wyre Councillor Frank Townend and his wife said goodbye to the Queen at the end of her Lancashire day out

FOR centuries the Kings and Queens [of] England have owned vast estates of ri[ch] farm land in the Fylde.

These acres, worth a Royal ransom on t[he] open market, are part of the Duchy [of] Lancaster.

In 1980, the Queen, Duke of Lancast[er] came north to meet the farmers and the[ir] families who rent her farms.

Controlled from offices in Lancaster, t[he] sprawling Duchy estate is centred on five area[s]

A smiling Queen Elizabeth with tenants from Wyreside, Dolphinholme. At Lee Farm, Bilsborrow (right) the Queen chatted with her tenants' children

# visit!

Down on the farm at Winmarleigh when the Queen came to the Fylde in 1980. This was at Snapewood Farm as the Royal cavalcade pulled in

The Queen learned more about the water scheme at the Franklaw water treatment works in Catterall Lane, Garstang with George Mann, then chairman of North West Water. She then unveiled a plaque marking completion of a £58 million scheme to link the rivers Wyre and Lune together by tunnel

ome are in the Myerscough-Bilsborrow listrict near the internationally-famous Myerscough agricultural college

Others are sited around Salwick near Kirkham and there are large holdings in he Winmarleigh area north west of Garstang.

Still more occupy land at Dolphinholme and the beautiful hill country near Whitewell, north east of Garstang.

On that Royal day the Queen also went to the Franklaw water treatment works in Catterall Lane, Garstang.

She declared open an ambitious scheme which had linked the river Lune to the river Wyre and meant that water could be diverted to prevent flooding.

It had been a huge civil engineering project . . . but it was to have a tragic outcome in the village of Abbeystead four years later.

Prince Charles unveiled a plaque in the Grand theatre foyer (left) after he had been greeted by Mr & Mrs Geoffrey Thompson and John Broadbent, chairman of Friends of the Grand (right)

# Charles

The royal theatregoer met the stars of the show. Behind Petula Clark and Danny la Rue is Blackpool comedian Lennie Bennett

ONE of Blackpool's most glittering theatrical occasions came in May, 1981, when Prince Charles arrived in the resort for a gala opening of the Grand Theatre.

It was the climax to years of hard work by campaigners who had fought to save the venue from demolition and find a way in which it could become a viable theatre again.

Record-breaking results this year have shown how successful their efforts have been.

The beautiful Victorian venue, designed by Frank Matcham, has survived.

But even after the lavish re-opening it was years before the Grand got on to a sound financial footing.

Campaigners lobbied Blackpool town hall where Coun Tom Percival, then leader of the council, put forward a package of measures designed to give the theatre a financial lifeline and councillors agreed to give the project support.

Prince Charles meets the crowds in Blackp

The Prince met more VIPs in the theatre's circle bar

Diana went on an impromptu walkabout at Warton (right) talking to planemakers in 1989. She wore a three quarter-length tailored cerise coat and carried a navy blue umbrella in the rain

Blackpool clairvoyant Angerlena Petulengro met Princess Diana after she flew into the Fylde in 1983. At the time, Prince William was one year old. Angerlena predicted a total of four children and said the next would be a girl with another boy and girl later

# and Di

SOME Royal watchers from the Fylde coast first saw the Princess of Wales on Lancashire soil when she opened the Royal Preston Hospital in 1983.

On that occasion she spoke with Blackpool clairvoyant Angerlena Petulengro who was in the crowd.

The Princess had been talking to some children when she looked up and saw Angerlena's striking figure.

A security man attempted to block the Romany soothsayer's attempt to shake hands with the Princess who was deeply tanned from a trip to the Caribbean.

But the Princess moved the security man away and clasped the well-wishers hand.

She remarked that the Blackpool woman had chosen a red dress just as the Princess had.

Later Angerlena predicted that Diana would have two sons and two daughters and the next child would be a girl. At the time the Royal couple had one son, Prince William,who was a year old.

But she added prophetically: "There will be upheaval on the male side of the family."

Many more Fylde folk saw the Princess of Wales when she flew into Warton in 1989.

She met local VIPs on the windswept tarmac at the British Aerospace base then drove off to Preston again.

But before she boarded the aircraft , the Princess charmed the crowds of planemakers who braved the rain to catch a glimpse of her.

She went on a walkabout to talk to them and flashed that brilliant smile to bring a ray of sunshine into a wet and windy day.

In 1985, four years after Prince Charles officially re-opened the Grand, campaigners made a successful bid for cash from Blackpool Council

Long-serving local councillor Richard Spencer of Freckleton met another Spencer when the Princess opened a sheltered housing scheme for deaf and disabled people. He was chairman of the North and East Lancashire Welfare Association for the Deaf

Diana flew to Warton on a March day in 1989 and met Fylde council officials including Mayor John Tavernor

# 16 die

ABBEYSTEAD DISASTER
IN LOVING MEMORY
OF THOSE WHO DIED
FOLLOWING THE DISASTER
OF THE 23RD MAY 1984
JAMES ROWLAND BIRTWISTLE
FRANK COUPE
MARK EDMUND ECKERSLEY
PAULINE ELIZABETH ECKERSLEY
HERBERT CHARLES GARDNER
GEORGE ALAN LACEY
GEOFFREY STANDING
ALBERT TOMLINSON
EDNA TOMLINSON
EDITH FREER TYSON
PENELOPE ANN WEILD

**Abbeystead from the air – the idyllic setting of a terrible tragedy**

**A plaque at St Michaels Church now commemorate s the disaster**

**Pat Kaylor recovers in hospital after the Abbeystead tragedy**

## *I wrote*

TIME has healed the physical and emotion scars for Abbeystead victim Pat Kaylor. Pa 66, who still lives in St Michaels, was one 28 injured when the horrific explosion rippe through an underground water pumping station Abbeystead on May 23, 1984. Sixteen others died

Two days later, a heart-rending picture of h badly-burned face appeared on newspaper fro pages worldwide.

The mother of two, now a grandmother ar retired, was at Abbeystead with a party of village from St Michaels worried about flooding.

Her injuries put her in hospital for four wee and it was two years later that she was signed off b doctors at the burns unit.

Like other survivors she has got on with her lif but forgetting the anniversary doesn't mean sh doesn't care. It is just a mark of passing time.

"Every year, up until this year I had been church, around that time. Even though I am not churchgoer, it was my way of saying 'thank you' fo my life and to remember those who had died.

"Not that I am ever going to forget.

"It was a lovely May day, I remember that. I we up to Abbeystead with George Tyson and h mother and Elsie Rawlinson. I had been floode like the others, and we were hoping for som answers.

# in tunnel blast

The awesome force of the blast blew away tons of debris in a moment

A plan of the water scheme

An early visitor was the Duke of Westminster, owner of the Abbeystead estate (right)

ON a beautiful summer evening 15 years ago a group of men and women left the ancient Fylde village of St Michaels and headed for the hills.

Their destination was the hamlet of Abbeystead in the hills around the Trough of Bowland.

A few hours later telephones started to ring in St Michaels and horrified relatives learned that their loved ones had been killed, maimed and burned in a giant explosion in the heart of the countryside.

The culprit was Mother Nature herself, compounded by human error. The explosion claimed 16 lives and damaged many more, including 28 who suffered grievous injuries.

In 1980 St Michaels had been badly hit by flooding from the River Wyre.

So when North West Water built a tunnel to move water from the River Lune to the Wyre in the high country above the village, local people were worried.

The water authority invited a party of parish councillors, other local people, water company officials and various friends and relatives to the Abbeystead underground plant.

The 44-strong party went into the chamber and a telephone call to the operator at the Lune end started the pumps and sent the water on its way. But flows had been low and deadly methane gas had seeped into the tunnel.

It was formed in the same deposits that created the oil and gas-rich geology beneath Morecambe Bay.

The flow pushed the gas down to Abbeystead and it built up undetected in the pit below the see-through grating on which the party stood.

Maybe someone struck a match or scratched a spark with a bootnail. No one will ever know.

The blast blew the roof off the chamber scattering concrete beams like a giant's toys. It was amazing anyone survived.

Rescuers risked their lives to free survivors and heroic efforts at Lancaster Royal Infirmary saved many more in the crucial first few hours that night. But this was only the first chapter in a book of misery.

St Michaels was dubbed The Village of Tears as funeral after funeral was held and the the survivors struggled to come to terms with their loss, their injuries and their trauma.

The Health and Safety Executive said no one was to blame. But Mr Justice Christopher Rose thought otherwise. He presided over a 36-day legal hearing at Lancaster Castle.

Wyre Council and Lancashire County Council loaned the families money to finance their fight for justice. If they had failed some would have lost their homes to pay the debts. Mrs Thatcher's government turned down their plea for aid.

Mr Justice Rose divided the blame between the world-famous design firm Binnie and Partners who planned the tunnel scheme, Edmund Nuttall of London who built it and North West Water who ran it.

The villagers of St Michaels looked forward to sharing in a £3 million payout. But they still had months to wait.

The case went to appeal and the Lancaster decision was overturned. All the blame was placed on Binnie and Partners.

They wanted to appeal to the House of Lords but were refused permission. After four years the cheques finally arrived.

The Lune-Wyre tunnel was altered to ventilate the killer gas and the works was rebuilt.

A simple plaque in the Doomsday church of St Michael tells strangers about that night at Abbeystead.

But in St Michaels they need no reminder of a terrible time.

## *my will on the back of an envelope ’*

"When the explosion happened I was just a few feet inside the main door. Some people were in an inner room. Fortunately, I had not got that far.

"Then there was a noise, like when you are a bit late lighting a gas ring – a 'whoop', only much, much louder. A big, blossoming flame came from the inner door towards me. The next thing I knew I was blown off my feet and up into the air. I could feel people struggling underneath me and when I opened my eyes I was in the doorway with not a lot on.

"I had gone dressed in a jacket, sweater and skirt. I just had the remains of my jacket across my shoulders, my sweater was untouched, and all that was left of my skirt was the waistband and a few tatters.

"I never experienced any pain while were were at the site. I suppose I was numb. I was burned on my legs, hands, face and neck. My hair was melted into a lump and my head was burnt.

"After the explosion I wandered around and looked at all these people lying there and was wondering what had happened.

"A couple of other people joined me and later – it didn't seem all that long – things started arriving. It was a policeman who drove us by car to Lancaster Infirmary.

"The next day I was transferred to Withington Hospital burns unit and did a couple of TV and newspaper interviews. I didn't know what I looked like. I knew I had hardly any hair and my face was a bit puffy, but that was all I knew. No one would let me have a mirror.

"When I saw the photographs much, much later on I thought how awful it must have been for my children to see me like that.

" I was afraid I was going to die because of the pain. Having my bandages changed was like being skinned alive. They had to give me morphine. I wrote my will on the back of an envelope. It sounds so silly now.

"I thought even then that someone should pay and I don't mean that in the sense of money. We had been invited there by the water authority – we hadn't asked to go – and we felt they should have accepted responsibility and then fought it out amongst themselves over whose fault it was – the design, the operation, the building or whatever.

"We couldn't start to put it behind us until all the legal arguments were settled.

"It was such a big thing for a small village like this. It was like a bomb dropping.

"All the people who were at Abbeystead that night have a tie to each other, like those who have gone through a war. I suppose it will gradually dissipate . It really pulled the village together and we got wonderful support from everyone here and outside – a church in Blackpool brought food out every week and the council arranged for coaches to take our relatives to see us in hospital. It was wonderful.

"You read about so many awful things happening and this makes you realise that under the surface of this horrible world we appear to live in, people do care and do things, not just give money.

"I look back and think I never tried to help anybody. I suppose it was shock, but it is to my everlasting shame that I never looked to see what was happening. I saw somebody lying there with no clothes on and unconscious and I never thought : 'What should I do to help'? .

"The one thing that gives me an excuse for myself is that I was nude from the waist down and I was wandering about not thinking."

After the four-year legal fight for compensation had ended Pat said there was no real victory celebration. " It was more 'Thank God, it's all over'. Now, at last, you can put it behind you and get on with your life."

Abbeystead was a tragic disaster, but Pat says it doesn't haunt her.

"Very occasionally I think about it. Sometimes something will remind me. I am grateful and lucky to be alive."

Pat Kaylor at her St Michaels home 15 years after the Abbeystead disaster

This superb floral display by Blackpool Parks department, outside St John's Church, was part of the celebrations

Nostalgia time along the Golden Mile (right) as old trams trundled again

# Tramfastic!

THERE was a double summer of celebration on the Fylde coast in the mid-80s.

And it was the tramway link between the towns of Blackpool and Fleetwood that joined the two events together.

It all started in 1985 when Blackpool celebrated 100 years of trams.

And the resort had something to celebrate because when the tramway was inaugurated on September 29, 1885 it was the first in the world.

In the end it was the last in Britain – although cities like Manchester and Sheffield have got back in the act since then.

On the big day the opening of the tramway had to take second billing to the inauguration of the Blackpool lifeboat Samuel Fletcher – now surviving as a pleasure boat on Stanley Park lake.

But the trams rolled into history and huge crowds turned out to mark their 100th birthday. It was held on the actual anniversary and the sun poured down as if to join in the fun.

Crowds queued to ride on historic trams while others took a look behind the scenes at the Rigby Road headquarters of Blackpool Transport. A cavalcade of historic vehicles drove to Fleetwood along with some of the trams.

And that was how the traditional Tram Sunday event was born.

The following year, 1986, marked the 150th birthday of the town of Fleetwood and a group of local people joined forces to plan the celebrations.

They were sponsored by Lofthouse of Fleetwood – the family-owned company which makes Fisherman's Friend cough lozenges.

The company has invested thousands of pounds in the Fleetwood community including schemes designed to make the town look more attractive and in backing for local organisations and charity projects.

The 150 Project awoke Fleetwood's community spirit and one of the most successful aspects of a year of local events was the street parties.

Hours of work and a lot of hard earned cash went into them and the were held all over the town.

It was a time when more an more people were becomin interested in local history – an realising how much of the preciou past had not been photographed o recorded because it seemed s ordinary at the time.

Enthusiasts in the world o transport deserve credit for bein among the first groups to realise th importance of remembering the wa we were.

## ...and Fleetwood keeps the party on

The Blackpool celebrations of 1985 included showcasing old trams and vehicles in Fleetwood. The following year this became part of the port's 150th birthday party and has flourished since then. On the right is the very first Tram Sunday

A typical Fleetwood 150 street party and (right) some of the volunteers whoorganised the event

There was even a special birthday cake

A Fleetwood 150 balloon race sets off in Seymour Street

# the right lines

Tug of war teams towed trams in Foxhall Square, Blackpool. Among them was TV quizmaster Derek Batey (left)

**There was an open-day at the Blundell Street depot as part of the tram centenary celebrations**

Two local authors, both authorities on tramway systems, in 1999 produced books about those bygone days.

Steve Palmer of Fleetwood, a member of Fleetwood Transport Festival Committee, has penned Blackpool Centuries of Progress which tells the story of the resort's growth and development. It is available from local outlets including Blackpool Central Library at £5.99.

And Brian Turner of Lytham has come up with Circular Tour – Seaside Pleasure Riding By Tram which includes text and pictures about Blackpool. It is published by Rio Vista at 19 Norfolk Road, Lytham, at £18.95.

IT MIGHT be sandpie in the sky to hope that boffins will ever get around to controlling the British weather, but in summer 1986 Blackpool went tropical with what was then the ultra-modern Sandcastle Centre.

Brows were no doubt raised at the neighbouring Pleasure Beach when Town Hall tourism bosses hailed the £16 million complex as the resort's biggest and most significant development since the Tower.

The glass-fronted concrete fortress building was certainly a controversial eye-catcher, dubbed the Blackpool Bunker as it started to take shape on the site of a famous landmark built in the Roaring 20s – the Open Air Bath.

Built for those visitors of hardier days who did not mind swimming in cold temperatures, the old bath, opened in June 1923, was modelled on the Colosseum of Rome.

Over the years it provided a catwalk for thousands of bathing beauty queens.

In the early 30s it became a backdrop for the film Sing As We Go, whose star Gracie Fields signed the visitors' book with the message: "Now't wrong wi' Blackpool Baths."

In 1959, another movie star, Hollywood's Jayne Mansfield, visited the baths when she came to switch on Blackpool Illuminations. Her verdict: "Fantastic pool. I wish I could take it home with me."

But the picture had changed by the mid-60s. The bath was now a white elephant according to the resort's elected worthies and over the coming years there were various proposals from a sports stadium to pop concert venue, a killer whale show, even an ornate angling pool stocked with trout!

The bulldozers arrived in February 1983, reducing the site to rubble in just five weeks. The £16 million Sandcastle, backed by more than £4 million worth of grants from the EEC, opened its doors in June 1986.

At that time, such tropical centres were a novelty and, as Blackpool's version also housed a huge entertainment hall and nightspot, it was designed to keep the tourists happy whatever the hour. The hope was also to attract lucrative conference and corporate business out of the holiday season.

But as modern indoor fun pools mushroomed around the country, the novelty of spending hours inside one on holiday began to fade.

In later years part of the venue housed the enterprising hi-tech Crystal Maze attraction but this was scrapped when the whole of the "dry" side was converted into the ill-fated Magic of Coronation Street attraction, which closed at the end of the 1998 season.

Almost since day one the Sandcastle has been a political hot potato as ratepayers face the cost of propping up annual losses through the financial involvement of Blackpool Council.

But those who use it praise the facilities and the centre has built up a strong following of local supporters.

*The 1980s was the decade when the demolition men moved in on the Fylde Coast's Roman open air baths and the "inside seaside" was born on the prom.*

**Happy days (above) at the newly-opened Sandcastle**

**The giant pool in its heyday (left) but as its replacement (below) took shape it was dubbed The Blackpool Bunker**

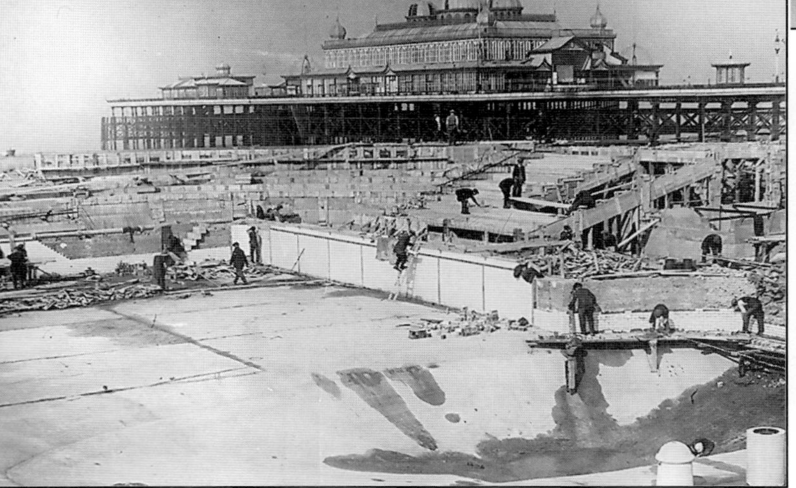

**This historic picture shows South Shore open air pool under construction. It opened in June, 1923. The biggest of its kind in the world it was designed by Blackpool Council architect John Charles Robinson**

Wore than 4,000 people queued to attend the opening of St Annes Roman Baths in June 1916

ST ANNES open air swimming had also lost its appeal by the time the '80s arrived – although as our picture from 1980 shows, sunworshippers gave the attraction one record breaking day in May.

Originally opened as the town's Roman Baths on South Promenade, the venue welcomed 4,000 people on its opening day in June 1916 and was hailed as unique in the north for having hot and cold filtered sea water all year round.

Attendances plummeted throughout the '80s and despite a 2,000-name petition to save the structure, the pool closed in 1988, lying derelict until it was finally demolished in 1992.

In April 1987, Fylde Council created a new indoor pool opened alongside the original baths site which over the years has been developed to become the Pleasure Island leisure complex.

Temperatures soared and sun worshippers gave St Annes open air baths a record day in May 1980

# the swim

Derby Baths was another Robinson design completed in 1939. It closed in 1988 and was knocked down in 1990

Protestors fought to save the Derby as a facility for local people and tourists

IT'S closure and ultimate demolition caused a political stir of Olympic proportions in the late 1980s.

Some observers still maintain today that the loss of the art deco Derby Baths – with its Olympic-sized pool, and where Hollywood Tarzan star Johnny Weissmuller appeared – was a major factor in the ousting of Blackpool Council's Conservative rulers.

Opposition parties and local residents mounted a spirited, if ill-fated, fight to save the doomed Derby on North Promenade.

But the doors were barred and bolted in 1988 and the building finally razed to the ground in 1990.

When the centre opened on the Pembroke Gardens estate in August 1939 it was described as "the largest and most luxurious swimming establishment of its kind in the UK."

But just over 40 years later, as the '80s got underway, a detailed report to the resort's tourism and leisure committee claimed it no longer had the atmosphere demanded by a new generation of leisure swimmers.

Some action would be needed to reverse the decline.

In 1983 permission was given to feisty American businesswoman Lloyce Boyd to create her Splashland aqua adventure attraction. Her 34ft-high Black Hole and Knucklebuster tubular water chutes, which ran inside and outside the building, flooded the complex with new business.

But Lloyce's later plans to transform the whole of the site into a South Sea island swimming and leisure complex were sunk by Blackpool Council when Lonrho, the then-owners of the neighbouring Pembroke Hotel (now the Stakis) won the £1 million contract to buy the baths for redevelopment.

Another political storm began brewing for the Conservative rulers when it was revealed the accepted bid had failed to meet specific council criteria.

Moor Park Pool at Bispham became a modest and modern council-owned successor to the Derby Baths.

But as history shows, no building on the Promenade materialised and today the former landmark is a grassed area with a modest children's playground.

The decision to scrap the Derby was a factor in the defeat of the Conservative council by Labour

The Fleetwood Open Air Pool was opened in 1925 and replaced in 1974 by the present indoor pool on the same site

*The St Annes statue that honours the brave men of the lifeboats*

THE FIRST lifeboat on the Fylde coast was established at Lytham in 1851 followed by Fleetwood in 1859 and Blackpool in 1864.

In those days lifeboat volunteers were local fishermen and the boats were powered by oars and sails.

But they achieved some amazing rescues – often in terrible weather. Sailing ships would be driven aground in a gale and the cockleshell craft would swoop through the breakers to grab survivors.

The Royal National Lifeboat Institution is one of Britain's favourite charities and has always relied on the public for the cash to keep the boats afloat.

The lifeboatmen prefer to keep their independence although they work closely with the Coastguard service.

National charity fund raising really took off thanks to the efforts of Charles Macara, a wealthy Manchester merchant who lived in St Annes.

He greatly admired the skill and courage of the lifeboatmen and after a terrible tragedy in December, 1886 he resolved to do something positive.

It happened when the sailing ship Mexico ran into trouble in the Ribble estuary in a night-time storm.

All 13 crew of the lifeboat, then based at St Annes, besides 14 from Southport, were drowned before the Lytham boat managed the rescue. A statue on St Annes promenade records the sacrifice of life at sea.

Mr Macara started modern fund raising so the lifesaving work could go on.

The courage and skill of modern day lifeboatmen has been recognised too.

On the day when the police officers were drowned at Blackpool, Coxswain Ian Fairclough took the Fleetwood lifeboat close to the seawall at North Shore.

The boat might easily have flipped over and the five men onboard been drowned. On the way to the scene a giant wave had already dropped on the craft like a bomb.

Today, the tradition on the Fylde coast continues. A new-style lifeboat has been stationed at St Annes and Blackpool has a splendid new lifeboat station and visitor centre.

Cash to build it came from a fund started in 1980 in a bid to buy the resort a new lifeboat.

Now, lifeboats are high tech and volunteers come from many walks of life. Often their rescue missions involve the growing number of leisure sailors.

But the sea has not changed. It remains as fickle, cruel and unforgiving as ever.

# DISASTER

THE sea has always been at the heart of the fresh air and fun image of the Fylde coast. But it has also proved to be a cruel, unforgiving man-trap.

It has claimed scores of lives and over the years there have been many hundreds of examples of courage from those who braved the worst weather in a bid to help others. Sometimes they paid with their own lives.

So it was in January, 1983 when 25-year-old Alistair Anthony from Glasgow left his parents holiday flats in Wilton Parade with his father Robert for a walk on the seafront.

Anthony threw a ball for Henry, his Jack Russell terrier, and when it bounced into the sea the dog followed.

Alistair, a hefty man and a good swimmer, stripped to his underpants and waded along the seawall apron.

A wave swept him off his feet but he swam to a concrete slope then found he could not get out of the water.

His father threw a lifebelt and Anthony used it to keep afloat while his Dad called for help.

PC Pat Abram went in first and got to within six feet of Anthony before his lifeline stopped him short.

He got back on to the slope with WPC Angela Bradley and PC Gordon Connolly. Then a giant wave washed them all off into the sea.

By now the wind was increasing, the tide rising and the sea was like a boiling cauldron.

PC Colin Morrison was also in the water by now. He lost his life while PC Abram tried to keep him afloat.

PC Abram nearly died himself when the only way rescuers could save him was to drag him out with a rope which had looped round his neck. He had no pulse when he reached dry land.

Earlier, PC Martin Hewitson was buffeted by waves when he went down the slope to try and throv lifebelt to the group in the water.

Police chief Roy Lenton stopp other officers from going in to sea in further rescue bids.

The Superintendent said later remember the awful realisation t we had a disaster on our hands. A yet they were so close to bring off the rescue."

Tributes to the courage of police officers came in from ma quarters and a memorial at Gynn marks their sacrifice.

Later, fire fighters, ambula crews and lifeboatmen who help were given certificates commendation by Lancashire Ch Constable Brian Johnson.

# . . . and on land

A child playing with matches turned an hotel into an inferno in April, 1988.

The blaze broke out at the Leber Mount Hotel in Dickson Road, Blackpool. And it claimed the lives of two adults and three children who were all related.

Other relatives escaped from the property which was used to house homeless people. In all 20 people got out safely.

The death toll might have been higher but for the prompt action of two local men who later received lifesaving certificates.

Bricklayer Gordon Moxon of Lord Street, Blackpool and builder Patrick Buckley of Dickson Road rigged ladders which helped survivors get out and guided firemen in saving vital minutes.

In the aftermath of the fire came a debate about the living conditions of homeless people and fire prevention in Blackpool's countless apartment buildings. It is a debate which goes on today.

**Vain fight for life: A six-year-old boy is carried out too late to be saved**

**A barefoot victim of the blaze is helped down a ladder to safety**

**A shocked survivor is helped from the scene**

# at sea

tormy seas lashed the oast as emergency ervices drove on to ne seawall

escuers elp a urvivor

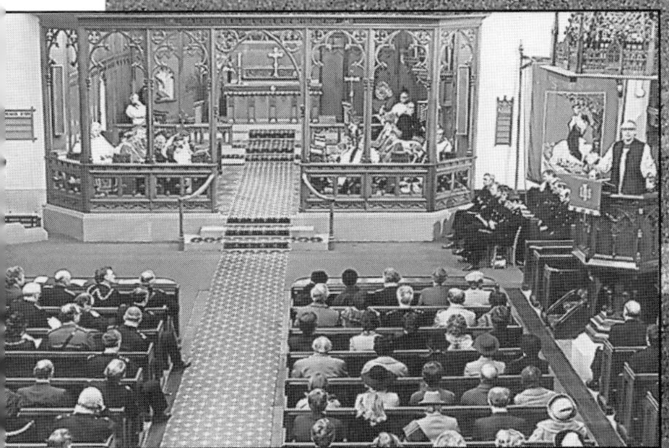

The Bishop of Blackburn, Rt Reverend Stewart Cross preaching at the Memorial Service for the three officers held in St John's Parish Church, Blackpool

Some of the lifesavers were honoured for their courage. Fleetwood lifeboatmen Steve Musgrave, David Owen, Andrew Griffin and David Bolland are on the right

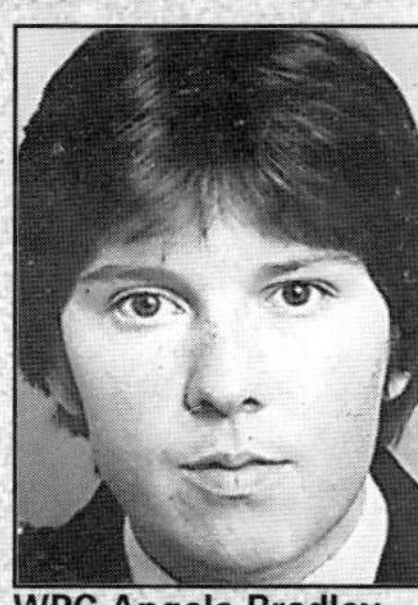

WPC Angela Bradley

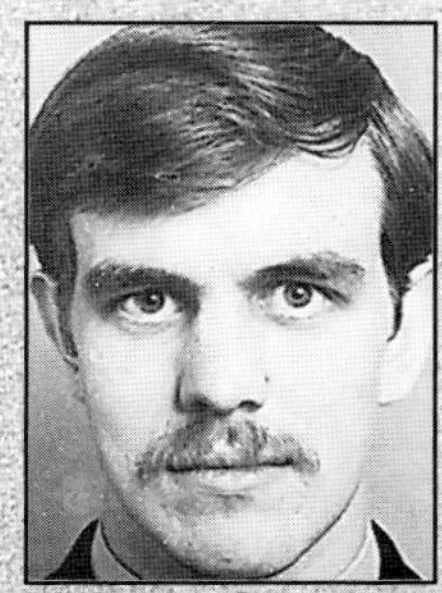

PC Gordon Connolly

PC Colin Morrison

Alistair Anthony with his Jack Russell dog

PC Pat Abram who was lucky to survive the incident at Gynn Square

# Rock on Tommy!

Comedians Cannon and Ball start the '80s Illuminations decade with a bang while one year later Earl and Lady Spencer lauded Blackpool and its attractions

THE ILLUMINATIONS were shining brigh and better than ever before. Summer s favourites Cannon and Ball, were the big dr for the 1980 ceremonials at the height of their fam

The decade included some unusual choices switch-on personality such as the self-effacing R Admiral "Sandy" Woodward, Falklands hero, in ' and Johannes Rau, Minister President of North Rh Westphalia in '84 – to mark the town's twinning w German industrial town Bottrop. Topical choi maybe, but not the biggest crowd-pleasers.

The cast of Coronation Street led by actress Do Speed who played Annie Walker, landlady of Rover's Return did the honours in '83 and broug the ceremony back into the full glare of the spotlig

BBC Children In Need presenter Joanna Luml before her own acting career's renaissance throu Absolutely Fabulous, turned on the Lights in ' followed by our own much-loved Lytham comic Dawson in '86, and BBC Holiday trio Ann Gre Kathy Tayler and Frank Bough in '87.

Composer Andrew Lloyd Webber, accompan by then-wife Sarah Brightman and a wh complement of entertainers clad as dancing mogg used the '88 platform as the opportunity to annou the coming summer's blockbuster musical at Opera House – Cats.

The show was to break the mould for the ven and the town's traditional variety mainstay, pav the way for other big attractions such as 42nd Stre Barnum, Joseph, Buddy and more. It led to h hopes of Blackpool rivalling Manchester as the b for some of Britain's biggest showcase productio albeit with limited success under First Leisur regime.

One of the most popular switch-on personalities the '80s was boxer Frank Bruno who threw the swi in 1989 – with Coronation Street stars back, yet aga in 1990.

But one of the most memorable and ma ceremonies was in 1981 when the Earl and Count Spencer – Prince Charles' new in-laws – switched the Lights and basked in their reflected glory.

The event turned into royal wedding fever all o again as the resort's biggest-ever street party chee the bride's father and stepmother.

Earl Spencer and the Countess stood on the to hall platform, beneath a giant portrait of their hon and pulled the double handle to send power along five-mile long display of 175,000 lamps.

The earl, referring to daughter Diana's weddi announced: "We are all very lucky to be alive duri the summer of 1981 which has been a wonderful y of happiness."

But he also proved a surprisingly loyal ambassa for Blackpool – having visited the town previously Blackpool Boys Club business and also to m legendary '50s footballer Stan Mortensen who, opined, "Blackpool FC needs again."

"My wife and I are delighted to be back Blackpool. We love coming here, we have been h several times and we'll be back before the year is o People should come here for a good holiday. Whet they live in Sweden, Switzerland or the Ou Hebrides, they will never have a better holiday than Blackpool.

"Here you have wonderful fresh air, very go shops , very good accommodation, very go restaurants and, above all, the best funfair in Europ

From left above: Falklands leader Rear Admiral Sandy Woodward –1982

Doris Speed pulled a pint in 1983

Joanna Lumley – 1985

Les Dawson – 1986

Frank Bough in 1987

**From left: Margaret Thatcher in Blackpool in 1981; checking for booby-traps on the Imperial Hotel car park; sniffer dogs trained to smell explosive were part of the massive new security checks; airport-style surveillance machines at the Winter Gardens**

# Iron fortress

WHEN terrorists struck at Brighton in 1984 an iron fist closed around Blackpool.

Tight security was thrown around the esort in 1985 to foil the IRA from repeating ts most spectacular strike against the British Government.

Conferences had helped put Blackpool on he world map and the Conservatives had een meeting in the resort since 1926.

Lancashire police had the task of devising the security blueprint for future conferences – to protect lives of delegates, residents and visitors.

They opted for a high-profile show of force. Police minutely checked out all venues – even to the extent of sealing manhole covers, placing snipers on rooftop surveillance, armed police stopping and searching vehicles, and – in 1987 – anchoring a Royal Navy minesweeper off the coast .

The no-nonsense policy drew angry criticism from some traders and residents who found the tight security irksome after the relatively free and easy atmosphere of conferences in the pre-IRA threat era .

The system for throwing the so-called security fortress around Blackpool evolved over time. Once the blueprint was drawn up to safeguard the conference, firearms experts, other branches of the police, Army and Navy were brought in to act as potential attackers and find possible loopholes.

In the light of their recommendations, the basic plan was modified and refined, and has since been used as a guide by forces policing conferences in Bournemouth and Brighton.

Ratepayers of Lancashire also had to pay out millions for the extra policing required but police chiefs asked 'What price democracy?'

The row over the bill raged for a decade _ until 1997 when Blackpool finally won its marathon battle for Government cash to help meet the massive security costs at both Conservative and Labour conferences.

# *Pub that cheated terrorism*

**Wyre MP Sir Walter Clegg who, with his wife Elise, escaped death in the IRA bombing of Brighton's Grand Hotel in 1984**

TERROR stalked a picturesque Fylde pub in 1983 – when the Irish Republican Army iscovered Weeton.

The carnage, had the terrorists' omb plot gone ahead, would have natched any atrocity or urban nassacre.

The original mission was to plant bomb at Weeton Camp to kill or naim British soldiers of the Second attalion of Light Infantry.

From April to September 1982 he unit had made a tour of duty in he notorious South Armagh border istrict of Ulster.

During the tour, 23 soldiers, ncluding an officer and NCOs, vere alleged to have looted property rom a school and homes.

The men were sent back to base t Weeton but gave the IRA motive nough for revenge.

A two-man active service unit of atrick Magee and Patrick "The ope" Murray – codenamed the Aechanic and the Minder – was ispatched to strike the blow.

The camp had to be checked out s a suitable target, and the IRA then, s now, had a network of mainland lotters to prepare the ground.

One of them was 50-year-old Raymond O'Connor who was Galway-born but had settled in Blackpool many years before and vorked in a resort cafe.

O'Connor alleged, at an Old Bailey trial three years later, that he was drawn into the bomb plot by a Dublin University graduate , a teacher living in Blackpool. But the teacher was later cleared of playing any part in the conspiracy and claimed he had been framed.

Whoever did check out the area for the IRA judged security too tight and concluded it would far easier to strike soldiers off-duty and off-guard.

The callous conclusion led to a simpler option which sat vulnerable and isolated nearby – the Eagle and Child pub at Weeton.

It was, and remains, a popular family pub which attracted limited numbers of squaddies – who tended to prefer the brighter lights of Blackpool or Kirkham for off-duty fun.

However it was a soft target for the terrorists. Magee and Murray arrived in Blackpool on April 12, 1983. They stayed at a flat on South Promenade, in Cleveleys, and checked out the pub from a Mark IV Cortina hired by O'Connor. They planned to plant two suitcases of explosives in the car and detonate them next to the wall of the gents' toilet.

But the bombers were unaware O'Connor had turned informer – and was relaying information to Special Branch.

In a covert operation dubbed Quicksand officers kept vigil at the busy pub, while Regional Crime Squad and Anti-Terrorist Squad members monitored the suspects' every move from unmarked cars and vantage points.

Licensees Joyce and Des McLellan had to tell curious locals that the hard-eyed newcomers who all but moved in to the pub were accountants!

Vigilant villagers also reported the Special Branch cars regularly to the local police.

The officers and terrorists continued the elaborate cat-and-mouse game as bombers swept the area before their intended strike.

Yet, just as the web seemed to be closing, communications broke down between Lancashire police and Scotland Yard. Pictures of the terrorists were not circulated to other forces. One local policeman claimed there was a delay in identifying Magee which stalled the arrest.

But it was widely believed Magee may have rumbled the operation.

In an event the bombers fled the Fylde on April 26 – evading police in a car chase. They abandoned their car at Preston railway station with the doors open and the engine running and took refuge in a safe house in Leyland before catching a ferry to Ireland from Fishguard in Wales.

Magee was caught only after he struck again – returning to the mainland in 1984 to kill five people and maim others in the bombing of the Grand Hotel at Brighton during the Conservative Party Conference – an attack which was to close the iron fist of security around Blackpool's political conferences.

Wyre MP Sir Walter Clegg and his wife Elise escaped the Brighton bombing with cuts and bruises. Magee was jailed for at least 35 years.

Murray was arrested on terrorist charges in France in 1989 and jailed for two years. He was later jailed for 10 years for carrying out a bomb attack on a British army barracks in Germany – a member of an IRA active service unit which planted a 330lb Semtex bomb next to where the soldiers slept.

Murray and two other gang members walked free four years ago after serving almost seven years in remand prisons in Germany and France.

The landlords at the time of the Eagle and Child bomb attempt went into retirement – and prayed for the peace process to work.

But it's not the end of the story. In 1987, 60-year-old stockman Michael McKenny was jailed for 16 years by an Old Bailey judge after plotting to bomb Blackpool during the height of the summer season.

Then, in 1991, Blackpool's Christmas shoppers were hit by a firebomb campaign in the resort – at the same time as an incendiary attack on Manchester. In all it involved 50 devices – 15 of which were found in the resort.

Early in 1992, the discovery of an explosive cache in Dead Man's Wood, Singleton, near Weeton Barracks, led to the hunt for a suspected IRA cell.

Lancashire trading standards officers have also long suspected links between the resort's sale of pirate videos and fundraising for terrorism.

An investigation by the Royal Ulster Constabulary in 1994 revealed the IRA received £1.5m from pirate video sales – to underpin the £10.5m needed to support the sinister network and fund bullets and bombs.

**Historical footnote:** the IRA attacked the Fylde back in 1939 , with bombs found at Blackpool General Post Office, in a dustbin outside Woolworths and in the grounds of Central Police Station, then at Albert Road. A bomb exploded in an empty bedroom at the North Euston Hotel, Fleetwood and at Blackpool town hall.

Wren Rovers of Blackpool clinched the 1981 Lancashire Combination Championship

Fylde Rugby aces Wade Dooley (left) and Steve Bainbridge played for England

IF Wembley belonged to Blackpool in 1953 and to England in 1966, in the 1980s it was Fleetwood's turn to fly the flag at the Twin Towers.

Over the years Fleetwood has been more famous for fishing than football. But in 1985 all that changed when the town's team became soccer stars when reaching Wembley in the FA Vase.

Unfortunately for Fleetwood's football romantics, there was to be no fairytale ending as they went down 3-1 in the final to Halesowen Town.

But it was still a day none of the 10,000 Fleetwood fans who made the trip to Wembley – outnumbering rival supporters in the 17,500 crowd, will ever forget.

And Fleetwood's players had more tangible memories to treasure after coming away with their losers' medals presented to them by Manchester United and England legend Sir Bobby Charlton.

It wasn't Fleetwood's only cup highlight of the 1980s. At the start of the decade there was a certain FA Cup date against derby rivals Blackpool.

Fleetwood were drawn out of the hat first. But after much debate and some on-off ground improvements at Highbury Avenue the tie was switched to Bloomfield Road.

And this was to be one David and Goliath cup tie without a shock ending as the Tangerines triumphed 4-0 to take their place in the second round.

But non-league opponents were to come back to haunt Blackpool, when Altrincham came to Bloomfield Road and upset the Seasiders – twice!

Altrincham won here in back-to-back seasons. The minnows triumphed 1-0 in 1984 and 2-1 in 1985 and were the only non-leaguers to knock Blackpool out of the cup in the 1980s.

There were happier times in the league Pool when they won promotion from t basement to Division Three in 198 clinching their move up a division with a 4 win at Darlington under long-term boss Sa Ellis.

In cricket Fleetwood's Aussie professio Mike Whitney had his own dream day wh he received a last-minute call-up to fa England at Old Trafford.

But the Test belonged to Ian Botham a Bob Willis as the home side staged a mira comeback in an historic series against t Aussies.

There was also a titanic struggle played c right here on the Fylde Coast – although had to wait an extra day than planned to s it.

Rain washed out Saturday's play at t 1988 Open Championship at Royal Lytha and St Annes. But little did golf watch know the treat in store on the extra Mond as two of the world's greats – Seve Balleste and Nick Price – went head to head.

In any other tournament, on any oth course, Zimbabwe's Price would have end up with the Claret Jug in his hands on the 18th green.

But this was Lytham, where the man fro Spain reigns. And after firing a reco equalling final round 65, Ballesteros lifted t famous trophy aloft at Lytham for the seco time in nine years.

Fylde had heroes further afield with rug union stars Wade Dooley and Ste Bainbridge were an integral part of Englan international side along with skipper F Beaumont whose team won the Grand Sla in 1980.

And down the road at Old Trafford the was a trophy to add to the cabinet wh Lancashire's county cricket stars won t Benson and Hedges Trophy in 1984.

# Fleetwood

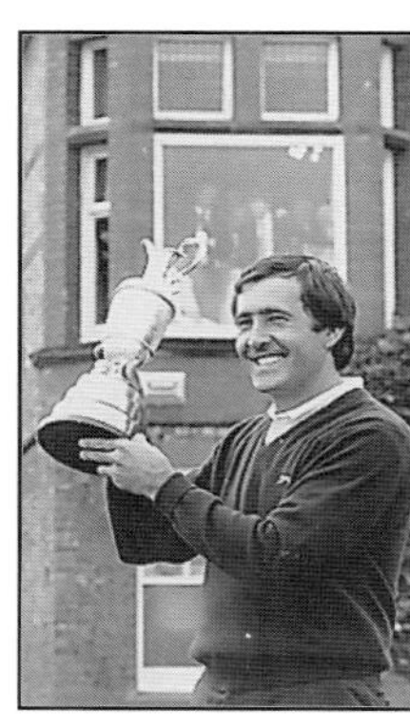

Nick Price (left) went head to head with Seve Ballesteros at Lytham in 1988 with the Spaniard (right) winning The Open claret jug at Royal Lytham

Australian cricket star Mike Whitney (right) with other Aussie players at his benefit match at Broadwater in 1981

The Lancashire cricket side which won the Benson and Hedges Cup in 1984

The Fleetwood squad of 1980 (left) take a vintage tram to Bloomfield Road for their FA Cup Clash with Blackpool. Above: Fleetwood's Stuart Robinson (right) keeps a close eye on Wayne Entwistle

Manager Alan Tinsley (left) leads the Fleetwood side on to the Wembley turf for the Final of the 1985 FA Vase. Below: Fleetwood fans at Wembley

# all aboard

eetwood lost 3-1 to Halesowen Town in the Vase but supporters braved the rain to elcome them home

FUNNY G
INTERNATIONAL COLOSSEUM
BLACKPOOL
ZH590
PLEASURE BEACH

## *Chapter Nine*

# *The Nineties*

# Resort rocks

IN May, 1991 the Labour group on Blackpool Council took control of the Town Hall for the first time in history.

Some members had previously played an important part in helping Labour gain control of Lancashire County Council.

However, it was not too long before Blackpool Council leader Ivan Taylor announced plans for the resort to go it alone. On April 1, 1998 Blackpool split away from Lancashire's umbrella control and moved back towards the old days when it had borough county status.

So the town regained direct control of its schools, social services, and highways services.

But responsibility for the emergency services remains with the County Council.

That was not the only change in town.

New landmarks like the Central Pier big wheel and The Big One on the Pleasure Beach sprang up.

So did For Sale signs on many of the town's guest houses as the tourism industry realised that changing trends meant too many beds in Blackpool for modern times.

But the crowds flocked in for Blackpool's night-time entertainment scene and changing trends in tourism included further expansion for Blackpool Airport.

As the decade drew to a close, another piece of local history was set for a major change.

The seafront Miners Home, one of the prime sites on the coast, was sold to be turned into luxury apartments. In the 10th and final edition of The Fylde Story we shall be featuring some recollections of life on the coast from people who have lived through the decades.

We began the series by looking back to the roots of our corner of Lancashire and we shall revisit those towns and villages to see how they have fared over the years.

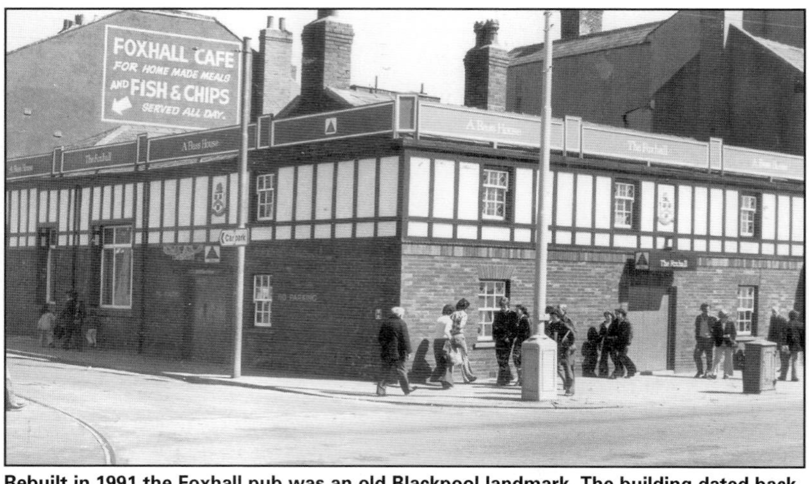


**Rebuilt in 1991 the Foxhall pub was an old Blackpool landmark. The building dated back to the 17th Century when it was a hunting lodge for the Tyldesley family**

**Another legendary seafront pub was rebuilt in 1996. The Manchester Hotel pictured before the £1.3m revamp**

*The weekend when terror came gift-wrapped for Christmas '91*

# Blackpool shop bomb blitz

**Long-serving Blackpool police chief Ken Mackay (left) at a press conference after the 1991 Christmas bombings. He said Blackpool police made a quick and effective response**

IT was the year terrorism came giftwrapped for Christmas.

In December 1991 IRA firebombers blitzed the very heart of Britain's top resort – and also struck Manchester.

Seven firebombs went off at the city's Arndale Centre and other devices, six of which ignited, were found in a rubbish bin half a mile away – believed dumped by fleeing terrorists.

Blackpool town centre was brought to a standstill while firefighters battled against the bombing blitz.

Streets were turned into no-go zones as police cordoned off shops where incendiary devices had been planted.

Fifteen fire engines with almost 100 men raced around town during the longest night of terror Blackpool has ever known.

Lefton's furniture store and warehouse in General Street was one of the worst hit in the spate of bomb attacks.

Devices were also left at the Town Hall, behind an arcade game on North Pier, in Marks and Spencer, on North Station land and at other shops and stores across town.

The firebombs had been slipped into jacket pockets, into a suitcase, even children's Christmas goods.

The callous act left property owners facing £1 million worth of damage and lost trade in the aftermath of the blitz.

But it could have been far worse – and valuable lessons were learned too.

The alarm was raised at 4.30pm on Saturday December 7 when police were informed =a young couple, staying at a local hotel, had found a firebomb in the suitcase they had bought at the Britannia Store, in Albert Road.

The 25-year-old guest and his girlfriend, on a weekend Christmas shopping trip from Crewe to Blackpool, made the shock discovery in their bedroom.

The 24-year-old woman described the device as "a rectangular object with wires attached."

Her boyfriend carried the suitcase downstairs and showed it to the landlord and landlady of the Tudor Rose private hotel, South Shore – who promptly raised the alarm. A young police officer carried the bomb away to the beach.

But it took five hours for police to alert stores using the traditional telephone ring-around alert system.

Some key holders could not be located and the bombs began to ignite from Saturday night through to Monday morning .

In all, 11 of the 16 incendiary devices exploded, leaving a trail of devastation and blighting Christmas trade. The weekend of terror caused damage and cost trade in excess of £1 million.

The delay in warning, which concerned major retailers, police and residents, led to the introduction of a hi-tech security early warning system within weeks.

Closed circuit TV also became a feature of town centre security within major stores and on the streets.

The IRA later claimed responsibility for the Blackpool firebomb attacks and warned the destruction would continue.

# on!

# ... with a return to old-style attractions?

HOWLS of protest greeted the decision to feature the Wolf Kids, Mexican brothers Larri and Danni Ramos-Gomez, in the first non-animal circus at Blackpool Tower in the summer of 1991.

The brothers, then aged 14 and nine, inherited a unique genetic abnormality from their grandfather which meant their bodies were covered from head to toe in a mass of dark body hair.

The booking ruffled the feathers of everyone from the animal rights protesters and the NSPCC to Lancashire County Council but their appearances went ahead as planned.

Circus impresario Peter Jay denied the brothers were being exploited or that it was a return to the days of Golden Mile "freak" attractions.

"They are unique and they are happy and they are an integral part of a family show – I cannot see anything wrong with that," he said.

Acrobat Neville Campbell, aged 20, from Stoke on Trent (left), was killed when he fell at Blackpool Tower Circus in a Wheel of Death accident in 1994. Showbiz partner Bryan Donaldson survived

Growing interest in nostalgia lead to projects like the heritage trawler Jacinta in Fleetwood docks

Julie Goodyear and Roy Barraclough from Coronation Street switched on the 1990 Lights

# Bright lights ahead

THE old-style Illuminations switch on ceremony was spectacularly short-circuited during the '90s and given a razzmatazz relaunch.

Coronation Street's Bet and Alec (Julie Goodyear and Roy Barraclough) had the fans in their hands for the first ceremony of the decade, followed by media celebrities Derek Jameson and Judith Chalmers.

In 1992 Rochdale songthrush Lisa Stansfield made a brief appearance for the Talbot Square crowds but later made more of a mark with outrageous behaviour when she threw torn-off bread roll missiles from the top table to her entourage at the civic supper in the Imperial Hotel.

The following year it was no longer deemed enough for a celebrity to simply pull the lever, give a wave and a smile and disappear back inside the Town Hall.

The waiting crowd deserved more, decreed the elected worthies, and a link-up with the Radio One Roadshow breathed new life into the ceremony with a show featuring current chart stars, before veteran rockers Status Quo took to the stage.

Unfortunately it was back to form in 1994 when Welsh diva Shirley Bassey declined to sing at all after a rousing performance by the National Youth Jazz Orchestra in an entertainment devised by newly-launched North West radio station Jazz FM.

But things came back on track the following year with those singing Gibb brothers the Bee Gees in what seasoned switch-on goers maintain was – and remains – the best Lights night ever.

Radio One did the honours that year and again in 1996 when girl group Eternal switched on the Illuminations.

Then, in 1997, the resort forged new links with the Radio Two Roadshow and that year's celebrity was West End musical star Michael Ball. The lady was in red, blue and every other colour last year when Chris de Burgh performed and, just a few months ago, in September 1999, the last switch-on of the century, indeed the millennium, was carried out by former Take That star Gary Barlow.

Shirley Bassey with comedian Stan Boardman

**1990:** Bet and Alec Gilroy, Coronation Street (Julie Goodyear and Roy Barraclough)
**1991:** Derek Jameson and Judith Chalmers
**1992:** Lisa Stansfield
**1993:** Status Quo
**1994:** Shirley Bassey, National Jazz Youth Orchestra
**1995:** Bee Gees
**1996:** Eternal
**1997:** Michael Ball
**1998:** Chris de Burgh
**1999:** Gary Barlow

Michael Ball switches on Blackpool Illuminations

Gary Barlow: Lights Switch-on 1999

In 1993 the Radio One Roadshow come to town with veteran rockers Status Quo

# Out with the old in with the new

Here's how Birley Street, Blackpool looked (above) before drivers were banned, and (right) the new as pedestrianisation continued in the town centre

BLACKPOOL turned back the clock to Victorian style in the Nineties for a £1 million scheme on the promenade that created new street lighting, kiosks, shelters and a stylish bandstand opposite Victoria Street.

Another new-look came in as pedestrianisation continued in the town centre – an idea which had begun in the Seventies when vehicles were banned from Victoria Street.

There was a bright new image for the old Lewis's store.

It was cut down in size and emerged as a brand new retail and leisure complex.

On the Golden Mile the Sea Life Centre opened its doors for the first time to provide a major new attraction with a different image than more traditional Blackpool delights.

It underlined a growing public interest in the natural world and the idea of protecting it from damage by mankind.

Two famed pubs on the seafront were rebuilt in modern fashion – the historic Foxhall and the Manchester Hotel.

A new landmark appeared with a Big Wheel on Central Pier.

But it was overshadowed by the giant Big One ride on the Pleasure Beach featured in more detail on pages 165 and 166.

This Victorian-style bandstand (left) was unveiled by Prime Minister John Major in 1994 as part of a £1m facelift of the Promenade

The re-vamped former Lewis's store (above) emerged like a butterfly in 1994 after a huge re-building project

The £5 million Sea Life Centre was a major new attraction in 1990. Inside, a giant tank filled with sharks is the biggest of its kind in Europe

What London does today Blackpool has already done – twice. Inspired by the memory of the Big Wheel beside the Winter Gradens, First Leisure opened a new Big Wheel on Central Pier in 1990. The resort's first monster wheel turned from 1896 to 1928. Central Pier had to be reinforced to take the Dutch-built wheel. It cost £750,000 and stands 108 feet high – roughly half the height of the original. It can carry 216 people in 26 carriages

**Safe to swim? Youngsters surfing on plastic debris from a storm-damaged sewer pipe on the Fylde**

**Everything was on a big scale for Operation Sea Change. This is the Dutch pipe-layer Merwede leaving Fleetwood in 1995**

# Clean start to 2000?

THE Battle for a Blue Flag on Blackpool beaches has been a big feature of the 1990s.

And the problem of making the sea off the Fylde coast clean enough to pass European Bathing Water Standards remains unsolved as the 21st Century dawns.

Providing clean drinking water was the job of the old Fylde Water Board which collected supplies from the hill country east of Garstang.

But for generations sewage was just dumped in the sea off the coast without any treatment at all.

North West Water took over responsibility for both these jobs and launched a £500 million scheme called Operation Sea Change to clean up the Irish Sea from the Scottish Border to Liverpool Bay.

Despite opposition from the Save Our Bay pressure group, they pushed through a bold plan to sort out the sewage situation on the coast.

A web of tunnels collects both waste and rainwater and takes it all to a giant treatment plant on the outskirts of Fleetwood.

Some of the gunge extracted at the works is buried on the giant refuse tips at Clifton Marsh, Freckleton or at Jameson Road near the Fleetwood works.

But the cleaned up water from the plant is pumped out into Morecambe Bay.

Recent test results have shown Fleetwood beaches getting cleaner.

But Blackpool is still failing the coveted Blue Flag test – receipt of which would be a big boost to tourism.

The responsibility for getting this right rests with the Government's Environment Agency and tests are going on to find out why the Blackpool beaches are still failing to pass.

**Some attempts to clean up the sea hit problems. The pipe-laying barge Holland XXIV ran aground at Cleveleys in bad weather during a 1981 pipeline project at Anchorsholme**

Deep below the Golden Mile as the tunnel system nears completion

The tunnels were cut by giant machines called Moles

One of the moles going in from a 100-foot deep shaft at Fleetwood

Technology has changed since this 1925 picture of local worthies, members of the Fylde Water Board. They are seen near Scorton where a reservoir was under construction

**If the fire had spread in the narrow streets of what was once called The Village, the damage would have been much greater**

**Overlooked by fire-blackened buildings the Foxhall Market was left as a skeleton of blackened girders**

# The Foxhall

IT was a September afternoon in 1995 when a column of black smoke began to rise into the sky from a complex of narrow streets just off the Promenade not far from Central Pier.

And so began what became known as The Foxhall Fire.

In the end it was thought the blaze had been caused by youngsters playing with lighters and setting fire to a display of gas lighters in a building called the Foxhall Market between Dale Street and Foxhall Road,

And it was estimated that damage costing £6 million was caused.

Mercifully, no one was killed or badly hurt in the fire despite the fact the area was packed with people working or visiting hotels and shops.

Firefighters faced tough conditions to stop the blaze spreading into what might have been a much bigger holocaust.

But there was nothing they could do to save one of Blackpool's most historic buildings.

The resort's first-ever department store was left a blackened ruin.

The first reports of a fire came in around 5.30 and when firefighters arrived they quickly requested reinforcements.

The number of machines alerted to the scene rose quickly to eight and then to 15 with fire crews called in from Preston and Lancaster.

By 6pm there were 100 firefighters on the ground.

Some of them were still at work 17 hours later.

The fire left many people homeless – both local residents and holidaymakers. Some were given emergency shelter at the Ibbison Court centre on Central Drive.

And, in the longer term, there was anger as local traders complained the incident had blighted the area and hit their livelihood.

Because of different landowners being involved it took more than a year before the whole area was cleared up. The site of the Foxhall Fire became a car park.

Later, a reconstruction at Lancashire Fire and Rescue Service HQ showed graphically how a display of gas-filled lighters could turn into an inferno in seconds.

The building destroyed in The Foxhall Fire had originally opened in time for Christmas, 1899 and was the talk of the town.

It was the first building in the resort with an electric lift and rivalled anything seen in a city with big plate glass windows to show off a wide range of household goods.

The Bickerstaffe family flag fluttered atop a domed turret and there was a clock using the 12 letters of the family name instead of numbers.

The Bickerstaffe family were at the heart of booming Victorian Blackpool and Alderman Tom Bickerstaffe put up the building on the site of the family ironmonger business which had opened in 1877.

Architects Garlick and Sykes used what was called modern renaissance style for the design.

The area around Foxhall Road was known locally as The Village and had once been officially termed Lower Blackpool.

It seems the Bickerstaffe operation closed down in 1924.

Later the building became the Empire Restaurant and was used by RHO Hills who had a large store in Bank Hey Street.

## *... and fun goes up in flames*

**At the height of the Fun House blaze on the Pleasure Beach**

DAMAGE estimated at £10 million was caused when fire ripped through the Fun House on Blackpool Pleasure Beach in December, 1991.

Even the famous laughing clown outside the building was destroyed – except his head which was in for repair.

The 57-year-old building was done in the Art Deco style – part of the huge revamp of the site which took place in the 1930s under architect Joseph Emberton.

Other attractions and equipment went up in smoke during the night time fire which was fought by 80 fire fighters using 1[illegible] machines.

When they arrived they found the building too far gone to save and they concentrated their efforts on stopping the spread of the huge blaze to the rest of the Pleasure Beach.

The Fun House was a big favourite with generations of Blackpool holidaymakers. Inside they slid down slides, whirled round on a giant turntable and rode in a revolving barrel.

Right away Pleasure Beach boss Geoffrey Thompson pledged that a new attraction would take the place of the Fun House and elsewhere in this magazine you can read more about it.

All that remained of the historic Bickerstaffe emporium after the Foxhall fire. It had been Blackpool's first department store in 1899

# Fire

Crowds turned out to welcome Princess Diana in July 1991

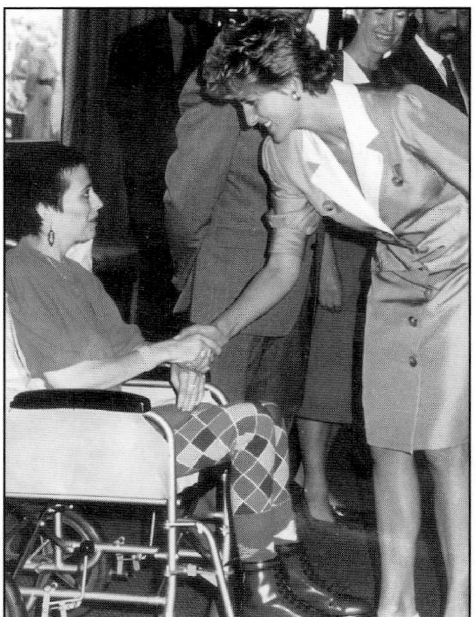

Diana renewed her links with Poulton student Louise Woolcock

Making new fr

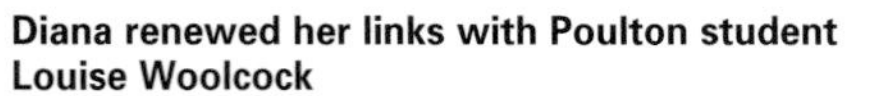

# The

THE death of Diana, Princess of Wales, in August 1997, touched the hearts of people across the Fylde just as it did across the world.

That famous smile had been turned on thousands of people on her visits to the coast over the years.

And she had often shown the caring and compassionate side of her nature.

It might be a special greeting for a pensioner in the crowd overco by the heat.

Or it might be by suppor words and a warm handshake patients at Trinity, the hospice the Fylde.

It was there in 1992 t Princess Diana renewed friendship with Poulton stud Louise Woolcock.

They first met in private Blackpool Town Hall wh Princess Diana visited the resor

The Queen made a visit to the Fylde in July 1990. She handed new colours

J's Cafe in Talbot Road

Meeting and greeting the fans

Princess Diana at Symbol Biscuits

In Blackpool in July 1992 Diana was full of concern when she spotted Madge Hargrave of Tarnway Avenue, Thornton. Madge was cared for by police when she felt faint outside the Winter Gardens

# Fylde and Di

July, 1991. She was impressed by the spirit of the bubbly young woman who fought bravely against cancer.

The Princess became a friend and corresponded with the family after Louise died.

During her visits to Blackpool Princess Diana impressed many by the genuine way she took an interest and talked sincerely to those she met – from workers at Symbol Biscuits to youngsters at CJ's Cafe on Talbot Road.

The Queen came to the Fylde in 1970 to present new colours to the Queens Lancashire Regiment at Weeton.

She was back in 1994 with the Duke of Edinburgh to mark 150 years of Rossall School at Fleetwood and 100 years of Blackpool Tower.

Once again the crowds were delighted as the Monarch went 'walkabout' and chatted to people who had waited hours to see her.

Sunshine turned to a downpour as the radiant Princess went walkabout

Queens Lancashire Regiment at Weeton

When Rossall school was 150 years old in 1996 the Queen and Prince Phillip joined in the celebrations with headmaster Richard Rhodes

# Two tall

■ Blackpool Tower opened in 1894, three years after the foundations were laid on the site of Dr Cocker's Menageries and Aquarium
■ It is 518ft 9ins (158.12 m) tall with a letter box at the top
■ Nine tons of paint are needed to cover Blackpool Tower
■ Each of the two Tower lifts travel about 3,500 miles per year
■ Winds on the upper levels have reached 75mph
■ A massive King Kong was brought from San Diego, California for the Tower's 90th anniversary celebrations in 1984
■ Time Lord Dr Who, alias Jon Pertwee, presided over a time capsule ceremony in the ballroom in 1991 to mark the centenary of the foundation stone laying
■ Princess Diana unveiled a commemorative mirror for the £14 million refurbishment of the seafront landmark into an indoor theme park in 1992
■ The Queen and Prince Phillip visited in 1994 to mark the centenary of the opening.
■ The glass-floor Walk Of Faith lets visitors walk "on air" 380ft above the Prom

BLACKPOOL'S world-famous holiday par atmosphere reached new heights in the mid-'90s w Two Tall Stories. That was the slogan for Festival the year-round celebration which gave a giant boost to k attractions in the resort.

The landmarks linked by the two tall stories tag were t newly-built world's tallest, fastest roller coaster, the I One, and the seafront's other steel monster Blackp Tower, which celebrated the centenary of its opening literally going for gold courtesy of a team of abseili painters.

Another centenary party, marking the laying of t Tower foundation stone, was staged three years earl when the guest of honour was Dr Who actor Jon Pertw and there was even a Royal visit by Diana, Princess of Wal to mark completion of a huge refurbishment in 1992.

But back – or rather forwards – to 1994 when there w unprecedented national and international media covera and a substantial increase in visitor numbers at a time wh many other UK resorts were suffering badly because of t effect of the economy.

Blackpool Pleasure Beach enjoyed a 30% increase in t number of early season visitors while Blackpool Tow figures were up 15%.

The Grand Theatre was also celebrating its o centenary success with a 20% boost in bookings, while was cheers, with raised glasses, at Yates Wine Lodge Talbot Square, where a similar milestone was being mark

But not everyone was happy with the party noise. petty as it might have seemed to resort revellers, so hoteliers complained the noise of fluttering festoon str bunting was keeping visitors awake!

The sky around Blackpool's already golden Tow became a blaze of colour as a fireworks spectacul marking the Grand Old Lady's 100th birthday, bu around her.

Thousands of partygoers stood open mouthed at t marvel of it all while inside the resort's best-lov attraction, Victorian-dressed visitors enjoyed three no stop days – and nights – of events. These included a Gra Centenary Ball, staged by Blackpool Conservati Association, where the guest of honour was someone w as recent events now suggest, was no stranger to the wo of "tall stories". It was Lord Archer.

Still with the world of politics, that same week, t Pleasure Beach's hopes of nationwide publicity through

The Tower went gold (left) to celebrate the special occasion and the Queen rode to the top in 1994 to meet the maintenance crew – known as Stickmen– who work on the structure

# stories

A glamorous launch for Valhalla, the Pleasure Beach's big new attraction for the millennium

**WHAT a difference a decade makes. In December 1991, even as 80 firemen continued dampening down in the early hours, Blackpool Pleasure Beach boss Geoffrey Thompson pledged that something bigger and better would fill the yawning gap left by the destruction of the five-storey 1934 Fun House building.**

**And, as reported then, he revealed a new attraction, though some years away, would be a dark ride based around a log flume.**

**Valhalla, the Viking-themed £15 million attraction which is Britain's biggest privately-funded Millennium project eventually opened in June, 2000.**

**Geoffrey Thompson is expecting 10 million visitors to the seafront park in the year 2000 on the back of the new attraction which will carry up to 2,000 riders per hour.**

ecial media trip on the yet-to-open Big One mmed when the spotlight fell instead on the eath of the-then Labour leader John Smith.

But soon after, hundreds of Fylde Coast fans ipped school to watch short-lived pop nsations Bad Boys Inc officially launch the eel roller coaster.

Disaster struck just over a week later when mputer failure was blamed for a crash in hich coaster carriages ploughed into a ationary train close to the ride station. The rst train had stopped at a braking point and a il-safe emergency brake had slowed down but iled to stop the second train following behind.

The ride was out of action for the peak mmer months and lost the fun park the udos of a previously-arranged sit by Prince hillip when he companied the ueen to the sort for a cen- nary trip to e top of ackpool ower.

The Dominion, Bispham, opened in 1938

Demolished in 1986 the Regent was Fleetwood's last cinema

The Waterloo was redeveloped for shopping

Built in 1912 in St George's Road, St Annes, the Empire

The Palladium in Waterloo Road, South Shore

The Imperial stood on Dickson Road, Blackpool

# Golden age of the silver screen

THE launch of the Odeon super cinema complex in Rigby Road, Blackpool last December, underlined the fact that the curtain ıs not fallen on the movies in the Fylde.

Ironically, it was not too far away, in gby Road, that the town's first regular nema stood in 1906.

The cinema was a large wooden ıilding called the Coliseum which had en part of the Raikes Hall Pleasure ardens. Later it was used as a garage and ıve its name to the now-defunct oliseum coach station off Lytham Road, ıuth Shore.

Nearby the Royal Pavilion became the wn's first purpose-built cinema in 1909.

There was a rash of cinema velopment in Blackpool before World 'ar One.

In 1914 the Tivoli – above Yates's Wine ıdge in Talbot Square and Blackpool's dest entertainment venue – acquired a reen.

The first talkie – Singing Fool starring l Jolson – was screened at the ippodrome (now the ABC cinema ımplex in Church Street) in April, 1929.

The march of the movie palaces went ı.

Also in 1929 the Empire opened in awes Side Road, Marton. Later it became e Sands Casino and Cabaret Club and is ɔw a bingo hall.

The Oxford by Marton traffic lights and e Dominion on Red Bank Road where ainsbury's is now had also arrived by 'orld War Two.

And, in 1939, the splendid Odeon on ickson Road was opened with it's tiled t deco frontage.

That now stands empty after the new Odeon development on Rigby Road opened its doors.

But the old cinema is set to play a new role in Blackpool;s entertainment story.

When the Dickson Road Odeon was still brand new there were cinemas from one end of the coast to the other.

Even little towns like Knott End and Thornton had their Verona cinemas and Poulton the Rialto.

St Annes had three cinemas, Lytham one and Kirkham had the Empire which survived until modern times.

Cleveleys had three, Fleetwood four and other venues, like the Grand Theatre, sometimes showed films.

The slump started in the 1950s.

In 1954 the Tatler news theatre on Church Street, which showed short travel and news films, became a furniture store.

Slowly but steadily through the '60s and '70s the cinemas went dark.

Some became bingo halls, like the Victoria on Poulton Road at Fleetwood.

Others survived longer by showing blockbuster films for the season like the Palladium on Waterloo Road.

Others became nightclubs like the King Edward on Central Drive and the Princess on North Promenade.

It looked as though television and home video had killed off a once-popular form of entertainment.

It was cheap enough for many people to go at least twice a week and the programme often changed twice a week. Youngsters had fun with the special Saturday shows.

Then a new generation of super cinemas began to emerge and a new generation of film lovers discovered that going to the pictures is even more fun than it used to be.

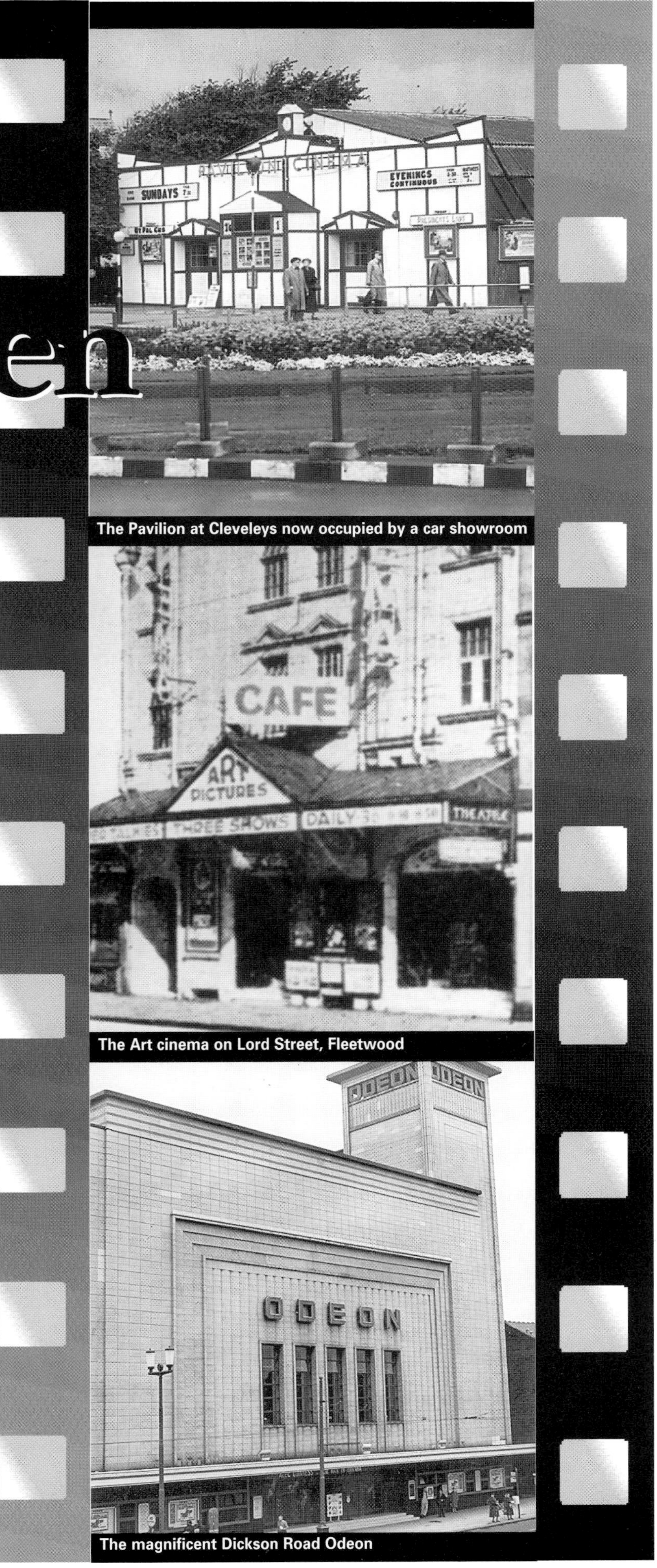


The Pavilion at Cleveleys now occupied by a car showroom

The Art cinema on Lord Street, Fleetwood

The magnificent Dickson Road Odeon

Protesters outside Kirkham's Empire Cinema battled in vain against its closure

*Nineties Blackpool is alive to changing trends*

# In the pink!

THEY should call Blackpool – Basil Pool! Gay nightclub king Basil Newby's tongue-in-cheek comment reflects his stake in the town's success – and the seaside significance of the so-called Pink Pound.

It took Basil's investment in town, back in the late '70s, to put Blackpool on the map as a gay-friendly resort but it was his developments, through the '90s, that really made the Pink Pound welcome here.

Basil has probably done more than any other figure to help engender a climate of tolerance towards gay locals and visitors.

His empire has also boosted the spread of gay-friendly hotels and other establishments catering for a specific clientele.

It was all very different 20 years ago – almost to the very day – when Basil bought the Flamingo nightclub on Talbot Road . . . an area which has recently been earmarked for sweeping changes as part of the transformation of the town centre.

But while Basil is at a crossroads, his empire is going from strength to strength.

He vows the Flamingo, whatever its location, will go on, along with Funny Girls, the burlesque transvestite showbar he opened in the '90s to cater for the mainstream market.

Both have had phenomenal success. He started out with the top floor of the Flamingo, bought the whole property, developed the bottom floor as well, bought Pepe's on the way, then, in '92, opened the stylish Basil's on the Strand, which proved the cornerstone of the renaissance of once-chic shopping street, Queen Street, which had, by then, fallen on harder times.

It marked a turning point in public attitudes too. Basil had to go to Crown Court to fight for his right to a late licence – pointing to his trouble-free record and the ease with which straight nightspots won licences.

He won, and with honours – told by the judge that the case should have never gone to crown court.

**Crowds queue to see the Funny Girls burlesque show**

Basil was pleased with the acceptance of his business in Blackpool.

"It's never been terribly homophobic although when the Aids epidemic hit, in the late '80s, it put it all back about a decade. I couldn't even get a plumber to fix the plumbing – it took time for the public perception to change with proper knowledge and information about the health risks."

Now, he admits, with a smile, it's "gone the opposite way" – he gets a lot of straight clients, especially women, at the Flamingo, while Funny Girls, opened in '94, has become world famous. All of his venues, including the Flying Handbag pub, which opened in '96, have raised hundreds of thousands of pounds for local charities, and kept the boyish nightclub king in the style to which he has become accustomed: living in luxury in an 18th century hall in rural Fylde.

While he owes his rise to fame and fortune to the Flamingo, Funny Girls burlesque she-boy showbar in Queen Street, has become the showcase of his empire – thanks to the talents of singing and dancing diva Betty Legs Diamond (aka Simon Green), dj Zoe and the r of the team.

And Basil has big plans for future too – including a stylish n eight-level nightspot-cum re aurant complex , for a mainstre clientele, at Queen Street wh opened in the summer of 2000.

**BASIL'S BREAKS**

Basil lays claim to having giv superstar Lily Savage "her" first break – when Paul O'Grady v part of a drag act called t Playgirls. Diana Dors also appea at the Flamingo, besides singer Dawn – Coronation Street's V Duckworth. The late Beryl Reid v a personal friend, as is Su Polla Boy George has also appeared th – and the woman who took a sw at former TV chat show host Russ Harty : Grace Jones.

# Disaster averted

Warton men struggle to pull wreckage from the sea at Blackpool after the 1996 Tornado crash

The controversial Hawk trainer (above). Sales from Warton brought protesters to the site over the use of the planes in strife-torn East Timor in the Far East

The first flight of the Eurofighter (below). As the decade dawned, planemakers at Warton looked forward to job security through development of this new generation of warplane. The picture below right shows work on the prototype in 1990

IT could have been an accident of terrifying proportions. But when a jet fighter dived to disaster over the town of Blackpool in September, 1996, it missed the Golden Mile and smashed into the sea instead.

It seemed to people who saw the plane that pilot Paul Hopkins from Lytham managed to get the nose up a little as he headed for the beach.

And that could have given him just enough height to clear the Golden Mile and the busy seafront.

The Tornado jet was on a routine test flight from BAE Systems Warton and Mr Hopkins and navigator Al Reynolds, aged 47, managed to eject safely despite the fact that the aircraft was so low.

It had flown over South Shore following Squires Gate Lane and people on the ground realised the aircraft was in trouble.

Rescue workers raced to the beach and found the two airmen safe.

Their first words were about getting in touch with their families to let them know all was well.

Mr Hopkins wife Linda was expecting twins and he was worried the shock would bring on a premature labour.

Immediately after the accident a team of Warton workers were drafted in to rescue chunks of wreckage from the beach as the tide came rushing in.

The Tornado crash was not the only problem facing boffins at the base in the 1990s.

Protesters regularly visited Warton over the site's involvement with the building of Hawk jet trainers.

It was the use of the planes in troubled East Timor which upset the peace campaigners.

But there was good news on the job front with orders for the Eurofighter – the new generation of warplane developed at Warton for use by the RAF and the airforces of other European countries.

The decade finished with the opening of a new chapter in the Planemaker Story.

In a £7.4 billion deal British Aerospace joined forces with Marconi Electronic Systems, the defence arm of GEC. The new company, BAE Systems, is the second biggest defence contractor in the world.

## *The agony …*

FAILURE: Dave Bamber misses a vital penalty at Wembley in 1991, while centre-forward Andy Garner contemplates defeat

## *The ecstasy …*

ECSTASY: Fans and (right) Dave Bamber celebrate the big win in 1992

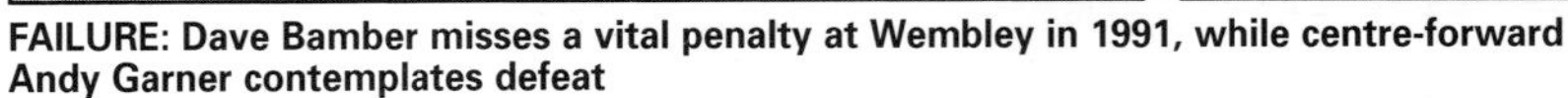

PRIDE: The winning Blackpool team that won promotion as the football league structure changed

# The UPS

FOOTBALL fans know all too well that following their favourite side means strapping themselves to an emotional rollercoaster with no chance to get off. And for Blackpool fans the 1990s resembled the Big One!

Three key moments in the decade saw them plunged into despair in 1991, only to rise up in delight a year later, before suffering an all-time low in 1996 which would shape the rest of their Millennium.

For the Seasiders the start of the decade was all about Wembley. They hadn't been there since the club's famous FA Cup triumph in 1953. Yet the Tangerines would journey to the Twin Towers twice within a year.

On both occasions more than 13,000 Blackpool fans followed the Seasiders to the capital to experience starkly contrasting emotions.

In 1991 they saw their side beaten by Torquay in the basement division play-offs before making amends and winning promotion to the now Division Two in incredibly similar circumstances when triumphing over Scunthorpe 12 months later.

First time around Blackpool favourite Dave Bamber was cast as the villain, missing the all-important spot-kick in a penal shoot-out decider after the sid had been tied at 2-2 after ext time, Paul Groves and Dav Eyres the Seasiders scorers.

A year on Bamber was the her netting in normal time in a 1 draw with Scunthorpe before t drama again unfolded in a penal shoot-out. Seasiders keeper Ste McIlhargey saved one spot-ki before Scunthorpe missed the decider.

The scenes of Blackpool bo Billy Ayre embracing h players will long remembered and more th made up for the previous yea disappointment which Ay

Mathew Ellis brought an ABA title back to the resort in 1995 while Fleetwood's Jane Couch (right) broke new ground by becoming the first female licensed boxer in Britain

Brian Duncan lifts the Waterloo crown green bowling trophy for the fifth time and (right) Andrew Flintoff hits out for club, county and country

# ...and the agony again

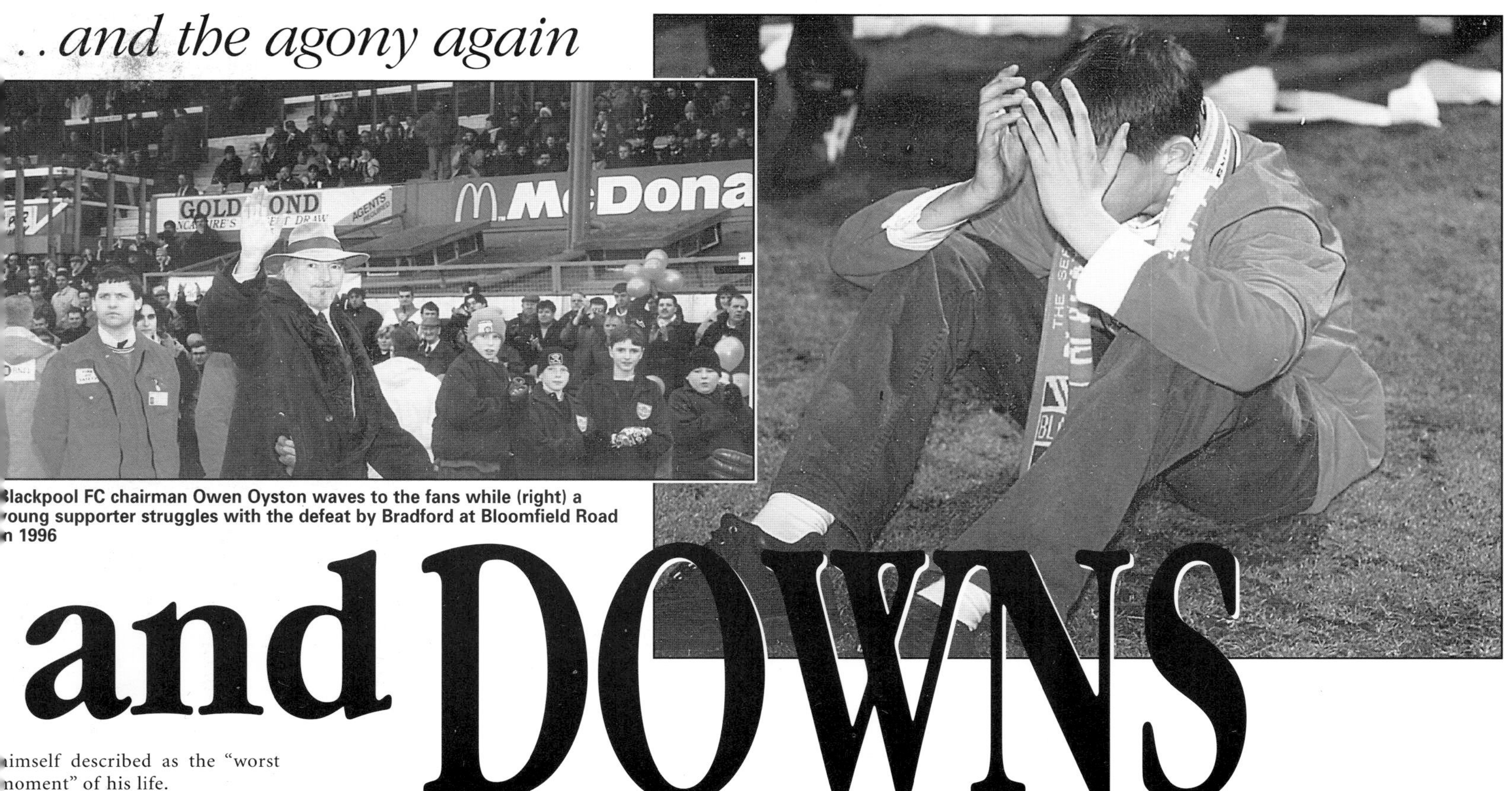


Blackpool FC chairman Owen Oyston waves to the fans while (right) a young supporter struggles with the defeat by Bradford at Bloomfield Road in 1996

# and DOWNS

himself described as the "worst moment" of his life.

Little did anyone connected with the Club then know the catastrophic events which would hit them in the summer of 1996.

Blackpool went into the final weeks of the season seemingly on course for certain promotion, at one stage 14 points clear of rivals Oxford United, with Swindon Town already assured of top spot.

But Blackpool collapsed in spectacular fashion Devon Loch-style in the run-in, to allow Oxford to pip them at the post for the second automatic promotion place.

Even then the Seasiders looked sure to book themselves a return trip to Wembley when winning the first leg of their play-off semi-final 2-0 at Bradford City.

Incredibly, Blackpool again pressed the self-destruct button, beaten 3-0 at home in the second leg on May 15 in front of 9,593 spectators. And before the month was out chairman Owen Oyston was jailed for six years. It was too much for many fans to take.

As Blackpool FC faces the new millennium with an uncertain future it is clear the events of the '90s have shaped the club – perhaps like no other decade.

It hasn't been all doom and gloom on the Fylde Coast sporting scene with the area having more than its fair share of success stories.

Former St Annes Cricket Club star Andrew Flintoff has risen from playing at Highbury Road to the Test arena, ending the decade playing for England in South Africa as well as being firmly established as a key player for Lancashire.

Both Fleetwood and Kirkham Grammar have celebrated the decade with cup visits to Twickenham, the former winning the Provincial Trophy, the latter enjoying their big day out despite losing in the Daily Mail Cup.

In the boxing arena, we have also packed a punch. Blackpool heavyweight Matthew Ellis brought the ABA title back to the resort in 1995.

Ellis has since moved on to the professional arena – next year aiming to bid for the British and Commonwealth title in the paid ranks.

Fleetwood's Jane Couch broke new ground by becoming the first female licensed boxer in Britain – she holds two versions of the world welterweight title.

Slowing the pace down, bowler Brian Duncan established himself as the greatest crown green bowler of all time. Duncan's mastery has been most apparent at the game's most famous venue, Blackpool's Waterloo Hotel green, where he won the title an unprecedented five times.

But if you like your sport a little faster, then how about trying to keep tabs on Preesall speedster Neil Wearden who looks to be going places in a hurry after marking 1999 with his maiden British Championship triumph when winning in Ulster.

The winning squad from Fleetwood RUFC which won the day at Twickenham in 1993

Flying to Victory: Neil Wearden gets his Vauxhall Astra airborne on his way to winning in Ulster and before celebrating at the Black Bull in Preesall

FR 5523

*Chapter Ten*

# *Celebrating the Millennium*

Blackpool students gathered at Bispham High School to rehearse their performance of Our Town, a mixture of drama and dance which they will put on at the Millennium Dome

# Sparkling Showcase at The Dome

THESE Blackpool youngsters geared up for the biggest performance of their lives so far.

A cast of 80 teenagers was hand picked to perform in the Millennium Dome on Friday January 14, 2000, where they told the story of Blackpool past and present.

A professional production team created a sparkling showcase performed at the Dome and using music, lights, sound and movement, the last 200 years of Blackpool came alive in front of the audiences.

The group took inspiration from the entertainment business and other aspects of the resort for their theme.

The project was set up to give every community in the United Kingdom an opportunity to tell their story locally as well as in the Dome.

Blackpool's story was performed in the specially built theatre within the Dome, which features an arch stage and professional sound and lighting rigs and will seat 500 people.

There was an exhibition area and video wall to present a display that will provide further insights into Blackpool and its people. Youngsters from Blackpool's schools became stars for the day when they were filmed voicing their hopes and dreams for the future. The films were then broadcast in the Dome on January 14.

Chief executive of Our Town Story sponsors McDonald's UK, Andrew Taylor said: "A cast of thousands combined to create an epic tale of the UKs history and hopes for the future.

"Every region in the UK looked forward to making their own mark in the millennium."

# Spreading the good word

**THE CHRISTIAN message of the millennium is a simple one.**

**It is that Jesus Christ was born 2,000 years ago to found a faith which has endured and will go on into the 21st century.**

**Members of Cleveleys Park Methodist Church in Cleveleys decided they would mark the millennium not just by special services but by a gift to the church folk of the future – the children.**

**A collection was made so that the Reverend David Tidswell could buy books published by the Scripture Union called Stories for 2,000.**

**These were intended for the 150 children who go to Cleveleys Park.**

**Mr Tidswell explained: "People were so generous we realised we had far more cash than we needed for the original plan. So we decided to make a gift of the books to all the children at the two local schools in our area – Manor Beach and Northfold.**

**Mr Tidswell went into the schools to hand over 800 copies.**

**Mr Tidswell said: "I think the Christian message of the millennium has been overshadowed by all the hype. I know that some of the children enjoyed the book and I hope they will keep their copies as a souvenir of this time of their lives and a reminder of the religious reason for this celebration."**

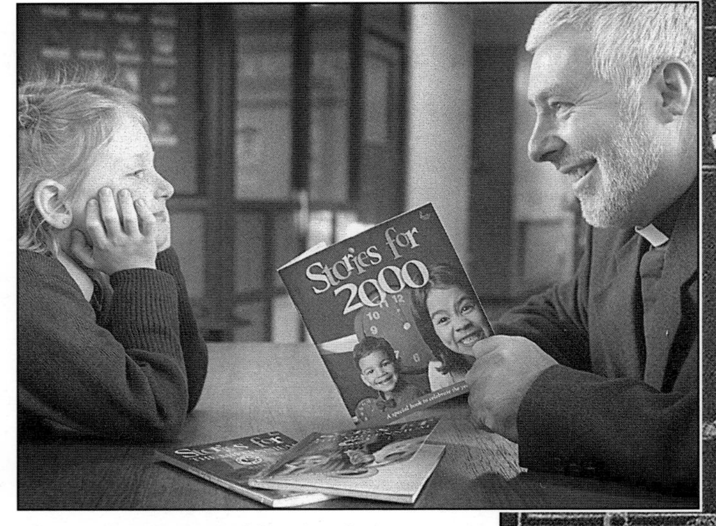


The Rev David Tidswell of Cleveleys Park Methodist Church reads to Manor Beach Primary pupil Jessica Dines from one of the millennium books presented to the school

# The story goes on

MEMORIES have poured in to The Gazette for this final chapter of The Fylde Story.

But of course, this is not the final chapter.

The story of Blackpool and the rest of the Fylde coast area is unfolding everyday in the pages of your favourite newspaper – six nights a week.

And if you are interested in the way we used to be don't miss our regular Memory Lane feature page every Tuesday.

In the Fylde Story local people have their say about some of the events that have shaped the life of the Fylde and its folk over the decades of the 20th century.

Perhaps it should be no surprise that our biggest postbag concerned wartime life and times.

From the memories of a World War One veteran to the poignant story of two brothers whose family was shattered by bombers over Blackpool, the huge conflicts of the century have made the biggest impact on local life.

And everyone's greatest wish as the new age dawns is that future generations will be spared the horrors of global battle.

As the millennium approached, we took a look at the way different parts of our area have changed and how they might develop in the future.

That belongs to the youngsters and we look at some of the young sports fans who are looking forward to winning their way into the 21st century.

## *Putting Christ at the centre*

JESUS, The Light of the World shined down on Blackpool's Millennium visitors.

Working from artist Graham Ogden's detailed sketches, craftsmen at the Rigby Road depot built a 21ft by 18ft eye-catching tableau of Jesus Christ.

The project was under the watchful eye of new Illuminations manager Richard Ryan, promoted from senior Illuminations engineer on the recent retirement of Keith Hall.

Richard said: "I am sure it will be well admired as the centrepiece of the new Millennium Lights section between Central and North piers."

The tableau has been blessed during a special service of dedication inside the workshops by the Bishop of Blackburn, the Right Rev Alan Chesters.

The £10,000 cost of the giant Jesus was helped by donations from churches across Blackpool, Fylde and Wyre.

A spokesman for the Diocese of Blackburn said: "This project marks exciting co-operation between Blackpool Council and Christian churches in Blackpool, Fylde and Wyre.

"Siting such a key symbol of the life and resurrection of Jesus in the centre of Blackpool Illuminations will remind people that Christ remains at the heart of the millennium for millions around the world."

The sequence starts with a single animated star cascading from the heavens to earth.

As it hits the surface of the globe, the world glows and the outline of Jesus, arms outstretched, slowly rises up from Earth against a background of radiating arcs and randomly lit stars.

The message spells out, a word at a time: Jesus The Light Of The World.

# Singing his way to war – aged 15

LIKE others of his generation, Nigel Bernstein of Poulton grew up with echoes of both world wars in his life.

He was 17 in 1971 when his grandfather died but has recorded for posterity some of the old man's recollections of his experience in World War One.

Allen Evans lied about his age to join the army. Many years on he did not dwell on the horror or play up his part in the fighting.

But, thanks to Nigel, he is a powerful witness to a terrible conflict.

Soldier boy Allen Evans was just 15 when he managed to enlist. The first time he tried to persuade the recruiting sergeant to sign him up he was told to go away and grow up a bit. But determined Allen tried again and within weeks he was in France. He was supposed to be 18.

Travelling by train in 1914 the young soldiers sang lustily – one half of the carriage did Tipperary and the rest sang Pack Up Your Troubles at the same time.

Their introduction to the horrors of the front line was brutal.

In the trenches for the first time he and his mates from the Lancashire Fusiliers were told to keep down where the parapet was low. Someone in front of Allen failed to do so and was shot through the head.

Allen recalled: " The first night I spent in the front line the artillery made me so nervous that I could not sleep. Someone gave me my first ever cigarette. I felt more at ease and was able to sleep. I smoked from then on."

Sometimes the trenches were 100 or 200 yards apart. Sometimes so close it seemed that Allied and German men might reach across with their rifles and touch.

One night Allen went on a night raid to capture prisoners for interrogation.

"An advance party had staked out white tapes a foot above the ground leading across No Man's Land. We ran our hand along them so we did not get lost in the dark. If a flare was sent up by the Germans we had to stand stock still. We carried long tubes of explosive called Bangalore Torpedoes to blow a path through the enemy barbed wire. We jumped into their trench and took prisoners. The man who led the raid got a medal."

One night Allen was digging a trench in No Man's Land when he accidentally struck a friend a terrible blow with a pickaxe.

"He was taken away unconscious and I thought I had killed him. Many years later I met him by chance in the Isle of Man and realised he had recovered and survived the fighting."

Appalling losses were suffered at the Battle of the Somme.

Allen and his mates waited in a trench for the order to attack.

" The first wave went over the top and disappeared. We never found out what happened to them. The second wave was machine-gunned in No Man's Land. The third wave was also cut down.

" I was due to go over in the next wave but we were ordered to stay in the trenches."

After the carnage became known at home in Salford, Allen's mother wrote to his CO and asked that he be sent home. He was a seasoned soldier at 17 years of age and still under age. The CO replied that he could not be spared."

Mud like quicksand and the terrible poison gas attacks were among the problems faced by young men like Allen Evans.

"Some men could not stand it and to get out they would lie down, put a rifle to their foot, and shoot off their toe."

The only time Allen was in hospital during the war was when he got tannin poisoning drinking gallons of tea during a spell working in the stores!

He had one home leave and his mother was astonished to see him. He was home for just a weekend.

On the 11th day of the 11th month in 1918 Allen enter a ruined village recently occupied by the Germans.

" They had laid a huge mine all ready to explode so we were lucky not to be killed on the very last day."

Despite all he had seen Allen never doubted the necessity of the war which he believed was necessary because Germany had been the aggressor by invading Belgium. He believed the Allies might well have lost if the Americans had not come in.

Allen Evans started his working life as a trolleyboy on the trams in Salford.

He played rugby league and came to Blackpool in 1926 to join the Borough's own police force.

During World War Two he was the police officer in charge of civil defence and was a long-serving detective in the resort.

He reached the rank of Superintendent.

After retirement he served for years as a Liberal member of Blackpool Council.

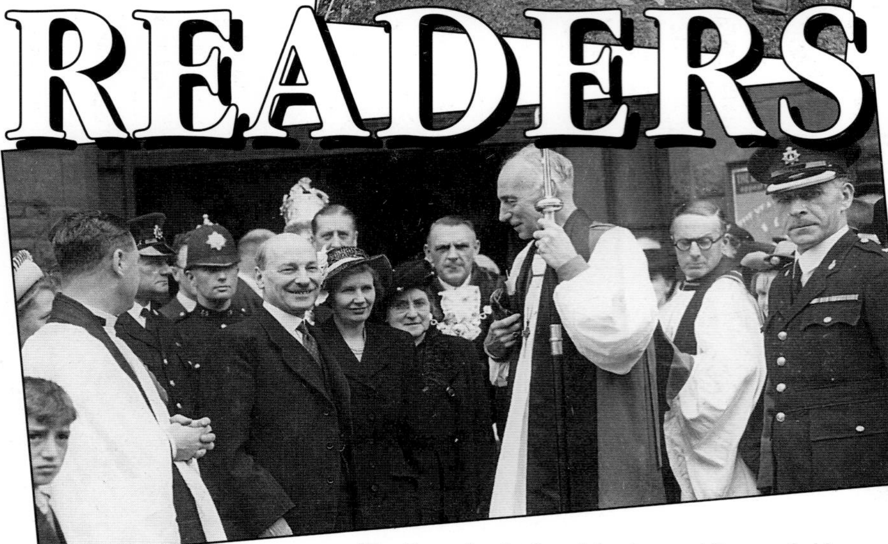


He had played cricket for the police and became an enthusiastic golfer. He was a Freemason.

For many years he and his wife Nellie lived in Lomond Avenue, Marton and had two daughters.

One was Mrs Ida Hampson of Corbridge Close, Marton.

She said: " My father had the quality of leadership. He was a fair man and he was as straight as a die in his dealings with other people."

**Allen Evans (centre top picture)as a soldier – probably soon after he enlisted at 15. At boot camp in 1914 the recruits had no uniform or rifles at first. They slept in circular bell tents with their feet towards the central pole.**
**In 1949, as Superintendent Evans (above) Allen was in charge of security when Prime Minister Clement Atlee was in Blackpool for the Labour Party conference**

# Father was king of carnival

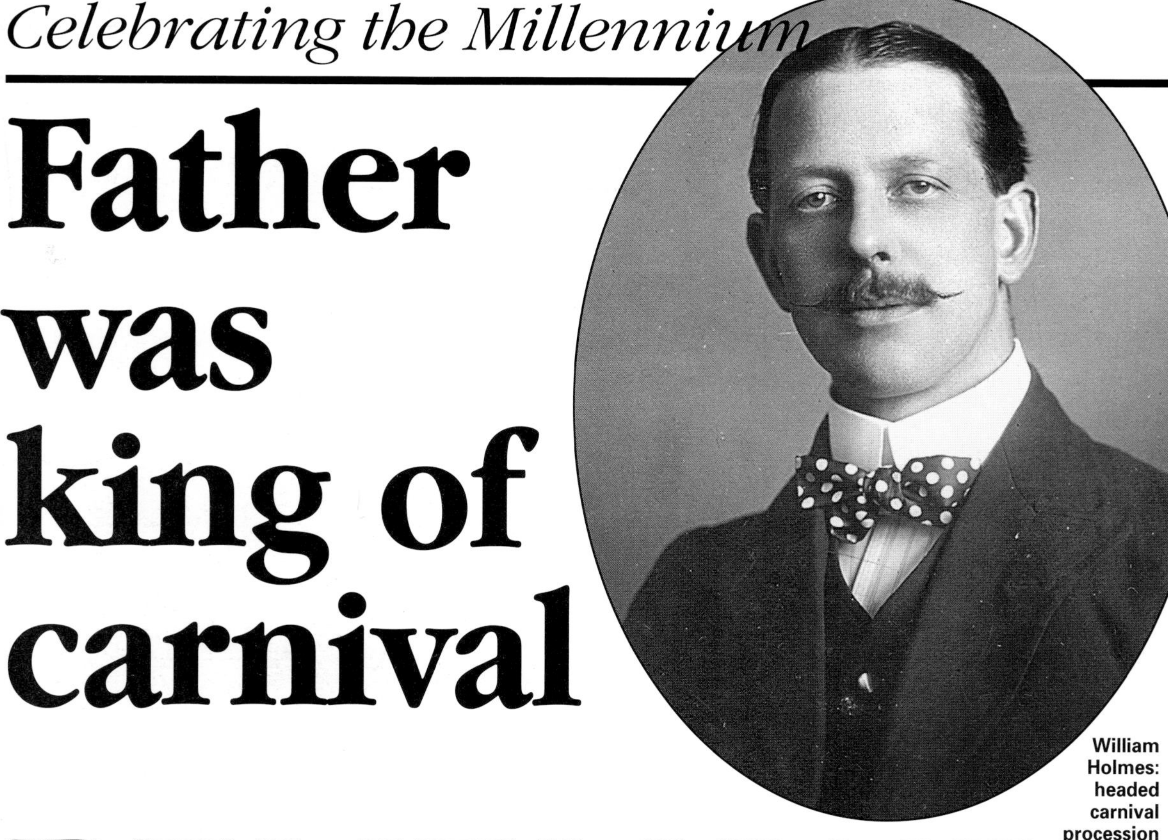

William Holmes: headed carnival procession

REMEMBER

OUR Thirties spotlight on the Blackpool Carnivals set Mrs JOYCE WATSON of Park Road, St Annes thinking about her father and the major role he played in the organisation of these major events.

He was William Holmes who was in business as an ironmonger and was president of the South Shore Traders Association.

He was also a great friend of William Bean, founder of the Pleasure Beach.

Mrs Watson remembered the Carnival times when she was a child attending Devonshire Road School.

In 1923 the school entered the carnival as The Wars of the Roses and she took part.

He father headed the procession in his car.

It was a two-seater Swift with a Dicky seat – additional seating that folded into the back of the vehicle like a boot.

He was dressed as a pierrot but it was inflated pigs bladders, not balloons, that revellers carried in those days.

Behind the car came some of the huge carnival heads – papier mache figures worn by Pleasure Beach workers.

The whole idea had come from Nice in the South of France and some of Blackpool's City Fathers had been down there to see for themselves.

The Blackpool events were successful at creating publicity and drawing in thousands of tourists but they were later marred by bad behaviour which created bad publicity.

However, in the times Mrs Watson recalls, the atmosphere was happy.

One of the French organisers from Nice came to Blackpool and Mr Holmes entertained him.

He also organised a workroom at the No3 Hotel where a team of seamstresses made costumes for the Carnival – and dresses for the ladies of the Holmes family to attend The Cotton Ball at the Winter Gardens.

In 1924 Mr Holmes opened a shop at the corner of Alexandra Road and Lytham Road and won a £500 prize from the Hardware Trade Journal.

HILDA HEATON of Beardshaw Avenue, Blackpool, has a souvenir book about the 1923 Carnival.

Her father in law is pictured in charge of a float from the railway company depicting Stephenson's locomotive The Rocket.

Hilda recalls: " The Pleasure Beach float was Noah's Ark with truly weird animals all making a gosh awful noise all along the Promenade."

Mrs DOROTHY NEWTON of Dawlish Avenue, Grange Park remembers when she took part in a Carnival parade and had to lead a live lamb .

She was placed near the front of the procession and moved along rather too quickly which meant she got mixed up with the band that was leading the parade!

After moving to Blackpool from Cleckheaton in Yorkshire with her family when she was a child Mrs RENEE FRANCE lived in Clifton Street.

For years it has been part of Blackpool's shopping centre but then their home had a front garden.

Born in 1911 she was at Claremont School at the time of the 1923 Carnival and is pictured in pierrot costume with her classmates ready to take part.

Mrs France now lives in Victoria Road, Poulton . She lived in Churchtown for many years and her late husband, Reg France, was the Lancashire County archivist for many years.

Before her marriage Mrs France worked at Woolworths on the Promenade.

She said: "In the days when everything was sixpence in the old money we used to sell cigarette cases that looked as though they were made of silver. Some had a picture of the Tower and others the Big Wheel. We had to order them 12 months in advance because they came from Japan."

Back in the 30s the Woolworth staff had to work 15 hours on a Saturday as part of their normal duties.

On New Years Day volunteers came in for a stock taking session. They got a 50p bonus in return.

Mrs France recalls: " It was hard work and long hours sometimes but it was a happy place to work and I made lifelong friends there."

All dressed up and somewhere to go. Mrs Renee France and school friends ready for the carnival parade

Workers at Woolworths in Blackpool nearly 70 years ago

Gordon and David Lea returned to Seed Street, Blackpool where they lived during the war when their house was bombed. Another survivor was a family pet bird, rescued from the rubble of the explosion

# READERS

# The two little boys who lost their mum

A BLACKPOOL pensioner has recalled the tragic night in Blackpool when German bombs robbed him and his brother of their mother and grandmother.

Gordon Lea and his brother David had a lucky escape themselves when the blitz came to Blackpool and blasted through a little street of terraced houses near the bus station.

But their relatives were not so fortunate. And the tragedy meant years of heartache for the brothers before their father was able to return home and care for them.

The family lived in Seed Street off Talbot Road and Mrs Mabel Lea worked nights at the Winter Gardens while her husband was in the army.

The boys were cared for by their grandmother Mrs Ada Howarth.

One night in September, 1940 Mrs Lea tucked up her sons in bed. Gordon was 10 and David five.

She went to work and when the boys were asleep their grandmother went to the home of a friend who lived just two doors away.

Gordon remembers waking up around 10.45 and he could hear the sound of the coal fire being poked downstairs. He realised his mother had returned from the Winter Gardens and went back to sleep.

Mrs Lea then went to the neighbour's to join her mother when 10 minutes later a stick of bombs fell across the nearby railway tracks and the little houses.

Gordon recalls: "There was an almighty bang and I sat up in bed. I could see the flames reflected on the wall through the window."

Then he realised the bed was covered in fragments of mortar and dust.

The boys sat there wondering what was happening.

Gordon said: "We weren't really frightened but then two men came into the house. It was lit by gas and they shone a torch on us. They wrapped us in blankets and took us to another house. When we got outside we saw the flames."

The next day the boys learned the terrible news.

Gordon reflects: "If Mum had been 10 minutes later getting home she would have missed it all.

"Perhaps it was fate but whatever it was we lost our Mum. People should never forget what happened in the war."

The boys were cared for by various aunts and uncles but later they were separated and had to live at two different addresses far apart in the resort.

At the age of 14 Gordon had to live in lodgings and the loss of his mother hit him hard then.

It was five long years before their father came back and the three of them made a new home in Grange Road, Layton.

Gordon , now 70 said: "Dad remarried and his wife had a daughter so it was like a family again. It was a happy ending."

He now lives on the Sunnyhurst Residential estate off Highfield Road, South Shore while his brother David, 65, lives in Torsway, Layton.

Mrs Shirlee Gledhill and her identical twin sister Mrs Betty Oliver went to Thames Road School, South Shore, during the Second

World War after moving from Leeds.

They lived in Withnell Road.

They were the first of three generations to attend Thames Road including the present day.

The twins looked so alike that even they could not tell themselves apart on photographs.

This led to a lot of confusion and practical jokes like swopping boyfriends.

As children however, Shirlee and Betty had to leave the school when an air raid alert came – not forgetting their gas masks which were carried in cardboard boxes that could hang round your neck on a string.

Those that lived a long distance from Thames Road went to the homes of other girls nearby until the all-clear sounded.

Later the twins joined the junior branch of the Womens Royal Air Corps. The uniform was: airforce blue shirt, black tie, grey skirt, grey jacket and a Glengarry-style cap.

Shirlee, of Hathaway, Marton, says the Junior WRACs met twice a week at Waterloo Road School, South Shore to learn skills including marching drill, aircraft recognition and Morse code.

She remembers: "We tried, without success, to blow our bugles. Our Mam sent us to the beach to practise because we made an horrendous noise."

In 1945 they joined other north west teenagers at a garden party held at the Cheshire home of Lady Leverhulme for junior WRAC members.

Betty now lives in Southport.

When we published this photograph in the Forties edition of The Fylde Story we wondered where The Mount was.

A Gazette reader thinks the picture was taken in Exchange

Street, North Shore.

The Mount was kept b[y] Thomas and Bertha Wright wh[o] retired to Laxey in the Isle [of] Man. Later Mrs Wright lived i[n] Sandringham Avenue, Thornto[n] until her death in 1997.

# Resort's RAF regiments

RESEARCH into the way Blackpool coped with thousands of RAF personnel during the Second World War has been carried out by two local historians.

Robert Gregson of Albany Road, Ansdell, is a retired lecturer at Blackpool and the Fylde College who carried out a study of wartime RAF photographic training in Blackpool.

Some of the training in the resort was recorded in a different way.

The war artist Charles Ernest Cunbdall painted The Morse School showing morse code training in the Spanish Hall of the Winter Gardens. This is at the Imperial War Museum.

And the Polish artist Felix Topolski drew his fellow countrymen on a church parade on the seafront in the summer of 1940.

Top ranking RAF chiefs praised Blackpool landladies for looking after the chaps but it wasn't all plain sailing between the RAF and the council.

Plans to turn the Pelham Mount Club on Park Road into an officers mess were turned down at the town hall. The club was much used by staff from the Transport Department.

Stan Rowland of St Martins Road, South Shore, has traced many locations all over Blackpool.

They ranged from the cellars of the Gynn Inn where gas mask lectures were given to a car showroom in Church Street where coffins were stored. The Tower itself was used for radar and radio work.

Stan discovered that RAF personnel going off duty from huts which had been placed on the flat roof of the tower buildings had to pass the backstage entrance of the Tower Ballroom.

Many broke the rules and slipped in unnoticed for a dance instead of paying their ninepence admission.

But the recruits were expected back in their billets by 10pm or they had to face the wrath of the famous Blackpool landlady.

# REMEMBER

Evelyn Coleman looks back on her memories as a bus conductress during the 1940s

# On the buses

DIGGING out a snowbound bus in the blackout on the way from Poulton to Blackpool is recalled by former conductress Mrs EVELYN COLEMAN of Kingsland Grove, Blackpool.

There were some bad winters during the Forties and Evelyn remembers holding a torch while the driver dug out the wheels after borrowing a shovel from a house nearby.

She remembers: "I nearly wept that night. My feet were wet and frozen when we arrived back from our trip along country roads where the snow was piled high against the hedgerows."

By the next day it was all forgotten and Blackpool Transport kept rolling to get the war workers to the factories on time.

The bus crews walked to and from work – ready to start at 6.30am and sometimes going home at midnight.

But Evelyn recalls summer days on the Staining run.

The drivers wife supplied delicious currant pasties and the crew had a 15-minute break for a flask of tea and a snack in sunny Staining.

She says: "The first time I went on the Blackpool-Fleetwood route it was pitch dark, no street lights lit, head lamps dimmed against any German bombers that might be lurking around.

" In time I grew to recognise every bump and turn just as I imagine a blind person would."

Evelyn remembers the navy blue uniform and the fact that everyone always wore their regulation caps on their heads.

The buses were busy and she often had to signal to the driver that the vehicle was full by ringing the bell three times.

The driver was isolated in his cab at the front and often used to sing to himself as he drove along ≠ no one could hear him!

Evelyn was sacked in a row over being 10 minutes late because she had walked to work in wellingtons which had blistered her foot!

It was the only time in a varied working life that she was dismissed but she looks back on happy days on the buses.

MRS DOROTHY ROBINSON of Drummond Avenue, Layton, took a flight in the last Wellington bomber made at the Vickers factory on Squires Gate Lane.

She recalls: "We stood up inside the plane and looked out through the dome in the middle as the plane flew round the Tower – it was so thrilling!"

She had been working as a bookbinder at the firm of Ayre and Seniors and reckoned her wage of 155 pence for a 48 hour week was a good deal for the time.

Then Dorothy was directed to work at the bomber factory.

She enjoyed her time at Stanley Park best – now Blackpool Zoo – where she remembers a happier atmosphere than at Squires Gate.

Mrs ROBINSON met her husband Fred in 1945 when she was working at the Clifton Hotel and he dropped in for a beer.

The couple married just over a year later and had four children. Fred died last year.

Mrs QUEENIE HANCOCK of Chepstow Court on Clifton Drive, South Shore made her debut performance as a pianist during World war 2 – and she didn't get a chance to rehearse.

By the time she was 15 Queenie had studied piano for five years and become an Associate of the London College of Music.

The hall of Holy Trinity church in Dean Street, the parish church of South Shore, was pressed into service for RAF duties.

It was also used to entertain hundreds of RAF men stationed in the resort.

Queenie helped out making tea in the kitchen but she admired the professional entertainers who trod the stage of the well-equipped hall.

Then, one Sunday night, there was a technical hitch which held up the start of the show.

Queenie was asked to go front of curtain and keep the boys in blue amused with some singalong songs.

She said: " Imagine the feelings of a 16-year-old girl stepping through the curtains to be met by the sight of row upon row of blue uniforms and 400 pairs of eyes gazing up in anticipation. Then a great rush of cheering came from all those delightful men – what an exhilarating moment."

After five years of Chopin and Beethoven Queenie set to work on Roll Out the Barrel and Run Rabbit Run – later the signature tune of Dad's Army.

So Queenie became an artiste like the rest.

Aircraft builders at the Stanley Park factory

She played a warm up spot every Sunday and was invited to take part in many other musical events and to play piano in local hotels which were billets for the servicemen.

Although he now lives in Bolton-le-Sands, PETER NORRIS spent the war years as a pupil at Waterloo Road primary school.

He started there on the day after war was declared.

And he lists some of the things he recalls from those times in Blackpool.

Watching soldiers camped where Palatine High School is now

Seeing a collection of huts at the terminus of the No13 bus where British Home Stores is now.

Sheltering under the stairs with mother during Blackpool's mercifully few air raids.

Travelling on single deck busses with a gas bag on the roof and double deckers towing a gas-producing trailer to save precious petrol.

Childrens show at The Empire cinema on Hawes Side Lane which cost two old pence to go in and one penny for a bottle of pop.

Missing school in the heavy snowfall of 1940

Undergoing a gas mask test in a special van which visited the school. Peter's friend's mask didn't fit properly and he came out suffering the effects of tear gas.

Food parcels from America. They were delivered to school and divided up for each pupil.

Sharing a banana with 10 other children. There were none in the wartime shops but Peter's uncle, in the Merchant Navy, brought a few home.

GATHERED IN: Through the centuries the church collected payments called tithes and used some of the value to help the sick and needy. Tithe goods like corn were stored in this tithebarn where the Teanlowe car park now stands in Poulton

READERS

# Happy days in old Poulton

THE days when Poulton was a market town surrounded by farming country rather than bricks and mortar are recalled by Mrs ADA O'HARA of Juniper Close, Preesall.

She and her family moved from Manchester to a bungalow at Highfurlong near the site of the present Collegiate High School just after World War One.

With her two sisters and their brother she walked to school near the Castle Gardens pub.

When the Smith family of Blackpool started a bus service the fare was half an old penny.

Ada says: "We only used it when it was raining. Sometimes the driver stopped to give us a lift."

Ancient St Chad's Church was shrouded then in a thick belt of trees full of noisy crows.

Among the residents of a lodging house in an alley nearby was a World War One veteran suffering from shellshock. Always muffled in layers of clothes he trundled an old pram and sometimes let it roll down the street causing traffic chaos.

The streets were often full of animals being herded to the auction market behind the Golden Ball hotel.

One day a bull literally finished up in the china shop – Hartley's china shop – but the farmer backed it out.

When Ada wanted a bike, on sale for £2.50 at Brimelows, her father said she could have it if she could get the price down to £2 – which she managed to do.

Near Ada's home were farms kept by the Poole and Drinkall families and at harvest time the workers ate in the fields. Local children like Ada helped out too and took food and drink to the workers.

They were happy times but not when Foot and Mouth disease struck and the farmer and his wife went away for a few days while their dairy herd was destroyed and burned.

Mrs VIVA SEVERNS (formerly Midgley) of Limerick Road, Bispham, has happy memories of the Tower Ballet shows at the Tower years ago produced by Pauline Rivers. The star of the youthful cast was "Little Emmie."

Another favourite was the Childrens Pantomime which Viva and her brother appeared in.

She was born next door to Pablo's Ice Cream Parlour in Back Charnley Road.

Viva recalls: "Mr Pablo wore a white stetson hat and drove a large American car.

"He was very generous. At the end of the season all the local children got free ice cream, the staff had a party and he took them on holiday – everything provided."

Viva was paid sixpence a week (two and a half pence) to appear in song booths on the Promenade run by impresario Lawrence Wright and her brother played drums there too.

The crowd thought she had volunteered to step up on the platform and sing to promote the sales of sheet music.

Mrs MILDRED HALL of Bostonway, Marton, says the origins of Harcourt Road, South Shore, lie in a cart track known as Piccadilly around 70 years ago.

Old-style wooden caravans and huts sited there were replaced by houses and bungalows and the name was changed to Harcourt Road off St Annes Road.

Mrs Hall remembers that in those days Blackpool seemed like a ghost town in winter and many who had seasonal jobs were thrown out of work and suffered great hardship.

Men received food vouchers in return for three days a week spent digging in Stanley Park.

At Christmas, the Chief Constable's Clothing Fund issued poor families with clothes and shoes.

She remembers Parkinsons, the local building firm, getting 200 applications for one job.

Mrs Hall writes: "I think Blackpool has come a long way since then but the old times were happier – no grumbling, stealing or drunkenness and everyone at peace with one another."

MemoriesS of happy holidays in Blackpool when she was growing up in Oldham are recalled by Mrs MARIAN HESKETH.

Mrs Hesketh of Bromsgrove Avenue, Bispham, has lived in Blackpool since 1956 when her husband took a job at British Nuclear Fuels at Salwick near Kirkham.

She published her own book of childhood recollections and her experiences must have been shared by hundreds of thousands of others.

Oldham shut down for the Wakes Week holiday and everyone went to Blackpool.

Marian's family stayed on the apartments system where they bought their own food and the landlady cooked it.

She said: "My ambition was to afford full board because their food always looked more appetising tha ours!"

On the sands the childre watched Punch and Judy and rod on the donkeys. In Fairyland on th Golden Mile they travelled i chariots through the Fairy Grotto.

On the eve of war the famil stayed at a guest house where th husband worked for Blackpo Council.

He came in the diningroom on night looking tired . . .

" What a day we've had," he an nounced. "Trying to get the Towe under the pier out of the way o Hitler – but we couldn't manage it!

# Wartime snapshots

Men of the 405 Coast Battery rigging equipment at Fleetwood. Off duty, other soldiers posted to the port pose with a friend

THESE wartime photographs were taken in Fleetwood. According to a note on the back, the young lady was a holiday-maker. That shot was taken somewhere near the seafront boating lake. But whoever sent us the pictures enclosed no covering letter. They were posted in the Teesside area.

# REMEMBER

## Family shop rolls on

A PIECE of Blackpool history is set to drive into the 21st century. It is a mobile shop which was operated for years in the Marton area by the Banks family.

In 1980 Uncle Arthur Banks died when thieves broke into his home on School Road, Marton.

Paperwork relating to the 1935 vintage shop vehicle went missing.

No one knows which firm built the shop bodywork on to the Bedford chassis but the old engine is still going strong.

The mobile shop now belongs to Joe and Ethel Davis of Garstang Road, Pilling, who saw it at a vintage vehicle rally and decided they had to add it to their collection. The couple already own a variety of tractors and memorabilia of the past including a 1904 fairground organ. They are strong supporters of the Fylde Countrylife Preservation Society which has a museum at Farmer Parr's World of Animals at Fleetwood.

Apart from some work on the brakes and a bit more restoration on the shop section, the Bedford is ready to roll for next year's summer season of events.

Mrs Davis said: "I think there will be a lot of interest in the Banks family shop."

A reference book on historic Bedford vehicles says it is probably unique.

## The day Geoff took a trunk call on the forecourt

WHEN former Blackpool councillor Geoff Silcock tells people about the day he met some elephants in Talbot Road they sometimes look a bit sceptical.

But Geoff, of Bristol Avenue, Bispham, really did meet the gentle giants one morning in 1949.

After leaving school at 15 he started work at Beaumont Brothers garage opposite the old North Station goods yard. The Flamingo club now stands on the site.

Arriving for work one morning he was told to remove the battery from a car parked outside and it was when he looked up from his work under the bonnet that he found the biggest elephant he had ever seen standing just six feet away.

Geoff remembers: "I shouted to my boss, Maurice Beaumont, who was inside the garage that I was pinned in by an elephant. He told me not to be cheeky and get on with the job."

One by one, five other elephants came down Talbot Road and each linked its trunk with the tail of the one in front.

By this time Maurice had come to the garage door and told Geoff not to move.

Geoff said he wasn't planning to.

Suddenly a man came running up to the garage asking to use the phone.

Geoff said: "I told him not to bother about the phone but to get rid of the monsters."

The elephants were in transit from Germany to the Tower Circus and had wandered off after arriving by train because their trainer had fallen between the platform and the moving goods wagons and lost a leg.

While he was being looked after, his charges went walkabout.

The final chapter in the story was also tragic. After the summer season the elephants set off again by train in December this time for Birmingham.

But Tarka the lead elephant, went berserk as the train neared Preston.

The animal, said to be 50 years old and worth £3,000, seized a keeper in its trunk and threw him bodily through the window of the van.

The creature smashed up the van and had to be put down. This was done by soldiers from Fulwood Barracks who shot the elephant dead. Animal rights activists demanded an inquiry into the incident.

# The day that Ann became limbo champ

READERS

## ...and met Lonnie Donegan!

MEMORIES of happy days on holiday in Blackpool came flooding back for ANN HAYNES.

Cleveleys-born Ann lived in Fleetwood as a child and still has relatives there including her mother, Mrs Eleanor Green of Pharos Street.

But the family moved to Manchester when Ann was five and she grew up and married there.

She said: " We came to Blackpool for a week's holiday about 1962 when I was 22.

"I did judo three times a week and I was into dancing so I entered a competition on the beach for limbo dancing."

Ann proved agile enough to pass under the bar at just 22 inches. She won a trophy and £25 cash in the contest run by a national newspaper.

She also met showbiz star Lonnie Donegan who presented the prizes.

Ann, who has travelled the world since those days working as a nanny recalls: They were happy days. At that time you could have a lot of fun with £25!"

## *Memories come flooding back for Stephen*

STEPHEN McCULLOUGH is now the Field Sales Manager in the Gazette's Display Advertising department.

But back in 1979 he made the front page when he was just eight years old.

Stephen, of Kipling Drive, Marton, was out for a walk with his grandfather after torrential rain had flooded the soccer pitch in Lancaster Road where he should have been playing for his team of those days Clifton Rangers.

Instead, Stephen ended up posing for a Gazette picture to illustrate the floods.

He remembers: "The water was so deep across the field there was a man in a canoe paddling along."

## The days when Michael Morley minded the family oyster stall

WHEN he saw this photograph by Blackpool lensman Alfred Gregory, Gazette reader Pete Boland realised he was looking at one of his old schoolmates.

He believes the youngster in the photograph is Michael Morley who lived in the Ibbison Street area and attended St John Vianney RC Secondary school in Glastonbury Avenue, Marton.

Pete, who lives in Marton, left the school 37 years ago when he was 15.

Pete said: "Mike came from quite a big family and was slightly older than me. I last saw him in a local pub about four years ago. I think he works in the building trade – maybe as a roofer."

The name on the mobile seafood stall in the picture is Morley so perhaps Michael was working for his father or another relative.

Pete said: "Lots of families around Ibbison Street in those days worked in jobs to to do with the seafront or the Golden Mile – on stalls, on the sands, the landaus or whatever."

Pictures by Alfred Gregory were featured in the 1960s edition of The Fylde Story.

Alfred, then a Blackpool travel agent, took photographs of life in the resort around the '50s and '60s.

A top mountaineer he was part of the successful British Everest expedition and later became a professional photographer.

# REMEMBER

# Round and round on the re-built Big Dipper

IRVING and MAUREEN ANDERSON of Clifton Drive, Blackpool were in the cast of the Ice Parade shows at the Pleasure Beach in the 1950s.

They recall standing on Harrowside Bridge and watching a fire which wrecked the Big Dipper ride.

Irving recalls: "We were understandably relieved when we realised that it wasn't the Ice Drome which was on fire."

There were more than 100 skaters in the show in those days, when the Pleasure Beach was run by Leonard Thompson.

After the Big Dipper was rebuilt some of the skaters were invited to take a trip on it along with Mr Thompson and his wife Doris.

The carriages went round not once but about 10 times and photographs were taken as the cars plunged down the first steep drop after rounding the new tower.

Mr and Mrs Anderson were right in the middle of the picture and a blown up copy is now on display in the Coasters American Diner in the Ocean Boulevard section of the Pleasure Beach.

Irving says: " All our family, five grandchildren included, are always proudly pointing this out to friends and relatives when they visit Blackpool and dine at Coasters."

Trophies of a champion. Blackpool boxer Ronnie Clayton with the belts he won in the ring. A portrait of the fighter as a young man hangs behind him

# When soccer stars meant something else

DON RUTTER of Common Edge Road, Marton, remembers meeting other showbiz personalities – on the British Rail soccer pitch in Hampton Road, South Shore.

He was then a fireman on steam trains and recalls Sunday morning friendly matches against the likes of Tommy Steele, Frankie Vaughan and Don Arroll who later compered the hugely-popular TV variety show Sunday Night at the London Palladium.

Don said: "When they built a clubhouse at Hampton Road stars came down to put on a cabaret that night. The singer Yana did the actual opening ceremony."

Born in Manchester, Don finished his schooldays at Highfield, South Shore, then a secondary modern school.

In 1952 the headmaster was George Ford and a Miss Bloomer was in charge of the girls department.

At 15 he worked for Loxham's Flying Services at Squires Gate. Two of the flying instructors were called 'Dixie' Dean and Cliff Ashley and they let Don ride in the back seat on flying lessons after he had swung the prop to start the Auster aircraft.

Their most famous pupil was the American film star Bonar Colleno. He later played a flyer in The Way To The Stars with John Mills.

Don remembers George Whittaker who sold motorcycles on Cookson Street hiring an Auster from Loxhams for a trip to France.

He ran into bad weather and tried to land in a field.

But the wing tip caught a tree and the plane flipped over and caught fire. Luckily, George and his passenger escaped.

Don later worked for George making Igloo Speed Freezer ice cream machines in a workshop in Back Cunliffe Road.

He adds: "I wonder if any of those machines are still around?"

# READERS

# The champ who ran home

ON a winter's night 65 years ago a Blackpool schoolboy entered a boxing contest at Blackpool's Central Workingmens Club.

Ronnie Clayton – who died in December 1999 – didn't tell his parents where he was going when he left the house that night but he told them where he'd been.

The plucky little boxer – his feet did not reach the floor from the stool in the corner of the ring – ran home to tell his family how he'd won three bouts to become boys champion of the tourney.

Ronnie, who trained as a sheet metal worker alongside his father Jack and served in the Fleet Air Arm, was the first Blackpool boxer to fight for a national belt.

He was British featherweight champion from 1947 to 1954, British Empire featherweight champion 1947 to 1951, and European featherweight champion 1947 to 1948.

Later he ran his own gymnasium in Princess Street.

Blackpool beauty queen Julie Duckworth, 19, became Miss England 1980. The only Fylde girl ever to win the title, she went on to compete in the Miss Universe contest in Seoul, Korea.She is the eldest of three beauty queen sisters. Middle sister Jane became Queen of the Lights in 1980, and youngest sister Dawn was Miss Wyre.

# *Doris was the first Blackpool Hotel Queen*

MRS DORIS COLLINSON of Glenmere Crescent, Norbreck, made history in 1952 when she was chosen as the first-ever Blackpool Hotel queen.

The contest was run by the Blackpool Hotel and Guest House Association.

Then, in 1953, she won the all-England Hotel Queen title and held it for 12 months.

The most important event of the 1950s for Doris was the birth of her only son but she also recalls going to the Royal Command Performance show at the Opera House with her sister Joan and seeing the Queen and the Duke of Edinburgh there.

Her father in law was a member of the orchestra that night.

# *Out for the Count as Jeffery keeps a star's secret*

**Count Basie, with cigarette, in his Blackpool dressing room**

JEFFERY MACHIN of Poulton Road, Blackpool, never forgot the time he met the great jazz musician Count Basie in the Fifties.

Jeffery worked at Sharples music shop at the corner of Church Street and Adelphi Street and helped to maintain 20 pianos kept in an underground store at the Winter Gardens and used for various shows.

He and colleague Natt Boyer were paid overtime to attend Sunday evening concerts at the Opera House and Palace Theatre to make sure the pianos were all right.

Jeffery was watching the Count Basie band in action from the wings at the Palace when the Count left the keyboard and slipped off stage for a smoke!

He lit up under a large No Smoking sign then asked Jeffery: "Will you hold this cigarette for me? I have to play a few more bars."

He must have realised that Jeffery was worried about the strict No Smoking rule and added: "Just tell them it's mine. I'm sure they don't want me to bring the whole band off so I can have a smoke!"

Jeffery said: "He went back to the piano and I, full of confidence, had a puff of his cigarette!"

# REMEMBER

# 'Look, but don't touch' on the Golden Mile girlie show

**John Gavaghan (right) with owner Jimmy Ainsworth at his rifle range, and John with pal Colin Fisher**

WHEN JOHN GAVAGHAN got a job running the Montmartre Theatre girlie show on the Golden Mile his boss gave him a warning . . .

John, a red-blooded 21-year-old was told: "If you touch the girls – you're dead!"

The strict instructions came from Wilf Probin, owner of the show.

John recalls: "He was a very powerfully-built man and when he said this to me he moved in really close. He was not a man to be ignored – and he wasn't joking."

Business boomed at the Montmartre Theatre – housed in one of the few buildings that still retains a vestige of the old-look Golden Mile.

To get a pitch, or crowd, John went outside on the forecourt with one of the girls from the cast.

He said: "She had very long legs and was dressed in next to nothing. She wore a blindfold and I carried a large sword."

The holiday hundreds who surged past wondered what this was all about and they never found out because it was just showman's hocus pocus to get them inside.

John recalls: "I've seen the crowd build up so much there were people all across the Prom and on to the tram tracks. It interfered with traffic and trams and every now and again the police booked me for obstruction. But they always gave me a sporting chance – they let the audience go inside first!"

The punters paid half a crown to enter the theatre.

They saw a series of tableaux in which naked girls posed on stage.

The law said they must not move or the act was illegal.

John said: "The tried every trick to make them move or laugh and that included firing pea shooters and catapults at them."

Apart from the four leggy lovelies there was a middle-aged woman named Sonia, whose body served to make the younger girls look more attractive, and a midget called Beryl.

In those more gullible days the crowd were told her diminutive size resulted from the debauchery of her parents.

Sometimes, things got out of hand with the audience.

Says John: "The worst was the boozer's pitch – about 10pm at night when they were full of beer."

During the show he stood at the front by the stage and acted as master of ceremonies.

"I had a lever which dropped a steel shutter closing off the stage like a guillotine, and keeping the girls from the crowd. I often had to use it. I then escaped through a security door."

This left the audience to the tender mercies of Freddie, a giant of a man who was stationed by the exit doors.

When the shutter dropped he kicked the doors open and ordered them out – perhaps 200 people. Some were not happy that the show had been cut short but Freddie brooked no argument.

John said: "Lads from the south of England were the worst. They always wanted to join in on stage."

John served his apprenticeship at Jimmy Ainsworth's rifle range on Central Pier.

Punters fired .22 rifles at targets but when Glaswegians arrived there could be trouble.

John said: "Some of the girls had razor blades hidden in their hats for use in a fight. The boys loaded the rifles then sprayed the booths like a machine gun. It was hair-raising but luckily for everyone else on the pier the rifles were chained down so they could not be turned away from the targets and hit anyone. We normally did not give prizes – it was a test of skill. But we always gave the Glaswegians a pack of cigarettes and they went away happy."

John's pal Colin Fisher worked on the nearby bow and arrow stall and they went down to London together. John got a job selling vacuum cleaners door to door but Colin came home after a few days.

But there was another attraction in London for John.

It was the home of Eve, one of the girls from the show and the couple got married.

Now John lives in South Croydon. A career in sales led him to his own company. He sold out and retired.

He says: "I have family in Blackpool and I've enjoyed recalling those days on the Golden Mile. They were happy times."

**Freeport Leisure (left) draws millions of visitors to Fleetwood with a shopping and leisure village on the old docklands site. Above and below: contrasting designs for the shape of a supermarket yet to come for the port**

# This way to

## *WYRE*

THE Sixties saw the beginning of a building boom in Wyre with areas like Thornton, Cleveleys, Poulton, Preesall and other Over Wyre villages beginning to expand for the first time in decades.

The dream of a retirement bungalow at the seaside fuelled the growth which also created the Larkholme and Rossall estates at Fleetwood.

But the port was hard hit when the distant water fishing industry collapsed. For generations Fleetwood had been all about fishing and the town went through a decade of decline before government grants were secured and a partnership involving local companies began to create a different atmosphere and hopes of a brighter future.

The Lofthouse family, makers of Fisherman's Friend lozenges, proved major benefactors to the local community.

And Freeport Leisure draws millions of visitors to Fleetwood with a shopping and leisure village on the old docklands site.

Now, two development companies are bidding to rebuild the Cop Lane area at the heart of Fleetwood.

This could see a Morrisons or an Asda supermarket built there.

Down the road in Poulton the ancient market town could see major changes with plans for a 600-home private estate and the possibility of a supermarket nearer the town centre.

Cleveleys has become a busy shopping area but thousands of jobs have gone with the rundown of the ICI Hillhouse site at Thornton.

However, a bold new plan for housing and shopping on part of the site has been mooted.

Across the Wyre, country towns like Garstang are looking to increased earnings from tourism as more and more people seek to explore the countryside.

## *BLACKPOOL*

A MULTI-MILLION pound redevelopment plan for a big chunk of Central Blackpool is set to give the resort a hugely different look in the new millennium.

London-based Chelverton Properties has a scheme for a 14-acre development in the Talbot Road area.

It would see an end to the Talbot Road bus station, nightspots like the Flamingo and the Tache/Barny's and pubs like the Wheatsheaf and the Hop Inn.

In their place would be an eight-screen cinema with restaurant and other entertainment facilities, a food store and a giant car park.

Like other, similar schemes in the Fylde, hundreds of new jobs are promised if the project goes ahead in a couple of years time.

Blackpool has had to face tough challenges in the latter part of the 20th century.

High unemployment, areas of poor housing, declining trade in the town centre and a downturn in traditional seaside holidays.

The resort has attracted millions of pounds worth of government grants aimed at creating jobs through effective training and improving housing conditions.

And hoteliers who have invested to upgrade their hotels hang on to traditional holiday business. They point to the personal and friendly service they can provide.

But the resort has seen a growth in American-style lodge-type accommodation.

The traditional Wakes Weeks are long gone and the Illuminations period is now a vital earner.

But Blackpool still has its reputation for fresh air and fun and for top class entertainment.

Not to be left behind, even the airport has taken off with the addition of a brand-new terminal.

**Pedestrianisation underway earlier this year in Church Street at the heart of Blackpool. On the right, the town gets its first multiplex cinema – with plans for more . . .**

The new elegant shopping centre at St Annes Square

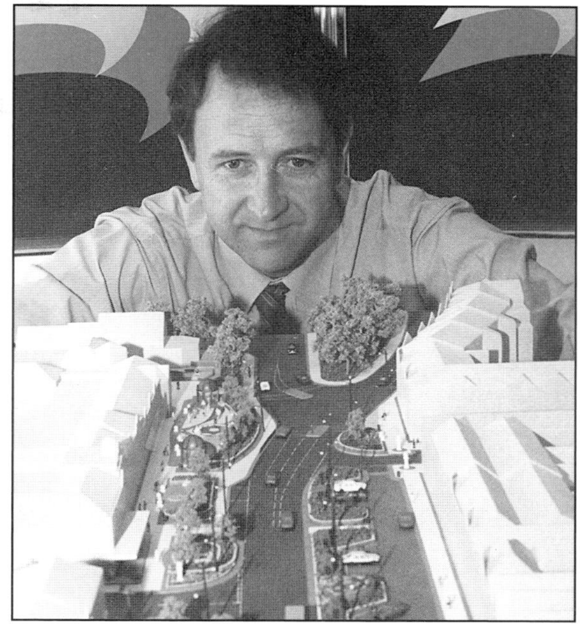

Chief Development Control Officer Paul Drinnan with a model of plans for the future of St Annes centre

# the future

Seashells in the shopping streets for the resort, as part of the town's modernisation. Closed circuit cameras (above) add to the sense of security

## *FYLDE*

THE march of bricks and mortar has changed the face of the Fylde area in the last 40 years. Acres of land once owned by the Clifton family of Lytham Hall were among the first to be covered by new housing.

In more recent times, villages like Warton, Newton and Freckleton have seen plenty of building.

The reputation which St Annes enjoyed as an elegant shopping centre has been dented but a £2 million regeneration project has given the Square a new image.

Five ornate pavilions not only provide places for people to congregate but also have exhibitions and band concerts. All follow a central theme which is 'garden town by the sea', a permanent link with the age when St Annes was born.

And in Ansdell the cash-strapped Fylde Rugby Club has sold off part of The Woodlands site possibly for a supermarket development.

Out in Kirkham, the building of a Safeway store has given local shopping a shot in the arm.

After its decline as an industrial centre, ancient Kirkham has been boosted by new homes which have made the place a commuter base for people working in the Fylde and other parts of Lancashire.

Although civil service jobs on the coast have dwindled other major employers have survived the recession and related economic factors.

British Nuclear Fuels at Salwick near Kirkham and BAE Systems at Warton continue to generate jobs for hundreds of people living all over the Fylde and so does AXA, the company which took over Guardian Insurance in Lytham.

The district breathed a sigh of relief when the global giant decided to keep the Lytham centre open.

Blackpool Seagulls Ice Hockey Team into cold storage and (left) unsettled outlook at the Waterloo Bowls

# Watch this

FORMER England inter national rugby star Wad Dooley said the 1999 Rugby World Cup – the last grea sporting spectacular of th millennium – was so lacking i atmosphere that the nex tournament should be played o the moon!

And while the towerin Blackpool bobby's comment were certainly tongue in cheek, i makes you wonder where th great sporting moments of th next millennium may be playe out.

Blackpool FC fans will fee they've already had more the their fair share of space-ag

**October 1993: Blackpool chairman Owen Oyston shows Sir Stanley Matthews the proposed Bloomfield Road super stadium**

# space!

stadium plans to last them another 1,000 years!

A more down-to-earth re-building programme at Bloomfield Road is now the preferred option after years of sky-dome style plans for floating pitches and retractable roofs.

The main hope for Seasiders supporters has got to be that the club manages to survive the football revolution which fast threatens the prospect of poorer clubs being left to go to the wall.

Can we really be say, with confidence, that we feel Blackpool FC will have a home in 2010 or 2100, let alone the next Millennium in 3000?

Already we've seen several Fylde Coast sporting clubs fail to make it to the new millennium, biting the dust as sport's rich-get-richer mentality takes its stranglehold.

Sadly Blackpool Borough rugby league club didn't make it into the new era, its greyhound track also being bulldozed along with the pitch and stand. The only reason you go to Borough Park today is to visit the new Odeon cinema.

Switch codes to rugby union and down the road at Fylde things are no more certain. Part of the club's Woodlands Memorial ground were ear-marked to become a Superstore.

And while such a development will solve the club's immediate financial problems how confident can we be that this small corner of Ansdell will always play host to sport as well as a supermarket?

Blackpool Seagulls ice hockey team was also put into cold storage long before the millennium milestone. These days the Pleasure Beach arena instead plays host to the ever-more-popular summer shows.

Even Crown Green bowling's hallowed home – Blackpool's Waterloo Hotel –- was at the centre of speculation over its future earlier this year.

Which leaves Royal Lytham and St Annes Golf Club as one of the last bastions of sport on the Fylde Coast – and perhaps the area's top sporting arena in terms of the calibre of sporting stars it hosts.

How ironic that, bar the famous ivy-clad clubhouse and surrounding buildings, it should be a simple strip of sandgrown'un land which makes this venue so special.

Raise a glass at the 19th to all our sporting homes, may they prosper and flourish alongside new modern arenas in the new millennium.

Because I, for one, don't much fancy a Saturday afternoon trip to the moon!

**The last bastion? Royal Lytham St Annes Golf Club**

# *The sports stars of the future?*

**THE future of Fylde sport looks to be in safe hands as a wealth of school-age talent is breaking through the ranks.**

**Young stars are emerging in almost every sport there is – from boxing to badminton and rugby league to rock climbing.**

**Boys and girls the length and breadth of the Fylde coast have shown their skills on the local, national and international stages.**

**The medals they have won would provide enough metal to re-cast Blackpool Tower.**

**And one Fleetwood teenager is hoping to add to the haul, Sarah Bainbridge, 17, from Broomfield Road, has been selected as part of the GB taekwon-do team.**

**Jim Murro, 12, from Sower Carr Lane in Hambleton, is the Britsh moto-cross champion for his age. He has been riding since he was six and competing in races since he was eight and recently moved up to 100cc bikes.**

**In cricket, 16-year-old Daniel Thomas from Ash Drive in Thornton, forced his way in to the Lancashire under-17 squad and played for the Palace Shield under-17 side as well as representing the Northern League's under-17 and 18 sides and finishing the season in the top 20 Northern League batting averages.**

**One of the brightest stars on the football field is goalkeeper Ryan Yeomans. An excellent all-round athlete who holds a host of school records, 13-year-old Ryan, from Lytham Road in Blackpool, plays for Manchester United.**

**Sarah Bainbridge**

**Jim Murro**

**Daniel Thomas**

**Ryan Yeomans**

# Seeing in the

**SILVER PLATED: Jessica Watts and Katy Seaman join in the Talbot Square celebrations**

**HATS OFF: Gina McAdam sees in the new year on Blackpool promenade**

A MIGHTY millennium roar echoed throughout Blackpool town centre at midnight as more than 20,000 party revellers packed into the heart of the resort to celebrate the start of the next 1,000 years.

Party-goers and families mingled and hugged each other as the clock struck midnight and the skies were lit up with a massive cascade of colourful fireworks.

Roads were sealed off as thousands of people from all over Blackpool and the Fylde coast filled Talbot Square and most of The Promenade for the final festive countdown.

Tony and Lynne Hamer, of Larkholme Parade, Fleetwood, with their eight-year-old daughter Charlotte, cycled from home to witness the historic event.

Amid deafening cheers they said: "The atmosphere is brilliant, it was well worth the cycle. We are just glad we could all be here for the event."

Pete and Aileen Eave and their 10-year-old son Lawrence, toasted the new millennium with champagne and lemonade respectively - from a well-stocked hamper.

The Bispham family, who also cycled from home, said: "It was wonderful and we are really pleased that we made the journey after all."

School teacher Zoe Steele, 27, and her 30-year-old partner Lee Fairhurst, both of Runcorn Avenue, Bispham, decided to see in the new millennium in Blackpool rather than Edinburgh.

Zoe said: "We have made the right decision because this year's New Year's Eve party in Blackpool was the best ever!"

Pensioners Brian and Beryl Lowe, of Dover Gardens, Carleton, came to Blackpool with family.

Brian, 65, a former insurance worker said: "It's excellent value for money and a fantastic atmosphere."

Douglas Whitmore, 76, of Carr Close, Poulton, said: "I have never seen anything so spectacular, Blackpool is the best!"

# New Century

## Fireworks light up new era

THOSE who had predicted that a massive bang would herald in the new era were right - an almighty thud signalled the start of a firework spectacular in Blackpool.

Thousands packed The Promenade between North and Central Piers to watch the display, which was perfectly timed to start as the first second of the new millennium struck.

The significance of a single star in the story of the birth of Jesus Christ 2,000 years ago was highlighted in the show which coloured the skies above Blackpool. And as part of the backdrop, Blackpool Tower and the Promenade Millennium Lights also burst into a blaze of colour.

As the finale for the 10-minute pyrotechnic display a powerful firecracker was sounded and chants of "more" could be heard from the crowds.

**A PROMENADE SPECTACULAR:** Worshippers gather at the brightly lit Jesus, the Light of the World illuminations tableau on Blackpool seafront to hold a millennium service. Right, the Rev John Austin from Blackpool Christian Fellowship leads the service between Central and North Piers

**HEAD GEAR:** Sparkly wigs and silly hats in Talbot Square, Blackpool

**LET'S BOOGIE:** Revellers enjoy themselves in a packed Talbot Square

**FLYING THE FLAG:** Simon and Rebecca Sheldon with family friend Janet Parker

**SKY WATCHERS:** Crowds gather on Central Promenade to watch the firework display

# Let's Pa

HOOTER BLOWING: Luke Dickinson at the Argyll Road street party

THE people of the Fylde took to the open air to unite in welcoming in the 21st century.

Community spirit saw neighbours pitching in to organise the street parties - banners and balloons adorned the roads, and disco music filtered through the air combined with the sumptuous smells of barbecues.

Bad weather saw winter woolies and brollies out in force, but it did not dampen spirits at any of the parties.

At the stroke of twelve, more than 100 neighbours gathered in Jem Gate, Anchorshome for a Millennium conga.

The party, organised by Mary Faulkner, Marie Catlan and Marie Bishop, was also attended by residents from nearby Maida Vale, Fleetwood Road and Norbreck Road.

The skies were lit above Layton as fireworks were launched to coincide with the dawning of the new century.

Residents on Sherwood Avenue had spent the previous four months preparing a

PAINTING BY NUMBERS: Eight-year-old Katy Willis of Maitland Avenue at the Jem Gate millennium street party, Cleveleys

HEAD GIRLS: Stacey Harris and Jacqueline Hutchinson at the Brook Street party

mammoth party. An open-air party also took place on St Heliers Road, South Shore, starting with a children's get-together earlier in the night.

Organiser Mandy Hulme, whose father Harold cooked up a storm with his

LOOKING AHEAD: Partygoer Carolyn Holland dons a pair of truly spect-tacular glasses at the Argyll Road street party

# ty Like It's 1999

OUR DOING: Maggie Collinge and Amanda Reynolds, organisers of the Argyll Road street party

MINI REVELLERS: Preparations are well under way for the great St Heliers Road millennium party. Here mums Sue Izard, Denise Parkinson and Mandy Hulme are seen with some of the mini revellers

LET'S PARTY: An excited group of children at the street party on Argyll Road

barbecue, said: "I remember my first street party when I was eight years old - it was the Queen's Silver Jubilee in 1977. I have such good memories of that event that I decided it would be nice for my children and all the other people in the neighbourhood to have similar memories."

A barbecue and disco was enjoyed in Revoe, where organiser Brenda Cook said: "Lune Grove has always had street parties since the Queen's Coronation in 1953. So we thought we would not break out of tradition."

Neighbours opened their doors to their family and friends in Brook Street, Hawes Side, to drink, play party games and be merry.

Party organisers Helen Green and Joanne Dixon sealed off the terraced street and adorned every house with bunting.

Helen said: "We thought this would be the best way to bring everyone in the street together." Joanne added: "It's a great way to spend millennium eve because adults and children alike can have fun on their own doorstep."

Householders in Argyll Road, North Shore, were in high spirits as they sipped champagne and feasted on mince pies from 9.30pm onwards.

Organisers Amanda Reynolds and Maggie Collinge came up with the idea to get the whole street together. Maggie, who works at Claremont Primary School, said: "It's brilliant to see so many people for the first time."

Blackpool paramedic Amanda said: "I have lived here for years and have now made several new friends because of the party."

Two Sisters of the Charity of Jesus and Mary convent were also present to say a special millennium prayer just before midnight.

PARTY POPPING: Nicola Barnes, Helen Green, Darren Ing, Joanne Dixon and Aiden Raybold at the Brook Street party

PARTY TIME: Jem Gate millennium street party, Cleveleys

HANDS UP: Lune Grove, Blackpool, street party

LIGHTING UP: After several attempts in atrocious weather conditions, the beacon at Fairhaven is finally lit as crowd look on

# Just

BEACONS were lit on the Fylde coast as part of a national chain of fire to light up the new millennium.

And in Blackpool, the beacon also symbolised a burning desire for the Fylde coast to further cement its links with countries across the world.

Friends of Bottrop, a group which retains links with Blackpool's twin town in Germany, lit the Blackpool beacon on North Promenade opposite Lowther Avenue.

George Hill, a member of the Friends of Bottrop, spoke as the flame was lit.

He told how it was a sign of friendship.

George added: "The flame must eventually be extinguished, but our friendship with Bottrop with remain, hopefully not only through the new millennium but for many more years to come."

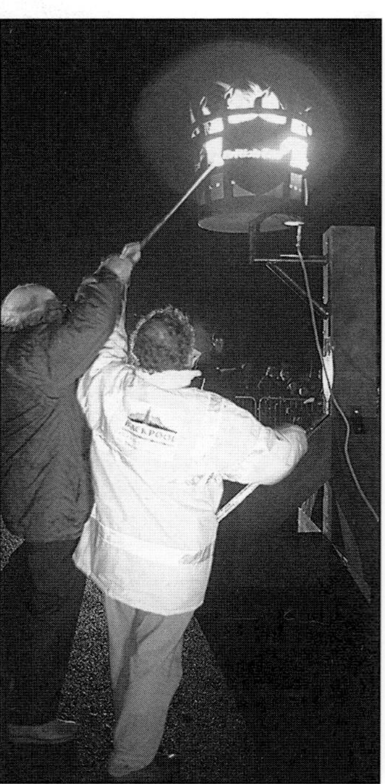

**HISTORIC MOMENT: Chairman of the Friends of Bottrop, Alan Jones, lights the Beacon at the highest point on Blackpool's Queens Promenade**

More than 200 people gathered on the highest point of the Fylde coastline to watch Alan Jones, chairman of the Friends of Bottrop, battle against the high winds and rain to light the flame.

To mark the occasion Blackpool Council gave £100 to the World Wildlife Fund, an official Beacon Millennium charity.

# Light That

**BRAVING THE RAIN:** The Millennium Beacon was lit on the highest point of Queens Promenade, Blackpool, at 10pm as crowds gathered round to watch

In Fairhaven it took members of the Lytham St Annes Twinning Association several hearty attempts to light the huge commemorative beacon near the beach at Fairhaven Lake.

More than 150 people from across South Fylde, battled the wintry elements to watch history in the making.

Georgina Coleshaw, secretary of Lytham St Anne's Twinning Association, said: "We arranged the event to coincide with other beacons right across the country. It has played an important part of the town's history and our twin town in Germany, Werne.

Fylde Mayor Coun Margaret Procopides, association president, said: "It's my honour and pleasure to light this beacon on millennium eve, and I wish everybody a happy New Year and millennium."

Graham Smith, 49, of Hungerford Road, St Annes, said: "I have been living here all my life and I love to see people from the area getting together for events such as this."

Morris and Christine Unsworth, of Hampton Court, Heyhouses Lane, St Annes, said: "We have come along because it's a way to celebrate the millennium with others."

Hotels across the Fylde coast staged their own parties while at Blackpool's Grand Theatre, the National Concert Orchestra - with soloists including Richard Swerrun, Patricia Leonard and Charlotte Page - were the stars of a celebration performance which continued into the new millennium.

**A GRAND TIME:** Mike Buchan, Patricia Leonard and star Richard Swerrun celebrate after starring in the Millennium Gala Spectacular at Blackpool's Grand Theatre

# Not too many casualties down in Casualty

As MIDNIGHT heralded the dawn of a new millennium staff surgeon "J" Jaiganesh welcomed in the new year with other doctors and nurses on duty in the accident and emergency unit at Blackpool Victoria Hospital.

Five and half hours earlier, and 6,000 miles away, his wife Vidya and their only child Sanju, four, had telephoned him from South Madras, India, as they joined family in celebrations to mark the start of 2000 there.

**HAPPY NEW YEAR: Dr "J" Jaiganesh shares a celebratory hug with Jackie Lawn**

J returned to Blackpool, leaving his family in India for an extended holiday, because he was working Christmas and New Year in A&E.

"I knew I was working and I thought they would have a happier time there," said J.

A cheer went up in the hospital as the new century began - but partying into the millennium was out of the question for the dedicated frontliners.

The doctors, nurses, administrative, ambulance and ancilliary staff were braced for action - whatever the biggest celebration of the century had to throw at them.

The Vic, which traditionally has one of the busiest A&E departments in the country on New Year's Eve, was ready for the challenges of the night.

A year of planning had ensured that it would be able to cope with a major incident. At 6pm 109 beds were available, almost 20 more than the target, and every member of A&E staff turned up for duty - many arriving early for their through-the-night shifts.

Three police officers were posted in the department to deal with any trouble-makers brought in.

Chief executive David Gill said: "We have been preparing for months, and are comfortable that all contingency plans will be effective."

He said he was grateful to staff for their willingness to give up their family time for the sake of the patients.

A&E nurses had taken their days off earlier in the week, and theatre nurses had covered for them, to ensure as many specialist staff as possible would be on duty for the big night.

One of the earliest casualties of the millennium party was Matthew Sumner, aged 11.

It was within minutes of arriving for the New Year celebrations at Jollies Bar that Matthew, of Duddon Avenue, Fleetwood, jumped into a ball pond and broke his ankle.

He and his mum, Liz, were rushed to the Vic by ambulance and within an hour he had been x-rayed, plastered up and was ready for home - proudly walking on crutches and sporting a patriotic 2000 hat and bravery badges given to him at the hospital.

"They're brilliant," said Matthew.

Matthew was shepherded through his trauma by Sister Larry Patterson, paedatric specialist nurse, who was having a busy night. "Most of the children w have had in this evening have had falls an boney injuries." she said.

Children and elderly people brought i to casualty were being admitted to warc as quickly as possible to keep as many A& spaces – including emergency overflo provision – free.

Specialist registrar Chris Brook volunteered for a shift which would tak him from one century to the next.

As part of the team who planned th A&E department's response for the nig he said: "I see it as an important part of m training to see what happens in a planne major incident. In a way, it is the fruitio of our labour."

It was just another working night fo triage sister Tara Brookes. Tara and h prison officer husband, Rob, caught 1 minutes together when he finished h shift and before she started hers.

"We'll celebrate sometime," said Tar looking forward to giving birth to the first child in July.

Volunteers from the St John Ambulanc Brigade put duty before party to be o hand to help at the hospital. Dawn Riddel 28, and Emma Whitney, 24, had n regrets. "We would much rather be here said Dawn.

As the revels on the streets of the Fyld peaked, the number of casualties rose mostly suffering from drink-relate problems, victims of fights, a few fractur and people with breathing difficulties an chest pains.

"We're coping comfortably," said chi executive David Gill, satisfied that th months of planning, coupled with super team work, had paid off.

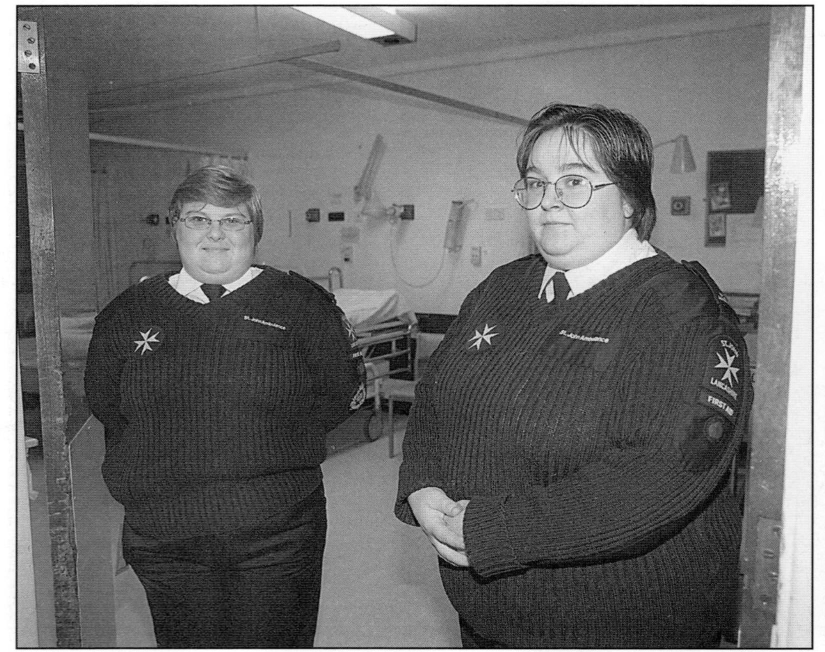

**VOLUNTEER FORCE: St John Ambulance volunteers Dawn Riddell and Emma Whitney who gave up their night to assist at the hospital — for free**

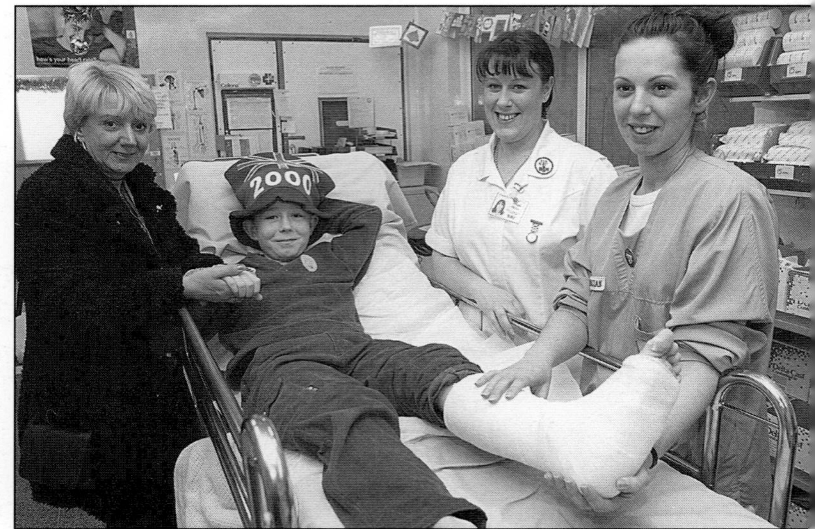


**MILLENNIUM BREAK: Casualty Matthew Sumner in the plaster room with his mum Liz, Susan Dicks, paediatric support worker and technician Joan Mahon**

**ON DUTY:** Triage sister Tara Brookes at work in A&E, at the stroke of midnight

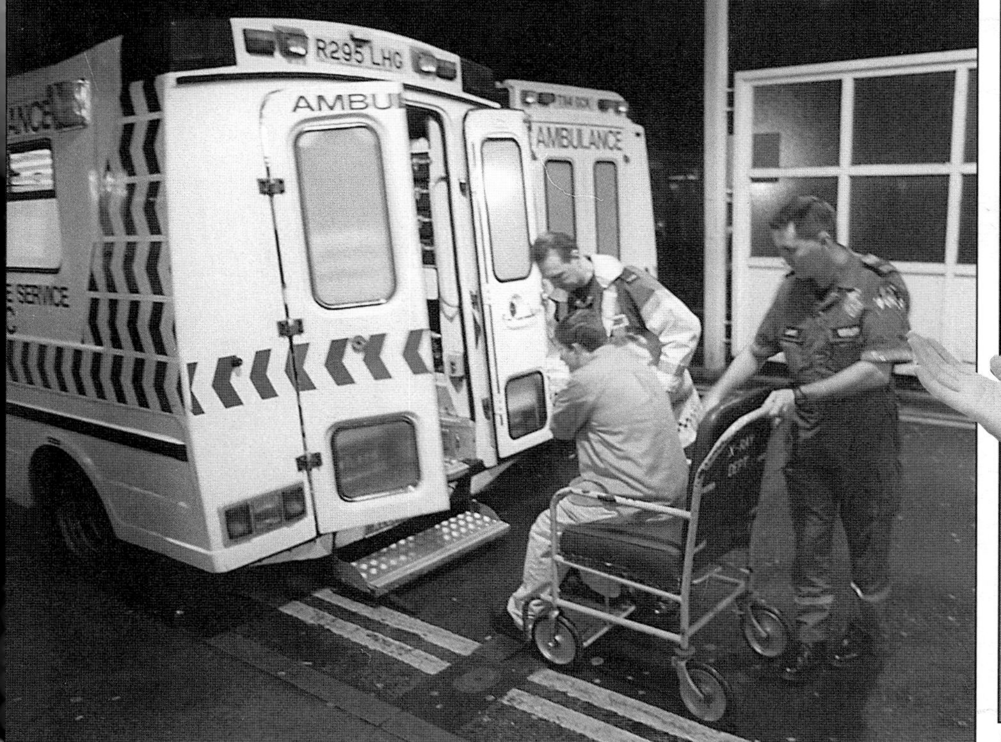


**WHEELCHAIR CASUALTY:** Another patient arrives at the A&E department

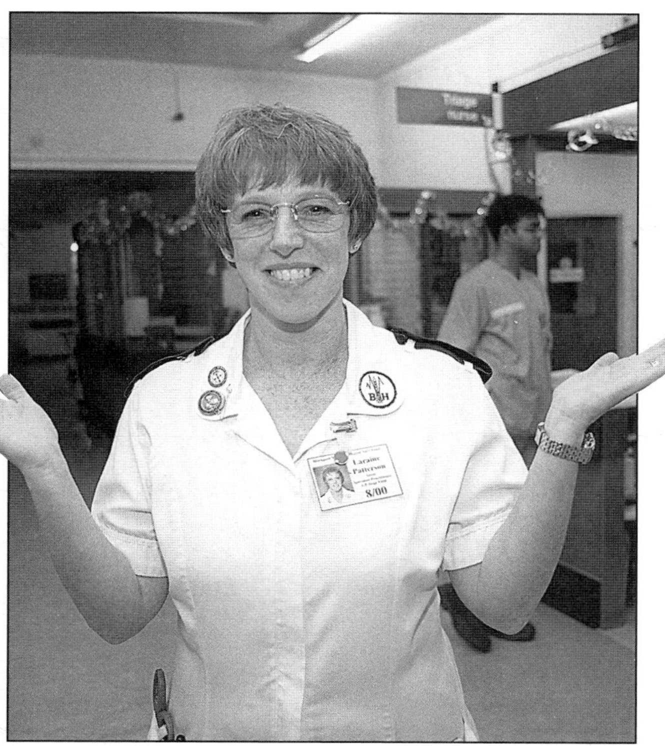

**HELPING HAND:** Sister Larry Patterson, paediatric specialist nurse who gave care and reassurance to young casualties

# Welcome to the 21st Century

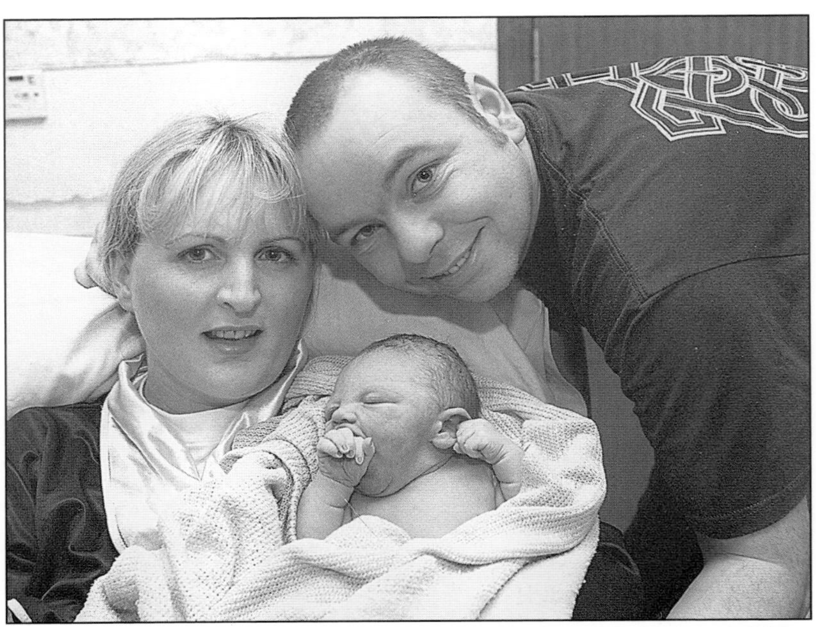

BABY BORN: Blackpool's first millennium baby – Erin with her parents Theresa and John

BABY Erin Wilson was Blackpool's first citizen of the new millennium. At exactly 21 minutes past midnight Erin secured her own place in history when, weighing in at 8lbs 1oz, she was the first Fylde baby born in 2000.

A daughter of the 21st century, she made her debut at Blackpool Victoria Hospital Maternity Unit to the delight of her mum Theresa and dad, John.

The couple, who live in Grange Road, Layton, were overjoyed with their precious little girl – a sister for their elder daughter, Shirley, seven.

Erin made a speedy arrival into the world – on the very day she was due. Her safe passage assisted by midwife Karen Swallow.

Theresa said: "We hadn't planned to do anything for New Year because of the baby and it wasn't until I had a bath at about 9.30pm that I started to feel pains.

"I timed them and rang the hospital when they were coming every few minutes."

Theresa and John's mum Celia Wilson got a taxi to the hospital while John ensured Shirley was settled with his dad Andy.

"Then I legged it up to the hospital, running all the way. I thought it would be quicker than trying to get a taxi," said bus driver John.

He stayed by Theresa's side throughout her labour. "We thought she wasn't going to make it into 2000 - but things slowed down a bit and she did.

"It is brilliant to have one of the first babies born in the new millennium. Very special," said John.

Mum Theresa, 31, looked radiant as she cuddled her newborn baby. "I feel wonderful, she is lovely," she said.

Psychiatric nurse Theresa and John, 30, moved to Blackpool from Scotland in April. John's parents had travelled from Glasgow to spend New Year south of the border.

"We're all from Scotland, Erin's born in England and has an Irish name. This is the best new year ever," said John's mum, Celia.

Staff at the maternity unit were thrilled with their early arrival. She was delivered with midwife Karen Swallow assisted by auxiliary Jean Birnie.

Karen said: "It was a perfect delivery – and a lovely baby."

Fellow midwife Stephanie Passmore also assisted Erin into the world.

For Stephanie it was her final shift at the maternity unit. After eight years in Blackpool she headed for a new job as an obstetrics nurse in Bermuda.

*Erin was the second baby born in Lancashire. The first, also a girl, was born to a Preston mum by emergency caesarean section at 16 minutes past midnight.

# *And as it ended, here's how the century began - a look back at how the resort welcomed in year 1900*

THE people of Blackpool took to the streets in their hundreds to welcome the dawn of the 20th Century.

Under the headline "The Birth of 1900 - How Blackpool dismissed the old and welcomed the New Year", The Gazette and News reported the festivities in its January 2 edition.

The commentator tells of a town thronging with people flocking to churches for quiet reflection or to meet up in Central and Talbot Squares.

Talbot Square, with the Lifeboat Band, hosted by far the biggest crowd where they joined in singing hymns of hope.

As the year 1899 approached its end The Gazette reporter of the day wrote: "And then we watched the hands of the clock in the turret get closer together, it was five minutes to midnight. The bells of the Parish Church were pealing in muffled tones their knell of the dying year. The parting year! What a year that has been for some of us!

Hurrahs

"What memories of the past 12 months it awakens, when you are watching the old year take its last, few fleeting breaths, the funeral bells tolling its death.

"Then we remember that the New Year, full of hope and the joy of birth, is knocking at the door, eager to be with us and we are glad 1899 is dead."

As the hands of the clock join at midnight and a new century starts and the reporter enthuses:

"The New Year is come. Hurrahs echo through the square. The throats of brazen instruments swell with the strains of merry, rollicking music 'Hail, smiling morn'. The bells from the church clash out joyfully. Ring, happy bells!

"A spirit of love and happiness is everywhere."

# Subscribers

Renee Andrew
Christopher B. & Kathleen S. Arkwright
Betty and Malcolm Ashworth
Mr James Aspinall
Arthur Atkinson
Kirk Atkinson
Gwenda Ayrton
David S. Bain
Mrs Rebecca Bamber Carr
C. Barker
Alan Barnes
Derick Barnes
Mrs E. Battersby
Mrs D. Beck
Ronald L. Bell
Arthur and Christine Bennett
Mrs M. Birch
Susan & Alan Bottomley
Sheila Boyes
Avril Braithwaite
M. Brandon
Alex Brown
H. J. Brown
Mrs D. Bryning
Gerald Burgess
Jane Candy
Kenneth Cardwell
Ada Carr
Doreen Carr
Barbara Challoner
Tom Clark
John Terence Cooper
J. Croker
M. R. Croker
Bill Cropper
Mavis and Alan Cross
Audrey Crossley
Douglas Dagger
William Dagger
Jean Davies
Joan Dawes
Mr A. Dawson
D. De-Lillo
Uncle Tom Devere
Barbara & Jim Diveney
K. Dodds
Robin & Beryl Donnelly
Margaret Dowling
Patricia Duerden
Patricia Earnshaw
Harold Eastwood
Mr A.E. Elliott
Bruce Evans
Lilian Farrar
F. Fell
Mrs V. Fisher
Lyndsey Fleming
Steph Fleming
James & Margaret Fletcher
Cleve Fortt
Conor Sean Peter Gilligan
Sinead Paige Gilligan
Andrew Gladwell
Jon Gomm
Robert Gomm
Rebecca Gooden
Mrs Yvonne Gregitis
Mike Hallett
John & .Lily Hallsworth
Mrs F.P.M. Hallworth
P. S. Hardman
Doreen Hardon
Craig Harvey
R. B. Harwood
Christos Hatjoullis
Marion Hatton
Mrs B. Haughton
Mr P. K. & Mrs J. D. Hay
Anne Hennessey
Robbie Heywood
Andy Higgins
T.C. Hill
Douglas M. Holmes
John Holmes
H. Hood
Brian Hornby
Anita Houton
E. Hudson
Mr & Mrs Hutchison
Colin Huttley
S. D. Isherwood
Fred Ives
Mr Jackson
Peter A. Jackson

Michael James
Mr J. Jenkinson
Mrs I. Johns
J. Johnson
Tina & Peter Kenniford
Mrs D. Kinsella
Gerald M. Kitchener
Gary Kirkham
Maria Kyle
Ian Lavelle
Mr David Lea
Gordon Lea
Rory Lee
May Ledger
Ms C.M. Leigh-Baker
Pauline Anne Leyland
Ted Lightbown
Steven James Lonsdale
Mr James Lord
Sandra & John Lucius
Marie McCabe
Mrs Norma McElwee
Karen McGee
Robert McKinnel
Mr Geoff McLellan
Jonathan McNicholl
Terry Mackness
Colin Edwin MacLeod
Alex Maitland
Geoffrey Males
Mrs J. Mason
John James Massey
Peter & Beryl Moran
David Morley
F. E. Morley
Rose Morley
Mrs R. Morris
Eric Morrison
Derek Moulding
Tony Moulding
Jill Murfin
Lilian Owen
Malcolm D. Owens
Juanita R. Oyston
Sharon M. Oyston
Mary Parkinson
Hazel Parr
David Allan Parry
Mathew Pearce
Susan Pearce
Mrs Marion Percival
R. Perry
Mr R. Pilkington
Jacqueline Catherine Pinder
Mrs Plits
Mr G. Pope
Mrs B. L. Potts
Barbara Quinn
M.F. Raines
Mrs M. Richardson
Mr Rose
Mr & Mrs K & D. M. Rose
Ruby & Don Rutter
Mrs M.A. Sanderson
Freda Sandiford
Valerie Sawyer
Mrs Scragg
Seabreeze Guest House
Colin Shaw
Harry Shaw
Mary Shaw
Mr Shaw
Jill Shepherd
Geoff Silcock
Linda Sinclair
Mark Singleton
Steve Singleton
Victoria Singleton
Andrea Smith
Richard Spencer
Amy Steedman
Christine Stevens
Leslie Street
Peter Swift
H. Swinton
Mrs H. Taylor
Mr Kenneth Taylor
Vera Todd
Mr Ron Twemlow
Linda Viney
Nigel D. C. Wall
Ian Walsh
Mr & Mrs F. Watson
Joyce M. Watson
Ronald Wilkinson
Alfred G. Wilson
John Wilson
Katrina Wood
Neville Woods
Mr S. Woodward